Inventing Congress

Inventing Congress

Origins and Establishment of the First Federal Congress

Edited by Kenneth R. Bowling and Donald R. Kennon

PUBLISHED FOR THE
UNITED STATES CAPITOL HISTORICAL SOCIETY
BY OHIO UNIVERSITY PRESS • ATHENS

Ohio University Press, Athens, Ohio 45701
© 1999 by Ohio University Press
Printed in the United States of America

Ohio University Press books are printed on acid-free paper ∞

05 04 03 02 01 00 99   5 4 3 2 1

Library of Congress Cataloging-in-Publication Data
Inventing Congress : origins and establishment of first Federal
Congress / edited by Kenneth R. Bowling and Donald R. Kennon.
     p. cm.
     "Inventing Congress represents the papers from the first two
conferences sponsored by the United States Capitol Historical
Society in its series, 'Perspectives on the History of Congress, 1789–
1801'" — Cip's pub. info.
     Includes bibliographical references and index.
     ISBN 0-8214-1271-X (alk. paper)
     1. United States. Congress — History — Congresses. 2. United
States — Politics and government — 1789–1797 — Congresses.
3. United States — Politics and government — 1797–1801 —
Congresses. I. Bowling, Kenneth R. II. Kennon, Donald R.,
1948–   . III. United States Capitol Historical Society.
JK1041.I58   1999
328.73'09'033 — dc21   98-46969
CIP

Contents

Preface

The United States Capitol Historical Society has sponsored an annual conference on American history since 1978. Under the guidance of the society's founder and first president, Fred Schwengel, and conference director Ronald Hoffman, the highly acclaimed 1978–93 conference series focused on the American Revolution. The more than 140 papers delivered and then published by the society dramatically altered in both depth and breadth the way we understand the Revolution.

As the bicentennials of the American Revolution and the Constitution drew to a close, Schwengel and Hoffman polled the scholars who had participated in the first series to discuss the future of the conferences. Several responses recommended a new conference series concentrating on the little-studied but critical Federalist Period, 1789–1801. In 1993 the society's chief historian, Donald R. Kennon, and its new president, Clarence J. Brown, following the advice of the society's executive committee, decided that two new conference series, one focusing on congressional history and the other on the art and architectural history of the Capitol, should be planned for the period from the bicentennial of the laying of the Capitol's cornerstone in 1793 to the arrival of Congress in Washington, D.C., in 1800. Kenneth R. Bowling of the First Federal Congress Project at The George Washington University was asked to chair the first series. Thus was born the society's 1994–2000 conference series on Congress before it moved to Washington, D.C., in 1800. This, the first volume from the series, covers the 1994 and 1995 conferences.

The 1994 conference entitled "Inventing Congress" looked at the creation of the institution itself. The papers presented were designed to raise broad questions concerning the interrelated intellectual, institutional, cultural, and political antecedents that contributed to the formation of the federal Congress. The Founders shared a common set of beliefs about how Greek and Roman legislatures functioned.

What were these? They understood far more accurately how the British Parliament functioned. Why did they reject it as a model? Many members of the Constitutional Convention had served in colonial and state legislatures as well as the prefederal congresses. What did they bring from that experience to the creation of the federal Congress? Questions about the structure and powers of the federal Congress affected the debate over the Constitution. What were the controversial issues?

Following President Brown's welcome and introduction of the new conference series, Sen. Robert Byrd of West Virginia spoke on "The Importance of Studying the History of Congress." The morning session covered non-American precedent. The first paper was delivered by Carl Richard of the department of history and philosophy at the University of Southwestern Louisiana. "The Founders and Classical Legislatures" investigated the origins of mixed government in ancient Greece and Rome as opposed to stressing British and colonial precedent. Richard concluded that the American concept of mixed government was based on Greek principles greatly modified for American conditions. Alison Olson of the University of Maryland's department of history concluded the morning session with "Thoughts on Why America Chose a Congressional Rather than a Parliamentary Form of Government." Her insightful musings stressed the symbolic as well as the actual role of the legislature in Anglo-American history.

The afternoon session covered American precedent. Donald Lutz of the department of political science at the University of Houston spoke on "Colonial Legislatures." Lutz provided an in-depth look at the structure of colonial legislatures, discoursing also on the role of political parties. R. B. Bernstein of the New York Law School spoke on "Parliamentary Principles, American Realities: The Continental and Confederation Congresses, 1774–89," arguing that it was Congress at which the Framers aimed their ire at the Federal Convention. John Kaminski, coeditor of *The Documentary History of the Ratification of the Constitution* at the University of Wisconsin, spoke on "Congress as an Issue during the Debate over the Constitution," focusing on whether the institution should follow the deliberative or representative legislative model. Charlene Bickford, director and coeditor of the First Federal Congress Project, concluded the conference with a paper entitled "The Media and the First Federal Congress," which summarized the long struggle in England and America for public access to the debates of the legislature. Her evidence indicated that cynicism, criticism, and Congress bashing are not twentieth-century inventions.

The 1995 conference, "A Vessel Just Launched: The First Federal Congress," was a day and a half in length and focused on the most important Congress in American history. Its awesome agenda breathed life into the Constitution, established precedent and constitutional interpretation that still guide us two hundred years later, and held the union together when sectional interests threatened disunion. Most significantly, it concluded the American Revolution.

After opening remarks by President Brown, Bowling presented a brief "Overview of the First Congress." R. B. Bernstein of the New York Law School opened the first session with a provocative paper, "A New Matrix for National Politics: The First Federal Elections." Using the House contest in Charleston, South Carolina, as a case study, Bernstein argued that even from the beginning popular electoral politics could be partisan, personal, and polemical, a far cry from the Federalist vision. First Federal Congress Project Director Charlene Bickford's paper, " 'Public Attention Is Very Much Fixed on the Proceedings of the New Congress': The House and Senate Get Organized," detailed the rules and proceedings that the two chambers evolved over their first two years, when they were, in the words of James Madison, in a wilderness without guidance.

Marie Sauer Lambremont, then an undergraduate at George Washington University, opened the afternoon session with "Rep. James Jackson of Georgia: Impassioned Orator and Southern Stalwart," arguing that Jackson, not Madison, should be viewed as the spokesman for the South in the first House of Representatives. William diGiacomantonio, assistant editor of the First Federal Congress Project, concluded the second session with his "To Form the Character of the American People: Public Support for the Arts, Sciences, and Morality." The paper revealed how the First Congress took steps toward fostering a novel and unique American character by encouraging the arts, sciences, and public morality under the new Constitution's "general welfare" clause and copyright and patent powers.

Pamela Scott, a historian of architecture, opened the third session with a paper and slide presentation entitled " 'Neat, Plain, or Elegant':

Housing Congress, 1774–1800," which described the buildings in which Congress met. Herbert Druks of the department of Judaic studies at Brooklyn College delivered a paper on "Religious Freedom and the First Federal Congress" in which he discussed the debate over whether the state or federal government had jurisdiction when religious issues came to the fore. Another George Washington University undergraduate, William Cowin, concluded the conference with a paper entitled "The Invisible Smith: The Impact of Adam Smith on the Development of American Economic Policy during the First Federal Congress."

Kenneth R. Bowling
Donald R. Kennon

I: Origins

Carl J. Richard

The Classical Roots of the U.S. Congress

Mixed Government Theory

HISTORIANS OF THE Founders of the United States have tended to emphasize the modern nature of the institutions they established. But the U.S. Congress owes its structure to a theory that, though modified in significant ways by the British Whig and colonial American perspectives, was ancient in origin. Classical mixed government theory provided the ideological framework through which the Founders judged both ancient and modern legislatures.[1]

The theory of mixed government originated in the desire of Athenian aristocrats to discredit democracy. Although democracy first developed in Greece, no one would have been more astonished by its current worship than the average Greek of the classical period. Hardly egalitarian, the Greeks were intensely concerned with distinctions between humans and animals, males and females, free people and slaves,

---

[1] Even those historians who argue that the Founders were "classical republicans" generally assume that they received the ideology from the works of British Whigs, via Machiavelli and Harrington. See Bernard Bailyn, *The Ideological Origins of the American Revolution*, 2d ed. (Cambridge, Mass., 1992), pp. 23–27, 44; J. G. A. Pocock, *The Machiavellian Moment: Florentine Political Thought and the Atlantic Political Tradition* (Princeton, 1975), pp. ix, 529–33; idem, "Virtue and Commerce in the Eighteenth Century," *Journal of Interdisciplinary History* 3 (1972):120, 133–34; Lance Banning, *The Jeffersonian Persuasion: Evolution of a Party Ideology* (Ithaca, 1988), pp. 13–18, 92–93, 273–74; Drew R. McCoy, *The Elusive Republic: Political Economy in Jeffersonian America* (Chapel Hill, 1980), pp. 189–95, 253.

men who owned property and those who did not, and, of course, Greeks and non-Greeks. Few Greek city-states possessed democracy before the fifth century B.C., when imperial Athens began pressuring its new allies to adopt political systems similar to its own.[2]

Democracy was a bold venture. One reason the Athenians were so elated by their victory over the Persians on the plain of Marathon in 490 B.C. was that it soothed their apprehension that the gods simply would not allow the overthrow of aristocracy—of a government controlled by men whose ancestry might ultimately be traced to the gods. The Athenians used the lot to select their officials partly because this system permitted the gods to play a role in what seemed to many people a most ungodly state.[3]

Members of prominent Athenian families resented the new democracy's dilution of their power and prestige and developed elaborate constructs to demonstrate its unacceptability as a form of government. It was these aristocrats who forged the basis of the anti-Athenian tradition that the Founders imbibed at an early age. The aristocrats maintained that Athenian democracy constituted the tyranny of the poor over the rich. The Athenian masses were irrational, unstable, ungrateful, and fickle. Pericles corrupted the citizens by offering them state pay for state service. Athens's situation worsened even further after the death of Pericles, when demagogues of lesser ability controlled the government. Athens was a horrifying example of what could happen if the inherent inequalities among men were disregarded and government were based upon a specious egalitarianism.

The leading forgers of the antidemocratic tradition that was to dominate Western political thought for over two millennia not only suffered from a class bias but also had personal axes to grind. Thucydides had been exiled by the Athenian people for a military failure during the Peloponnesian War. Although the historian praised Pericles, he did so largely in order to contrast the Athenian statesman with the "demagogic" Cleon, the man most responsible for Thucydides' exile. Thucydides (2.65.5–13) emphasized that Pericles "restrained

---

[2] Thucydides, *History of the Peloponnesian War,* 3.82.
[3] These ideas were derived from Jennifer Tolbert Roberts, *Athens on Trial: The Antidemocratic Tradition in Western Thought* (Princeton, 1994).

the people. . . . He was not led by them, but they by him." Similarly, Plato and Xenophon, already critics of democracy and supporters of a Spartan-style aristocracy, were devastated by the public execution of their mentor, Socrates. Hence it is not surprising that Thucydides' *History of the Peloponnesian War* featured hair-raising descriptions of the chaos and violence of Athenian democracy, that Xenophon's *Memorabilia of Socrates* was antidemocratic, that Plato advocated a simple aristocracy of guardians (led by a philosopher-king) in the (in)famous *Republic,* or that Plato's chief pupil, Aristotle, equated democracy with mob rule.

In the fourth century B.C., Plato identified three simple forms of government: monarchy, aristocracy, and democracy — rule by the one, the few, and the many. Each of these forms, he claimed (*Laws* 756e–757a, 832c; *Politicus* 291d–303c), deteriorated over time: monarchy into tyranny, aristocracy into oligarchy, and democracy into ochlocracy (mob rule). Plato suggested that the best form of government would be a mixed government, one that balanced the powers of the three orders of society. (The theory represented a marked departure from the one Plato had elaborated in the *Republic* more than a decade earlier.) Aristotle then immortalized mixed government theory, making it the centerpiece of his *Politics* (3.7), in which he cited numerous examples of mixed government in the ancient world.

In the second century B.C., Polybius provided the most detailed analysis of mixed government theory (*Histories* 6.5–18). The Greek historian agreed that the best constitution assigned approximately equal amounts of power to the three orders of society. He explained that only a mixed government could circumvent the cycle of discord that was the inevitable product of the simple forms. Hence only a mixed government could provide a state with the internal harmony necessary for prosperity and for the defeat of external enemies. Polybius claimed that the cycle began when primitive man, suffering from chaos and violence, consented to be ruled by a strong and brave leader. Then, as men began to conceive of justice (by developing the habit of putting themselves in others' positions), they replaced the strong and brave leader with the just leader and chose his son to succeed him, in the expectation that the son's lineage and education would lead him to emulate his father. But the son, having been accustomed to a special status from birth, possessed no sense of duty toward the public and, soon after acquiring power, sought to distinguish himself from the rest of the people. Monarchy had deteriorated into tyranny. When the bravest and noblest of the aristocrats (for who else would risk their lives in such an endeavor?) overturned the tyranny, the people naturally chose them to succeed the king as rulers. The result was an aristocracy, "rule by the best." Unfortunately, the aristocrats' children were not the best, but the most spoiled and, like the king's son, soon placed their own welfare above that of the people. Aristocracy had degenerated into oligarchy. The oppressed people rebelled against the oligarchy and created a democracy. But the wealthy, seeking to raise themselves above the common level, soon corrupted the people with bribes and created factions. The result was the chaos and violence that always accompany ochlocracy. When these reached epic proportions, sentiment grew for a dictatorship. Monarchy reappeared. This cycle, Polybius contended, would repeat itself in every society indefinitely until the society had the wisdom to balance the power of the three orders.

Polybius considered the Roman republic the most outstanding example of mixed government. He claimed that the Roman constitution, which had been constructed slowly through trial and error and had reached perfection at the time of the Second Punic War (218–201 B.C.), was the secret of Roman success. The interdependence between the one, the few, and the many minimized internal strife. The Roman consuls (in this case, "the two" rather than "the one") needed to maintain good relations with the senate because that body could block the flow of grain, clothing, and money to them in military campaigns; could replace them in the middle of a campaign if their year in office had expired; and could withhold triumphs and other prestigious awards. The consuls needed to maintain good relations with the people, since they could find fault with the account that the consuls were required to submit at the end of their term and could reject the treaties that they negotiated. Similarly, the senate and the people were bound to one another by the senate's control of lucrative contracts, by its dominance of the judicial system, and by the people's ability (through the tribunes) to veto senate legislation. Likewise, the people needed to maintain good relations with the consuls, since they served under them in the army. Presented with the need to explain to his dazed and defeated Greek compatriots how a group of Western "barbarians" had managed to conquer "the whole inhabited world" (the Mediterranean basin), the historian understandably turned to a well-established Greek theory.[4]

But such was the beguiling clarity and simplicity of Polybius's analysis that he convinced even the Romans themselves that their complex system of balances was the chief cause of their success. In the following century, Cicero (*Republic* 2.23–30) seized upon Polybius's theory to thwart the increasing efforts of ambitious Romans to consolidate their own power at the republic's expense. Although the historians Plutarch, Livy, Sallust, and Tacitus never formally endorsed mixed government, their sympathy toward the lost republic and criticism of absolute monarchy, combined with their disquisitions on the volatile nature of untutored mobs, suggested a strong sympathy for it.

It may be doubted that the Roman republic ever possessed a mixed government. Even at the peak of plebeian power, the patricians continued to hold the upper hand, for three reasons. First, since the patrician senate controlled the treasury, it could use financial leverage to prevent the enforcement of such measures as the Gracchi's land redistribution laws. Second, vast economic inequalities allowed the patricians to control large blocks of plebeian votes through a client system. Third, most plebeians could not afford to hold office, since officials were denied salaries. Hence, it is debatable whether consuls — who were almost always patricians, shared in the economic interests of that class, and generally had relatives in the senate — can be considered to have served as an effective counterweight to the aristocratic assembly. In addition, Polybius's "balances" between the consuls and the people were of unequal weight. A consul's fear that he might have a treaty rejected hardly balanced the terror felt by plebeians at the thought of opposing someone who, as a military leader, would have the power of life and death over them. Indeed, the imbalance between the patricians and plebeians was becoming much worse at the very time Polybius and Cicero were writing. The further inequalities produced by the growth of the latifundia — plantations in the conquered

---

[4]For an excellent line-by-line analysis of Polybius's sixth book, see F. W. Walbank, *A Historical Commentary on Polybius*, 3 vols. (Oxford, 1957–79), 1:635–746.

provinces worked by slaves (mostly prisoners of war) — increased the relative power of the patricians enormously.[5]

Nevertheless, mixed government theory dominated Western political thought for millennia, winning the support of such disparate theorists as Thomas Aquinas, John Calvin, and Niccolo Machiavelli. The mixed government tradition was not challenged until the rise of absolutism in the seventeenth century. Even the Roman emperors had generally cloaked their edicts in the language and forms of the republic. But monarchists Jean Bodin, Robert Filmer, and Thomas Hobbes, who were as revolutionary, in their own way, as latter-day democrats, attacked the hallowed theory of mixed government with great zeal. Although they disliked democracy as much as the mixed government theorists, the monarchists preferred to attack the most sacred model of mixed government, the Roman republic, than to join their opponents in kicking the dead horse of Athens. Taking care to refute Aristotle, Polybius, Cicero, and Machiavelli, Bodin denied the possibility of such a thing as mixed government, arguing that the Roman republic had been a simple democracy and Sparta a simple aristocracy. Since the only real choice lay between the simple systems, and since monarchy was the best of these systems (Bodin agreed with his opponents that democracy was the worst), reasonable men had no choice but to support monarchy. Filmer agreed. After grousing that the Greeks had possessed "learning enough to be seditious," Filmer made a halfhearted and dubious attempt to convert Aristotle into a monarchist. He then contrasted the paltry 480 years of the Roman republic with the millennia of ancient Middle Eastern monarchies. Even during those 480 years, the Roman republic's restlessness betrayed its inability to find a decent form of government. Contending that effective government demanded the concentration of sovereignty in a monarch, Filmer concluded that mixed government was a vain "fancy." Similarly, Hobbes assaulted the hallowed system of classical education that instilled the absurd belief in mixed government, writing: "By reading these Greek and Latin authors, men from their childhood have gotten a habit, under a false show of liberty, of favoring tumults and of [the] licentious

---

[5]H. H. Scullard, *From the Gracchi to Nero: A History of Rome from 133 B.C. to A.D. 68* (London, 1959), pp. 18–21, 27.

controlling [of] actions of their sovereigns and again of controlling the controllers, with the effusion of so much blood as I think I may truly say there was never anything so dearly bought as these western parts have bought the learning of the Greek and Latin tongues." The fact that Hobbes was not dissuaded by such sentiments from calling Thucydides "the most politic historiographer that ever writ" and translating his work into English does not reveal inconsistency. Thucydides never advocated a specific form of government, and his horrific depiction of Athens during the Peloponnesian War could be interpreted as a portrayal of Hobbes's state of nature, a state to which Hobbes believed any society without concentrated sovereignty would revert.[6]

English republicans responded to these unprecedented assaults both by reasserting classical arguments against the simple systems of government and by adding Great Britain to their list of successful mixed governments. The king, the House of Lords, and the House of Commons joined the Spartan and Roman governments in the pantheon of mixed government theorists. Seventeenth-century Englishman Harrington contributed the theory of "natural aristocracy," a concept essential to any American adaptation of mixed government theory. Harrington held that even in a new country like his mythical Oceana, which lacked a titled aristocracy, certain men would possess greater talent than others. In any free society this natural difference in talent would produce unequal wealth. Unequal wealth would, in turn, produce class conflict. Mixed government, combined with a few laws limiting the size of landholdings, was the only means of preventing violent struggles between the classes and the tyranny that inevitably followed these civil wars. Hence, Oceana's government consisted of a senate that represented the natural aristocracy, a huge assembly

---

[6]Paul K. Conkin, *Self-Evident Truths* (Bloomington, Ind., 1974), pp. 146–47; John Calvin, *Institutes of the Christian Religion*, 2 vols., trans. Henry Beveridge (Grand Rapids, Mich., 1970), 2:656–57; Niccolo Machiavelli, *The Discourses of Niccolo Machiavelli*, trans. Leslie J. Walker (New Haven, 1950), 1:212–15; Jean Bodin, *Method for the Easy Comprehension of History*, trans. Beatrice Reynolds (New York, 1945), pp. 179–87, 267, 282; Peter Laslett, ed., *Patriarcha and Other Political Works of Sir Robert Filmer* (Oxford, 1949), pp. 85–87, 91, 93; Thomas Hobbes, *Leviathan, Parts I and II* (New York, 1958), p. 175. For Hobbes's statements concerning Thucydides, see Paul A. Rahe, *Republics Ancient and Modern: Classical Republicanism and the American Revolution* (Chapel Hill, 1992), p. 367.

elected from the common people, and an executive to provide a balancing center of power. Harrington believed that such a system would produce good laws, which would, in Polybian fashion, produce good men. Algernon Sidney shared Harrington's respect for mixed government, writing: "There never was a good government in the world that did not consist of the three simple species of monarchy, aristocracy, and democracy [mixed together]." Mixed government theory was used to justify both the British system of government and the American colonial governments, which generally consisted of a governor, a few councilors, and an assembly elected by the colonists.[7]

The Founders had access to every level of this tradition. Hence it was only natural that, when confronted by unprecedented parliamentary taxation during the 1760s and 1770s, they should turn to the most ancient and revered of political theories to explain this perplexing phenomenon. Patriot leaders such as Richard Henry Lee, Samuel Adams, and John Adams ascribed the new tyranny to a degeneration of the mixture of the English constitution. Although the form of the British government remained the same, King George III had destroyed its delicate balance by using his patronage powers to buy the House of Commons and to pack the House of Lords. This corruption had then seeped into colonial governments, where royal governors generally possessed the power to appoint the upper branch of the legislature. As in the nations of antiquity, the source of tyranny was an inadequate mixture. As Gordon Wood noted: "The long wrangle with England, for all that it touched in the realm of politics, had scarcely contested, and indeed for most Americans, had only endorsed mixed-government theory." The theory was still so axiomatic among all but a few absolute monarchists and radical democrats that it was very rarely questioned.[8]

The framers of the new state constitutions that emerged from the American Revolution never doubted that their governments should be mixed. Rather, their dilemma was how to mix them in a society that no longer possessed a monarch and that had never possessed a titled

---

[7]J. G. A. Pocock, ed., *The Political Works of James Harrington* (Cambridge, 1977), pp. 459, 607; Algernon Sidney, *Discourses concerning Government* (1751; reprint ed., London, 1968), pp. 130, 139–40, 434.

[8]Gordon S. Wood, *The Creation of the American Republic, 1776–1787* (Chapel Hill, 1969), pp. 201–2, 211.

aristocracy. The framers decided that these essential roles should be played by an elective governor and a senate consisting of Harrington's "natural aristocracy." Ten of the thirteen states created a senate, nearly all of them establishing property qualifications for senate candidates that exceeded those for members of the lower house. North Carolina and New York even established special property qualifications for their senates' electors, a practice that won James Madison's approval as late as 1788. Maryland went even further, establishing an electoral college to select its senators. When Virginia chose to have its upper house elected in the same manner as its lower assembly, and when Pennsylvania chose to eliminate its upper branch altogether, the resultant furor engulfed both states. Unmollified by the creation of a long-termed Council of Censors (based on the Spartan ephors and the Roman censors) to monitor the single, democratic assembly, obstructionists finally crippled the Pennsylvania Constitution, forcing a new constitution that mimicked the mixture of the other state governments. Americans had decided that since education and talent often accompanied wealth, and since wealth (unlike either talent or virtue) could be easily quantified, property was the most appropriate criterion for identifying the "natural aristocracy" that would provide their governments with the necessary senatorial stability. The state senates were generally smaller than the lower houses, and senators generally served longer, staggered terms to diminish their vulnerability to popular pressure.[9]

Even Thomas Jefferson, the future champion of representative democracy, embraced the theory during the Revolution. Young Jefferson had devoted more space in his legal and political commonplace book to Montesquieu, the most famous modern advocate of mixed government, than to any other author. In 1776 Jefferson argued that "the wisest men" should be elected to the Virginia Senate and should be, "when chosen, perfectly independent of their electors." Experience taught Jefferson "that a choice by people themselves is not generally distinguished for its wisdom," a sentiment echoed in his literary commonplace book quotations. Hence he disliked the Virginia Constitution's provision for the direct election of senators. The final draft of his own proposed constitution established a nine-year, nonrenewable

---

[9]Ibid., pp. 203, 208, 213–14, 232–33.

term, so that senators would not always "be casting their eyes forward to the period of election (however distant) and be currying favor with the electors, and consequently dependent on them." Jefferson could even accept Edmund Pendleton's suggestion "to an appointment for life, or to any thing rather than a mere creation by and dependence on the people." As late as 1782 Jefferson was still complaining about the Virginia Senate. He noted: "The purpose of establishing different houses of legislation is to introduce the influence of different interests or different principles." But since both of Virginia's houses were elected in the same manner, Virginia could not derive "those benefits" of a mixed system that compensated for its inconvenience. Jefferson also deplored the weakness of Virginia's governor, remembering his own troubles as governor during the Revolutionary War. His proposal for a new Virginia constitution the following year favored the indirect election of senators and the elimination of all previous restrictions on the Senate's power to originate or amend any bill. He added that the governor should appoint the state's judges, in order to make the jurists "wholly independent of the Assembly — of the Council — nay, more, of the people."[10]

John Adams was the most visible and most persistent advocate of mixed government in America. As early as 1763 he claimed in "An Essay on Man's Lust for Power": "No simple Form of Government can possibly secure Men against the Violences of Power. Simple Monarchy will soon mould itself into Despotism, Aristocracy will soon commence on Oligarchy, and Democracy will soon degenerate into Anarchy, such an Anarchy that every Man will do what is right in his own Eyes, and no Man's life or Property or Reputation or Liberty will be safe." In 1772 he contended: "The best Governments of the World have been mixed. The Republics of Greece, Rome, and Carthage were all mixed Governments." In 1776 Adams published his *Thoughts on Government,* a series of essays urging the Virginia and North Carolina legislatures to establish mixed governments in their new constitutions. The pamphlet ex-

---

[10]Ibid., pp. 201, 213, 215, 436; Douglas L. Wilson, ed., *Jefferson's Literary Commonplace Book* (Princeton, 1989), p. 11. For reference to Jefferson's early support for Montesquieu, see Joyce Appleby, *Liberalism and Republicanism in the Historical Imagination* (Cambridge, Mass., 1992), p. 295. For Jefferson's complaints concerning the governor's lack of power, see Bailyn, *Ideological Origins of the American Revolution,* p. 293.

erted a tremendous influence on the framers of the state constitutions. In 1780 Adams played a leading role in the drafting of the Massachusetts Constitution, then widely considered the best of all state constitutions. Under the Massachusetts Constitution, representation in the Senate was based upon the amount of taxes paid by each district. A high property qualification was required for the senators' electors. An even larger amount was required for the governors' electors. The governor was a limited, elective monarch who possessed the veto power, a fixed salary, and broad powers of appointment. In 1787 Adams wrote *A Defence of the Constitutions of Government of the United States of America,* which remains the fullest exposition of mixed government theory by an American. He penned the three volumes partly in response to Turgot's *Letters,* which had endorsed the single-assembly government of Pennsylvania, and partly in response to Shays's Rebellion, whose supporters had demanded single-assembly government. Shays's rebels, Massachusetts farmers angered by foreclosures resulting from a shortage of paper money, knew that a single democratic assembly was more likely to yield to popular pressures to inflate the money supply.[11]

In the *Defence,* the first volume of which circulated at the U.S. Constitutional Convention, Adams claimed that since the time when Lycurgus (now considered mythical) first instituted mixed government in Sparta in the eighth century B.C., only three improvements had been made in the science of government: representation, the separation of power, and the executive veto. What Adams feared most were single-assembly governments, which would inevitably be dominated by a natural aristocracy of wealth, birth, and talent. Hence the natural aristocracy should be segregated in the Senate, where their talent could benefit the country, while their ambition could be checked by the one executive and the representatives of the many. The consequence of the

---

[11] John Adams, "An Essay on Man's Lust for Power," Aug. 29, 1763, and "Thoughts on Government," 1776, in Robert J. Taylor, ed., *The Papers of John Adams,* 7 vols. (Cambridge, Mass., 1977–), 1:83, 4:88; L. H. Butterfield, ed., *The Diary and Autobiography of John Adams,* 4 vols. (Cambridge, Mass., 1961), 2:58; Wood, *Creation of the American Republic,* p. 434; Adams to Thomas Jefferson, Oct. 28, 1787, Adams to Benjamin Hichborn, Jan. 27, 1797, Adams to Philip Mazzei, June 12, 1787, Adams to Richard Price, May 20, 1787, Adams to John Trumbull, Jan. 23, 1791, Adams to Samuel Perley, June 19, 1809, in Charles Francis Adams, ed., *The Works of John Adams, Second President of the United States,* 10 vols. (Boston, 1850–56), 8:458, 9:551, 553, 558–59, 572–73, 623–24.

states' failure to maintain such a balance would be a repetition of Greek history — that is, "two factions, which will struggle in words, in writing, and at last in arms." Having cited Thucydides on the barbaric acts of "the aspiring few" and "the licentious many" in many of the Greek city-states during the Peloponnesian War, Adams ascribed this class conflict to their single-assembly governments. He then pleaded: "In the name of human and divine benevolence, is such a system as this to be recommended to Americans, in this age of the world? . . . Without three orders, and an effectual balance between them, in every American constitution, it must be destined to frequent, unavoidable revolutions." Adams further contended: "The history of Greece should be to our countrymen what is called in many families on the [European] continent a boudoir; an octagonal apartment in a house, with a full-length mirror on every side, and another in the ceiling." He added that a nation the size of the United States should fear simple governments even more than the tiny Greek republics did.[12]

The simple government to which Americans were most apt to fall prey was, of course, democracy. Adams claimed that democracy never had a patron among men of letters, because the people applauded "artifices and tricks . . . hypocrisy and superstition . . . flattery, bribes, [and] largesses." "It is no wonder then," he added "that democracies and democratical mixtures are annihilated all over Europe, except on a barren rock, a paltry fen, an inaccessible mountain, or an impenetrable forest." Later in the same volume, Adams expanded upon his view of democracy:

> An usurping populace is its own dupe, a mere underworker, and purchaser in trust of some single tyrant, whose state and power they advance to their ruin, with as blind an instinct as those worms that die while weaving magnificent habits for beings of a superior order. The people are more dexterous at putting down and setting up than at preserving what is fixed; and they are not fonder of seizing more than their own than they are of delivering it up again to the worst bidder, with their own into the bargain. Their earthly devotion is seldom paid to above one at a time, of their own creation, whose oar they pull with

---

[12] John Adams, *A Defence of the Constitutions of Government of the United States of America*, 2 vols. (1787–88; reprint ed., New York, 1971), 1:i–vii, xii–xiii, 139–41, 183, 210.

less murmuring and more skill, than when they share the leading, or even hold the helm.

Democracy, Adams concluded in Polybian fashion, was a mere way station on the road to tyranny.[13]

Adams opposed the other simple forms of government as well. He marshaled an impressive array of examples, drawn largely from ancient history, to prove the crucial importance of a balance among the three orders of society. His favorite example of mixed government was Polybius's favorite, the Roman republic. Adams claimed that in the eighth century B.C. Romulus (another mythical figure) had created a mixed government in Rome modeled upon the Spartan government instituted by Lycurgus. Unfortunately, Romulus failed to give the Roman king the full executive authority and a veto on the senate's legislation, and failed to balance the aristocratic senate with a regular assembly of the people. As a result, the aristocracy overturned the monarchy, as it must when the monarch lacks the aid of a popular assembly. There followed a harsh oligarchy. The two consuls replaced the one king. The consuls were elected annually, thereby allowing the senate much influence in their selection. In addition, the consuls, like the kings before them, lacked full executive authority and the veto power. Nevertheless, after suffering numerous popular revolts, the senate granted the plebeians the authority to elect tribunes, who possessed the power to veto senate legislation. As a result, the Roman government finally achieved the rough balance of the three orders that served as the basis for the city's unparalleled stability, prosperity, and growth. But the people were dissatisfied and grasped for more power. Since the consuls were too weak to moderate between the few and the many, open warfare ensued between the two groups. The leader of the many (Caesar) defeated the leader of the few (Pompey), as he must when aristocrats lack the aid of a powerful monarch. The horrible dictatorship that ensued lasted five centuries.[14]

Adams also attributed the downfall of Carthage to its lack of a separation of powers and executive veto. Since the two Carthaginian suffetes, like the Roman consuls, shared executive authority with the

---

[13]Ibid., 1:xii, 104.
[14]Ibid., 1:101–2, 217–25, 335–38.

senate and lacked the veto power, they were too weak to moderate
between the few and the many. The popular assembly possessed too
much power, settling all legislative questions on which the senate did
not rule unanimously. The enormous power of the assembly was fatally
increased when the term of the state's popularly elected chief judicial
officers was reduced from life to one year. The dissension that resulted
from the ensuing lack of balance between the few and the many undermined the Carthaginian war effort against the Romans. This was the
reason the Romans "finally destroyed their rival power so effectually
that scarce a trace of it remains to be seen, even in ruins."[15]

Adams ascribed the fall of Sparta to the same imbalance, resulting
from the same causes. The Spartan senate, called the *gerousia* ("council
of elders") consisted of twenty-eight members of the nobility, aged
sixty and older, elected by the adult males for lifetime terms, and
Sparta's two kings. The gerousia had the whole executive power and
most of the legislative authority. The two kings were largely religious
and military leaders. The popular assembly could not debate but could
only confirm or reject senate proposals by acclamation. Hence the longevity of the Spartan constitution could not be ascribed to two other
causes. First, the five popularly elected ephors, who acted as the people's watchdogs over senate administration, swore an oath every month
to maintain the kings' hereditary honors, while the kings vowed to obey
the laws. These solemn oaths, though a poor substitute for a royal and
popular veto power, served to unite the kings with the people against
the senate. Second, and more important, Sparta's remarkable social
system instilled in her citizens a deep attachment to the republic. This
system featured "the equal division of property; the banishment of
gold and silver; the prohibition of travel and intercourse with strangers; the prohibition of arts, trades, and agriculture [by citizens]; the
discouragement of literature; the public meals; the incessant warlike
exercises; [and] the doctrine that every citizen was the property of the
state, and that parents should not educate their own children." Not
only was this system contrary to the personal happiness of the citizens,
but the Spartan conquest of Athens and the rest of Greece, by introducing luxury and foreign manners into Sparta, destroyed the values the

---

[15]Ibid., 1:212–15.

system had produced. The ephors, against their most solemn oath, killed a king. To Adams, the lesson was clear: proper balancing of the power of the three orders of society, not religious oaths or education, was the only practical method of achieving public happiness.[16]

Adams contended that Athens's downfall had also resulted from an improper imbalance of the orders. Athens was first ruled by an aristocracy of nine archons. By the seventh century B.C. the archons had become so tyrannical that Draco's harsh legal code allowed creditors to sell debtors into foreign servitude. Such laws would have incited revolution if Solon had not been made dictator in 594 B.C. Solon eased the plight of debtors and transferred power to the popular assembly. Though only the wealthy could hold office, because of high property qualifications, the majority held the supreme power. Adams wrote regarding Solon: "He had not, probably, tried the experiment of democracy in his own family before he attempted it in the city, according to the advice of Lycurgus; but was obliged to establish such a government as the people could bear, not that which he thought best, as he said himself." The inevitable result of Solon's democracy was the tyranny of Peisistratus and his son Hippias (561–510 B.C.). After a brief civil war, the Athenians returned to democracy, which again failed to last "above one hundred years" (actually, by a fairer reckoning, close to two hundred). Like the Spartans, the Athenians had toyed with empty solutions to the problem of tyranny, such as ostracism, a system of banishment that served only to exile Athens's best leaders. Adams asked: "What more melancholy spectacle can be conceived even in imagination, than that inconstancy which erects statues to a patriot or hero one year, banishes him the next, and the third erects statues to his memory?" The real solution to democracies' problems, Adams concluded, was their moderation by the other two orders.[17]

The U.S. Constitution was as much a product of mixed government theory as the state constitutions. At the Constitutional Convention, James Madison, the "Father of the Constitution," argued for a nine-year term for senators, declaring: "Landholders ought to have a share in the government to support these invaluable interests and to balance

---

[16]Ibid., 1:253–58.
[17]Ibid., 1:145–46, 262–85.

and check the other [the many]. They ought to be so constituted as to protect the minority of the opulent against the majority. The senate, therefore, ought to be this body; and to answer these purposes, they ought to have permanency and stability. Various have been the propositions; but my opinion is, the longer they continue in office, the better will these views be answered." It was useless to deny the existence of an American aristocracy, though there were no "hereditary distinctions," and though inequalities of wealth were minor by comparison with Europe. Madison continued: "There will be debtors and creditors, and an unequal possession of property, and hence arises different views and different objects in government. This, indeed, is the ground work of aristocracy; and we find it blended in every government, both ancient and modern." Madison concluded that even in his own day America could not be regarded as "one homogenous mass" and that there were recent "symptoms of a leveling spirit" that he feared might lead to "agrarian acts" (land redistribution measures) if not checked by an aristocratic senate. Four years earlier, when Madison chaired a committee to recommend books for congressional use, he had placed Aristotle's *Politics* at the top of his list of works concerning political theory.[18]

Madison reiterated his position in *Federalist* Nos. 47 and 63. In No. 47 he tied the success of the republic to mixed government and the success of mixed government to the separation of powers, writing: "The accumulation of all powers, legislative, executive, and judicial, in the same hands, whether of one, a few, or many, and whether hereditary, self-appointed, or elected, may justly be pronounced the very definition of tyranny. Were the federal Constitution, therefore, really chargeable with the accumulation, no further arguments would be necessary to inspire a universal reprobation of the system." In No. 63 Madison asserted that "history informs us of no long-lived republic which had not a senate." He then related how the Spartan, Roman, and Carthaginian senates, whose members possessed lifetime terms, had acted as an "anchor against popular fluctuations." Madison further

---

[18]Max Farrand, ed., *The Records of the Federal Convention of 1787*, 4 vols. (1911–37; rev. ed., New Haven, 1966), 1:422–23, 2:299; "Report on Books," Jan. 23, 1783, in *The Papers of James Madison*, 17 vols. to date (Charlottesville, 1962–77), vol. 6 (William T. Hutchinson and William M. E. Rachal, eds.), pp. 76–77.

argued that the danger of a republic's being corrupted was "greater where the whole legislative trust is lodged in the hands of one body of men than where the concurrence of separate and dissimilar bodies is required in every public act." The operative word here is *dissimilar.* Madison did not consider the Senate a mere redundancy, a democratic body that existed only to block any hasty legislation that might emerge from the other democratic body, the House of Representatives. Rather, it was obvious from the Senate's different manner of selection and much longer term of office that it would house a natural aristocracy. Thus, Madison took care to assuage fears that the Senate would convert the government into an oligarchy. He demonstrated that in Sparta, Rome, and Carthage it was encroachment by the representatives of the people, not by the senate, that had corrupted the republic. Madison concluded: "It proves the irresistible force possessed by that branch of a free government which has the people on its side." Evidently, the U.S. Senate was not the branch that was intended to "have the people on its side." In his notes for the essay, Madison cited Aristotle, Polybius, and Cicero as his sources. In his previous essay, he had also referred to "the dissimilarity in the genius of the two bodies" that were to form the U.S. Congress. In the same year, Madison warned Jefferson: "Wherever the real power of Government lies, there is the danger of oppression. In our Governments the real power lies in the majority of the Community, and the invasion of private rights is chiefly to be apprehended not from acts of Government contrary to the sense of its constituents, but from acts in which the Government is the mere instrument of the major number of the constituents."[19]

Alexander Hamilton was yet another Federalist who advocated mixed government. Hamilton's outline for a speech given at the Constitutional Convention on June 18, 1787, a speech in which he advocated lifetime terms (with good behavior) for both the president and the Senate, included these statements: "Here I shall give my sentiments of the best form of government — not as a thing attainable by us, but as a model which we ought to approach as near as possible. British

---

[19]*Federalist* Nos. 47, 63; "Additional Memoranda on Confederacies," Nov. 30, 1787, in *Papers of James Madison*, vol. 10 (Robert A. Rutland et al., eds.), p. 274; Wood, *Creation of the American Republic*, p. 410.

constitution best form. Aristotle — Cicero — Montesquieu — Neckar. Society naturally divides itself into two political divisions — the few and the many, who have distinct interests. If a government [is] in the hands of the few, they will tyrannize over the many. If [it is in] the hands of the many, they will tyrannize over the few. It ought to be in the hands of both; and they should be separated." Hamilton added that the voice of the people was not the voice of God. He concluded: "Nothing but a permanent body [a lifetime senate] can check the imprudence of democracy." Eight days later Hamilton opposed Roger Sherman's measure to reduce the senators' term of office, reminding him that the House of Representatives would act as "the democratic body." He further noted that the absence of legal distinctions in America between citizens did not mean that American society was homogenous. Inequality of property still "constituted the great & fundamental distinction in Society." Making an analogy between the United States and the Roman republic, he asked: "When the Tribunitial power had leveled the boundary between the patricians and the plebeians, what followed?" He answered: "The distinction between rich and poor was substituted." He concluded pointedly: "If we incline too much to democracy, we shall shoot into a monarchy. The difference of property is already great among us. Commerce and industry will still increase the disparity." At the New York ratifying convention, Hamilton declared: "There are few positions more demonstrable than that there should be, in every republic, some permanent body to correct the prejudices, check the intemperate passions, and regulate the fluctuations, of a popular assembly."[20]

Other Federalists endorsed the Constitution as establishing a mixed government. Gouverneur Morris, George Wythe, and John Dickinson championed mixed government at the Constitutional Convention. Morris warned of the usual "encroachments of the popular branch of Government" and suggested an absolute veto by the president as the remedy. Wythe echoed Morris's concern. Dickinson insisted that the Senate should "consist of the most distinguished characters, distin-

---

[20]Farrand, *Records of the Federal Convention*, 1:299–300, 308, 424, 432; Wood, *Creation of the American Republic*, pp. 557–58.

guished for their rank in life and their weight of property, and bearing as strong a likeness to the House of Lords as possible," a body that would combine "the families and wealth of the aristocracy" in order to "establish a balance that will check the Democracy." To ensure that the Senate possessed such a character, Pierce Butler and John Rutledge opposed the payment of salaries to its members. In a subsequent pamphlet, Dickinson argued that the ambitions of the popular branch were most to be feared, having killed the republics of Carthage, Rome, and Athens. Noah Webster claimed that there were a thousand examples of the failure of "pure democracy," contended that the Roman masses had "extorted" powers from the senate, and concluded that the U.S. Constitution was similar, though superior, to the illustrious mixed constitutions of Britain and Rome.[21]

Recognizing that mixed government theory provided the theoretical foundation for the Constitution, most Antifederalists either assaulted it vigorously or denied its applicability to the American context. "Centinel" (Samuel Bryan) turned Adams on himself, writing regarding mixed government: "Mr. Adams, although he has traced the constitution of every form of government that ever existed, as far as history affords materials, has not been able to adduce a single instance of such a government." Adams's own examples proved that the balance between the orders was constantly in jeopardy, if not wholly impossible to maintain. Centinel added that Great Britain, another highly touted example of mixed government, was also unbalanced. (Centinel was certainly correct on this point. Even as he wrote, George III's porphyria was undermining the British monarchy. In addition, the House of Commons remained a misnomer at least until the mid-nineteenth century as a result of high property qualifications for voting. Like Sparta and the Roman republic, Great Britain might more aptly have been termed a simple oligarchy than a mixed government.) Centinel concluded, in a fashion ironically similar to the seventeenth-

---

[21] Farrand, *Records of the Federal Convention*, 2:299; Herbert W. Benario, "The Classics in Southern Higher Education," *Southern Humanities Review* 11 (1977):16; Gordon S. Wood, *The Radicalism of the American Revolution* (New York, 1992), p. 292; Paul Leicester Ford, ed., *Pamphlets on the Constitution of the United States* (1888; reprint ed., New York, 1971), pp. 34, 43, 57–58, 65, 189–90.

century monarchists, that mixed government was a mirage. Furthermore, he argued, even if mixed government were possible, it would promote a lack of responsibility, since the various branches would blame one another for government inefficiency or corruption. By contrast, the most responsible government would be simple in structure, featuring one legislative body elected for a short term. The Articles of Confederation government, which the Federalists were seeking to displace, was, of course, just such a government.[22]

Other Antifederalists, stopping short of a complete repudiation of mixed government theory, merely contended that the United States differed too fundamentally from the ancient republics to warrant the adoption of their political theory. At the Constitutional Convention, Charles Pinckney responded to expositions on mixed government theory: "The people of this country are not only very different from the inhabitants of any State we are acquainted with in the modern world; but I assert that their situation is distinct from either the people of Greece, or Rome, or of any State we are acquainted with among the antients." Pinckney then moved from the general to the specific: "Can the orders introduced by the institution of Solon, can they be found in the United States? Can the military habits & manners of Sparta be resembled to our habits & manners? Are the distinction of Patrician and Plebeian known among us?" Pinckney recanted his position the following year at the South Carolina ratifying convention, supporting the Constitution precisely because it proposed a mixed government. He declared: "Among the other honors, therefore, that have been reserved for the American Union, not the least considerable of them is that of defining a mixed system by which a people may govern themselves, possessing all the virtues and benefits, and avoiding all the dangers and inconveniences of the three simple forms." He explained that the six-year Senate term would give "the system all the advantages of aristocracy—wisdom, experience, and a consistency of measures." James Monroe agreed with Pinckney's original argument that the United States was fundamentally different from the ancient republics.

---

[22]Herbert J. Storing, ed., *The Complete Anti-Federalist,* 6 vols. (Chicago, 1981), 2:138–39.

At the Virginia ratifying convention he claimed that although the Roman and British governments were based on mixed government theory, the American situation was entirely different, necessitating government "founded on different principles."[23]

But whatever disagreements existed among Antifederalists over the possibility of mixed government in the abstract, all agreed that the Constitution would not establish one. Rather, the Antifederalists claimed it would produce an oligarchy. Centinel called the Constitution "the most daring attempt to establish a despotic aristocracy among freemen that the world has ever witnessed." "Philadelphiensis" (Benjamin Workman) wrote that the "lordlings" of the Constitutional Convention were "unanimous in favoring a government that should raise the fortunes and respectability of the well born few, and oppress the plebeians." "Helvidius Priscus" (James Warren?) compared the Constitution with the "draconian code" of Athens, while "Sidney" compared its supporters with the Athenian aristocrats of Solon's day who sold debtors into slavery. Patrick Henry claimed that "similar examples are to be found in ancient Greece and ancient Rome — instances of the people losing their liberty by their own carelessness and the ambition of a few." "A Columbian Patriot" (Mercy Otis Warren) declared that it was every citizen's duty to "resist the first approaches of tyranny, which at this day threaten to sweep away the rights for which the brave sons of America have fought with an heroism scarcely paralleled even in ancient republicks." "An Old Whig" (George Bryan?) concurred fully with this assessment, comparing the American people, should they ratify the document, with the tree in Aesop's story that furnished the handle for the ax of a man, who then cut down the tree. He added: "If we perish in America, we shall have no better comfort than the same mortifying reflection, that we have been the cause of our own destruction." "John Humble" wrote, with overbearing irony, that the "skillful physicians" at Philadelphia, "through the existence of John Adams Esquire, in the profundity of their great political knowledge, found out

---

[23]Farrand, *Records of the Federal Convention*, 1:402; Jonathan Elliot, ed., *Debates in the Several State Conventions on the Adoption of the Federal Constitution*, 5 vols. (1879; reprint ed., New York, 1968), 3:218, 4:326–29.

and discovered that nothing but a new government consisting of three branches, kings, lords, and commons, or in the American language, president, senate, and representatives, can save this our country from inevitable destruction."[24]

Even the few Antifederalists who advocated mixed government denied that the Constitution would create one. "A Farmer" contended: "There is nothing solid or useful that is new. And I will venture to assert that if every political institution is not fully explained by Aristotle and other ancient writers, yet that, there is no new discovery in this the most important of all sciences, for ten centuries back." But "A Farmer" denied that the Constitution would create an Aristotelian mixed government. "The Federal Farmer" agreed, claiming that it would create an oligarchy. George Mason concurred. In the 1770s, he had proposed the indirect election of Virginia senators from among men who possessed estates worth two thousand pounds or more. In 1787, at the Constitutional Convention, James Madison recorded: "Mr. Mason argued strongly for an election of the larger branch by the people. It was to be the grand depository of the democratic principle of government. It was, so to speak, to be our House of Commons. . . . He admitted that we had been too democratic, but was afraid we should incautiously run into the opposite extreme. We ought to attend to the rights of every class of the people." Unsatisfied that the Constitution had created a mixed government, Mason opposed it thereafter, predicting: "The government will set out a moderate aristocracy; it is at present impossible to foresee whether it will, in its operation, produce a monarchy or a corrupt, tyrannical aristocracy. It will probably vibrate some years between the two, and then terminate in the one or the other."[25]

As proof that the Constitution would institute an oligarchy rather than a mixed government, Antifederalists generally cited the small number of delegates to be elected to the House of Representatives and, hence, the large size of their electoral districts. As William Gray-

[24]Storing, *The Complete Anti-Federalist,* 2:139, 269, 380; 3:58, 89, 118; 4:152; 6:103. For Henry's statement, see Elliot, *Debates,* 3:46. For the statement by "A Columbian Patriot," see Ford, *Pamphlets on the Constitution,* p. 4.

[25]Storing, *The Complete Anti-Federalist,* 2:238; 5:17; Bailyn, *Ideological Origins of the American Revolution,* p. 293; Farrand, *Records of the Federal Convention,* 1:48–49; Kate M. Rowland, *The Life of George Mason,* 2 vols. (New York, 1892), 2:390.

son put it: "If we look at the democratic branch, and the great extent of the country . . . it must be considered, in a great degree, to be an aristocratic representation." He feared that the House "might unite with the other two branches" against the people. Samuel Chase agreed. He asserted: "I object [to the Constitution] because the representatives will not be the representatives of the people at large, but really of a few rich men. . . . In fact, no order or class of people will be represented in the House of Representatives — called the Democratic branch — but the rich and wealthy. They will be ignorant of the sentiments of the middling (and much more of the lower) class of citizens." The large size of the House of Representatives' electoral districts was proof, Antifederalists felt, that the proponents of the Constitution were merely utilizing mixed government theory as a respectable cloak for shameless oligarchical schemes.[26]

The Founders received both their general political theory and their principal supporting examples for that theory from the ancients. Yet it was a theory substantially altered by modern innovations. Representation removed the people from direct participation in government. Based upon a suspicion of government alien to the ancients, Montesquieu's separation of powers balanced government branches rather than social orders. The executive veto injected a greater degree of monarchical power into modern republics than had existed in the ancient republics. Most significant was Harrington's concept of "natural aristocracy," a concept essential to the American adaptation of mixed government. The eventual replacement in the United States of England's hereditary king and aristocrats with an elective monarch and an assembly of wealth necessarily increased the nation's distance from the classical polity. But the Founders' general unwillingness to recognize the revolutionary nature of modern innovations to mixed government theory is one of many testaments to their reluctance to stray too far from the font of classical wisdom and authority.

By the 1790s James Madison and Thomas Jefferson, the leaders of the Republican party, had begun to distance themselves from mixed

---

[26]Elliot, *Debates,* 3:421; Storing, *The Complete Anti-Federalist,* 5:89–90. For use of the same argument by "The Federal Farmer" and Brutus, see Storing, *The Complete Anti-Federalist,* 2:273, 380.

government theory and to support a simple representative democracy. Madison based his defense of democracy on the argument he had first presented in *Federalist* No. 10. He argued that modern commercial republics like the United States possessed so many different factions that majorities must be weak coalitions, incapable of prolonged tyranny. As the years passed, Madison clung ever more fervently to this solution to the problem of majority tyranny, a solution that not only seemed more appropriate to the American context, but also justified a form of government more popular with the public. By contrast, Thomas Jefferson and most other Republicans based their defense of representative democracy on the tradition of classical pastoralism, a heritage as ancient and revered as mixed government theory. Republicans comforted themselves with the notion that the United States could safely adopt a democracy, however vilified by classical political theorists, because the abundance of land would allow a citizenry of Virgilian farmers. The ancient republics had been great not because of their mixed governments, but because of their pastoral virtues.[27]

By the first decade of the nineteenth century the Republicans had ascended to power. Faced with the increasing unpopularity of mixed government theory, John Adams's pessimism grew. By 1806 he had come to the terrifying conclusion that the mixed government established by the Constitution of 1787 was being transformed, in substance if not in form, into a simple democracy. Divisions between political parties were replacing the intended divisions between branches. Adams declared: "I once thought our Constitution was quasi or mixed government, but they have now made it, to all intents and purposes, in virtue, in spirit, and effect, a democracy. We are left without resources but in our prayers and tears, and having nothing that we can do or say,

---

[27] *Federalist* No. 10. Madison makes a similar argument in *Federalist* No. 51. For Jefferson's pastoralism, see Douglas L. Wilson, "The American Agricola: Jefferson's Agrarianism and the Classical Tradition," *South Atlantic Quarterly* 80 (1981):347–54; Karl Lehmann, *Thomas Jefferson: American Humanist* (Chicago, 1964), p. 181; Gilbert Chinard, ed., *The Literary Bible of Thomas Jefferson: His Commonplace Book of Philosophers and Poets* (1928; reprint ed., New York, 1969), p. 32; A. Whitney Griswold, "Jefferson's Agrarian Democracy," in *Thomas Jefferson and American Democracy*, ed. Henry C. Dethloff (Lexington, Mass., 1971), pp. 46–47. For reference to the pastoralism of John Taylor, see M. E. Bradford, "That Other Republic: Romanitas in Southern Literature," *Southern Humanities Review* 11 (1977):7–8. The influence of the pastoral tradition is explored much more fully in my book, *The Founders and the Classics*.

but the Lord have mercy upon us." By "they" Adams meant the Republicans, particularly President Jefferson, whose administrations he considered subversive of the intent of the drafters of the Constitution. Ironically, since Jefferson had quickly reinterpreted the Constitution as having established a representative democracy, he had come to the same conclusion about Adams. It was of little consolation to Adams that his interpretation of the intent of the drafters was more accurate than Jefferson's. It was Jefferson's that prevailed.[28]

Nevertheless, Adams's judgment was overly pessimistic. The modern American political system is a hybrid of democracy and mixed government. The rise of political parties, combined with other developments, has democratized American politics. (These other developments include the linkage of the selection of the electoral college with the popular vote, accomplished before Adams's death in 1826, and the ratification of the Seventeenth Amendment in 1913, which provided for the direct election of senators.) Yet, elements of mixed government remain. The Supreme Court, whose power has grown steadily, is still appointed for life by the president, who is still indirectly elected. The senators' larger electoral districts still foster a more aristocratic representation than the House of Representatives, while the equality of the states in the Senate favors the small states. Hence the passage of congressional legislation requires more than simple majority support. Ironically, in their effort to emulate the systems of Sparta, Rome, and Great Britain, whose status as mixed governments was dubious at best, the Founders of the United States may have created the first real mixed government in history—though mixed in a modern sense.

But classical mixed government, at least as defined by purists like Adams, was more the victim of its own fundamental inadequacy than of latter-day changes. The rise of political parties so soon after the inauguration of the new government, parties that failed to follow class lines and that received support from each branch of government, was proof that Adams's understanding of the interests that divided the

---

[28]Adams to Rush, Sept. 9, 1806, in Douglass Adair and John A. Schutz, eds., *The Spur of Fame: Dialogues of John Adams and Benjamin Rush, 1805–1813* (San Marino, Calif., 1966), pp. 66–67; Richard M. Gummere, "The Classical Politics of John Adams," *Boston Public Library Quarterly* 9 (1957):179.

United States was too simplistic. Adams failed to see that mixed government, in its rigid Polybian form, was unsuited to a modern commercial nation like the United States. James Madison was correct in noting that modern commercial nations were heterogeneous, possessing more than Polybius's two interests, the few and the many.

Nothing better exemplifies the Founders' shrewdness than their adaptation of mixed government theory to the American context. Though based on the same Greek principle of society's need for a balance of power among its factions, mixed government theory had undergone important changes. Thoughtful men, the Founders resisted slavishness. They refused to establish a simple democracy, despite the urging of leading philosophes like Turgot. Yet neither did they simply copy the mixture of the old colonial governments, borrow the proposals of Enlightenment philosophers, or ape the ancients themselves, though anxious to learn from each of the three primary sources that made up their collective "experience." Rather, the Founders established a political system that bears their own indelible stamp. It is, to borrow a phrase from Alexander Hamilton, "neither Greek nor Trojan, but purely American."[29]

---

[29]"Philo Camillus No. II," Aug. 7, 1795, in Harold C. Syrett and Jacob E. Cooke, eds., *The Papers of Alexander Hamilton*, 27 vols. (New York, 1961–87), 19:98. Hamilton's statement concerned American neutrality in the Anglo-French conflict.

Alison G. Olson

Thoughts on Why America Chose a Congressional Rather than a Parliamentary Form of Government

WHEN IT COMES to telling us why they preferred a congressional system of government to a parliamentary one, the Founding Fathers are not very helpful. Indeed, during the entire summer when they were drawing up the Constitution the Framers never debated the comparative merits of a parliament as opposed to a congress. The Virginia Plan, which Edmund Randolph submitted as a starting point for discussions in May, said simply, "The National legislature ought to consist of two branches" and this provision was approved two days later "without debate or dissent."[1] Thereafter the Framers never addressed the "character" of this national body: they referred generally to "the National legislature," the "1st branch and the 2nd branch," the "big house," and the "small house" before drifting into the title "congress" without debate.

If the minutes of the Constitutional Convention are not much help, neither is the dictionary. *Parliament* is defined as "the supreme legislature consisting of the monarch and two houses," *congress* as "the chief legislative body of a nation consisting of the collective body of repre-

The author thanks Whitman Ridgway, Donald S. Lutz, R. B. Bernstein, and Kenneth R. Bowling for advice and comment.

[1] May 29, 1787, James McClellan and M. E. Bradford, eds., *Jonathan Elliott's Debates in the Several State Conventions on the Adoption of the Federal Constitution*, 3 vols. (Richmond, 1983), 3:32, 39.

sentatives." From our twentieth-century perspective, there seems to be a clear difference here about the relationship of the legislature to the executive: the king is a constituent part of a parliament, whereas the president is quite separate from congress. And the king is not only a working part of the legislature; his calling them to session is the occasion that gives the meetings legitimacy.[2] Within rather sharply prescribed limits the monarch can decide when he wishes to dissolve the legislature and call for a new election. Once convened the authority of Parliament rests somewhere between itself, purely (the monarch and the Lords) and the electorate (the Commons). Congress, by contrast, derives its authority from the people, and the time of its election is determined by the Constitution.[3]

The distinctions look clear enough today, but it is less clear whether we can translate them back to the eighteenth century and identify them with particular legislative functions that would in turn have influenced the thinking of the Framers. In the twentieth century, "King in Parliament" means that cabinet members sit in the Commons, propose legislation, and focus debate. Defeat on a key issue, a vote of "no confidence" from the parliamentary majority, can prompt a new election; at the other extreme, ministers riding a crest of popularity can call an immediate election. All of this is quite different from the U.S. Congress, but we must remember that it is largely a matter of evolution rather than definition. The eighteenth-century Parliament was much looser: cabinet members were not necessarily in the Commons (by 1787 the prime minister was generally assumed to be in the Commons, but the secretary of state was likely to be in the Lords, for example); any member could propose bills (the bulk of legislation in England, as in the American legislatures, came from private bills); and a ministry losing its parliamentary majority was likely to regroup and seek a new coalition before they or the monarch considered dissolution. In addition, of course, the maximum term of any Parliament was, after 1688,

---

[2] See J. R. Pole, *Political Representation in England and the Origins of the American Republic* (London, 1966), p. 4.

[3] James Wilson, Dec. 4, 1787, speech before the Pennsylvania ratifying convention: "In every community there is supreme controlling power, which I call sovereign power, Sir William Blackstone informs us that this power is in the British Parliament. . . . [Here] it resided in the people" (*The Documentary History of the Ratification of the Constitution,* 17 vols. to date [Madison, Wis., 1976–], vol. 2 [edited by Merrill Jensen], p. 485).

always established by law (three years by 1694, extended to seven in 1715).[4] Distinctions in dictionary definitions, while seemingly very clear, nevertheless allow for such a variety of possible arrangements that they do not seem to have influenced the Framers' thinking.

Neither could the Framers have been influenced by questions about the compatibility of a congressional or parliamentary system with other constitutional features they considered essential. Both systems can be based on either a written constitution or one based on custom; both can function with either a limited franchise or universal suffrage (both the United States and England had a limited franchise in the eighteenth century and universal suffrage today). Both are compatible with federalism, as witness the commonwealth countries that have federal parliaments today. Both assume separation of powers. This might appear questionable since the king is "in Parliament," but when one looks at particular powers one finds they can be as nicely separated or joined in one system as the other. Take treaty making, for example: in both parliamentary and congressional forms of government the executive signs treaties, but legislation is almost invariably necessary to make the treaty work. Look also at particular functions that we actually exercise less separately under the congressional than under the parliamentary system: for example, the king cannot be impeached but the president can, and by the legislature acting as a court.

If the very openness and fluidity of both systems suggests that the Framers here did not think it very useful to compare their theoretical

---

[4]On this, see P. D. G. Thomas, *The House of Commons in the Eighteenth Century* (Oxford, 1971), esp. chaps. 5, 10–13; Kenneth Bradshaw and David Pring, *Parliament and Congress* (Austin, Tex., 1972); John P. Mackintosh, *People and Parliament* (London, 1978), pp. 210–12; Sir Lewis Namier, "The Circular Letters, An Eighteenth-Century Whip to Members of Parliament," in *Crossroads of Power: Essays on Eighteenth-Century England* (London, 1962). I am grateful to Kenneth Bowling and William C. diGiacomantonio for letting me see page proofs of volume 12 in the *Documentary History of the First Federal Congress*. In the debate on Hamilton's public credit report, Rep. Joshua Seney of Maryland referred to another member's earlier comment reflecting a general assumption that "the British parliament and Congress are bodies very different as to power; the former is omnipotent and unlimited as to objects of legislation; the latter is not so, but restricted and confined by the constitution which controls their power." Seney agreed with this but argued of Congress that "as to objects within their power, they were as much omnipotent as Parliament" (*Documentary History of the First Federal Congress*, 14 vols. to date [Baltimore, 1972–], vol. 12 [Helen E. Veit, Charlene Bangs Bickford, Kenneth R. Bowling, and William C. diGiacomantonio, eds.], pp. 448–49).

merits, then we must look for an alternative approach to explain how the Founders arrived at a preference for the congressional system. Could the Framers have been asking which kind of legislature was best adapted to the American experience? Which was the American populace most familiar with, and hence more likely to obey by habit? When Hamilton addressed the convention he emphatically referred to "an habitual sense of obligation."[5] John Adams, who was not at the convention, pointedly asked members just beforehand, in his *Defence of the Constitutions of Government of the United States of America:* "If we suppose English customs to be neither good nor evil in themselves, [but] merely indifferent, and the people, by their birth, education, and habits were familiarly attached to them; would not this be a motive particular enough for their preservation rather than to endanger the public tranquility, unanimity, by renouncing them?"[6] Burkean views, these, but shared outside the conservative circle of Hamilton and Adams by men who feared that introducing unfamiliar institutions to the new nation would inspire the populace to undertake political experiments of their own, possibly pushing the Revolution to a more radical stage.[7]

But institutional familiarity turns out not to have been an adequate distinguishing feature, either, for colonial Americans had had experience with both types of legislature. At the imperial level, policies affecting several or all of the colonies were set by Parliament; but at the provincial level, questions were left to the colonial legislatures, comprising two houses entirely separate from the governors. The upper houses were chosen in a variety of ways, the lower houses were elected.

---

[5] See, for example, Robert Yates's version of Hamilton's June 18 speech, Harold C. Syrett and Jacob E. Cooke, eds., *The Papers of Alexander Hamilton,* 27 vols. (New York, 1961–87), 4:196.

[6] Charles Francis Adams, ed., *The Works of John Adams, Second President of the United States,* 10 vols. (Boston, 1850–56), 4:300.

[7] Compare Adams and Burke, for example. Popular governments "will defeat themselves . . . if they aim at [change] by any other than gentle means and gradual advances" (Adams, *Works of John Adams,* 4:297). "Nations are governed . . . by a knowledge of [popular] temper, and by a judicious management of it; I mean—when public affairs are steadily and quietly conducted" ("Thoughts on the Cause of the Present Discontents," *The Works of Edmund Burke, with a Memoir* [New York, 1859], 1:157). See Forrest McDonald, *Novus Ordo Seclorum: The Intellectual Origins of the Constitution* (Lawrence, Kans., 1985), pp. 209–13.

But even here the legacy was unclear. Though structured on what was later to become the congressional model, the assemblies spoke as if they imagined themselves mini-parliaments and they had copied parliamentary procedure whenever they thought it was appropriate. The fifty-five men who showed up at the Constitutional Convention were men of note in state politics, but many of them were comfortable discussing British politics as well. The Framers had immersed themselves in parliamentary history, procedure, and law (they cited Hume and Blackstone at length, and in 1796 the U.S. Senate adopted Jefferson's manual of procedure, which followed parliamentary example); they knew the English opposition writers like Trenchard, Gordon, and Bolingbroke, and they delighted in translations of Enlightenment writers like Montesquieu and Voltaire, who extolled the virtues of Parliament.[8] The English merchants they had dealt with and the lobbyists who represented them before the imperial institutions were likely to be either members of Parliament (the lobbyists, certainly, by the 1760s and early 1770s) or closely allied with particular MPs. Many of the Framers read their English newspapers, too, though there is some question (more on this later) how much their knowledge of contemporary English politics fell off after the Revolution.

If the Framers and their constituents were familiar with the way both types of legislatures functioned, which did they think functioned more effectively? Here again the answer could not have been very clear. The successes of each in its two most important relationships — with constituents on the one hand and the executive on the other — were evenly matched.

Let us take first the legislative-constituent relationship. A quick glance would certainly suggest that the assemblies did better, hands down. Consider the franchise, for example. In England and America there was a tremendous variety in the suffrage requirements. In the

---

[8]Thomas Jefferson, "Jefferson's Parliamentary Writings," in *The Papers of Thomas Jefferson*, 2d ser., ed. W. S. Howell (Charlottesville, 1988). The imitation of parliamentary procedure is discussed in Mary Patterson Clarke, *Parliamentary Privilege in the American Colonies* (New York, 1943). Thomas Hutchinson, Speaker of the Massachusetts General Court, had described himself as "being little less than a Prime minister" in 1757 (Hutchinson to Israel Williams, Aug. 15, 1757, Israel Williams Papers, Massachusetts Historical Society).

colonies the norm—if one may call it this—had been a fifty-acre free-hold or personal property worth fifty pounds, but in smaller communities almost any free white Protestant male over the age of twenty-one could vote. In England the property requirement for the county franchise, the only measure consistent throughout the country, was the ownership of a freehold worth forty shillings a year, but the borough requirement varied from ownership of a hearth to payment of local taxes to membership in a guild, and some boroughs, of course, had no voters or almost none at all.[9] In general, however, the suffrage was considerably broader in the colonies, with a majority of the free white males eligible to vote as opposed to something like 25 to 33 percent in England.[10] Elections also varied in frequency in the two areas: in England the maximum period between elections was seven years for most of the eighteenth century; in most of the colonies it was considerably less, and some had annual elections.

In addition, the colonial assemblies were probably becoming more responsive to constituent demands than Parliament was. As the colonial assemblies improved their internal organization, enhancing the role of the speakers, regularizing the committee systems, and improving their record keeping, they were also able to respond more efficiently to constituent petitioning and instructions to members, and to make their deliberations known through measures such as publishing minutes and holding public hearings.[11] We need more comparative research on law enforcement in the two areas, but there would appear to have been relatively few riots protesting unpalatable laws and a relatively high degree of compliance with provincial laws in the colonies.

Just how well Parliament equaled this achievement is hard to say. Clearly it was attempting to strengthen its constituent relations, opening its galleries to the public, initiating the publication of debates, es-

---

[9] R. K. Webb, *Modern England from the Eighteenth Century to the Present* (New York, 1968), p. 47; Sir Lewis Namier, *The Structure of Politics at the Accession of George III* (London, 1963), chap. 2.

[10] J. H. Plumb, "The Growth of the Electorate in England from 1600 to 1715," *Past and Present* 45 (1969):90–116; Edmund S. Morgan, *Inventing the People: The Rise of Popular Sovereignty in England and America* (New York, 1988), p. 137.

[11] Alison G. Olson, "Eighteenth Century Colonial Legislatures and Their Constituents," *Journal of American History* 79 (1992):543–67.

tablishing growing numbers of select committees to respond to growing numbers of petitions.[12] With a generally narrower franchise, more
venal electors, more infrequent elections, and a looser committee
structure, Parliament had a weaker set of mechanisms for meeting
constituent needs. But MPs, like their counterparts in the American
assemblies, recognized that without more substantial police enforcement than either one had, compliance with the laws was largely voluntary. So they did, in fact, respond to constituent protest expressed as
riot or simple noncompliance by repealing laws or quickly allowing
that they were dead letters.

All of this would seem to suggest that colonial assemblies shared a
more stable relationship with their constituents and may have enjoyed
a more voluntary compliance with their decisions than did Parliament.
But there was a downside to their constituent relations. The broad
franchise and frequent elections produced an electorate with serious
flaws that had been obscured by the imperial system, and one doesn't
have to read far into the convention debates to discover the Framers'
profound distrust of the populace because of these flaws. As "Centinel" (Samuel Bryan), writing during the debates over ratification, put
it, "The great body of people will never steadily attend to the operations of government, and for want of dire information are liable to be
imposed upon."[13]

One problem was that it was doubtful how far their attention could
be extended beyond purely local issues. Only toward the middle of the
eighteenth century had their interests expanded to include some
provincewide issues as opposed to town, county, or neighborhood affairs. How could their energies, even their attention, ever be focused at
the national level? Would they ever accept the principle that by the

---

[12]There is some debate over how much members of Parliament were responding to
instructions by their constituents. Paul Kelly argues that instructions became important only in the 1780s and that normally Parliament as a deliberative, rather than a
representative body, felt no need to consider instructions ("Constituents' Instructions
to Members of Parliament in the Eighteenth Century," in Clyve Jones, ed., *Party and
Management in Parliament, 1660–1784* [New York, 1984], pp. 169–89). Edmund Morgan, by contrast, argues that they were common throughout the century after the
Glorious Revolution (*Inventing the People*, pp. 209–30).

[13]Oct. 5, 1787, *Documentary History of Ratification*, 2:161.

very act of choosing representatives they "delegate[d] away their own power" on continental issues? If they did, then the Framers' generation asked, "How . . . [the] representatives can [still] be accountable to the people."[14] Under the imperial system, Parliament had provided the legislation on intercolonial issues. What happened when the imperial structure was removed?

For another thing, the colonial electors were notoriously volatile: they had turned out to vote only intermittently and only on issues about which they had strong emotions. On these occasions they voted "with precipitation and inadvertency" for candidates or propositions that offered, for example, the possibility of revenging themselves on unpopular ethnic, religious, or economic minorities.[15] They could then produce an assembly that responded to such intemperate popular biases by passing legislation with "too hasty, careless, incautious and passionate proceedings; breaches of wholesome order and necessary form," severely penalizing various minorities.[16] Under the imperial system, colonial acts were subject to review by the Privy Council, which often disallowed egregiously discriminatory legislation. Again, what happened when the imperial structure was removed? "Nothing could maintain the harmony and subordination of the various parts of the empire," wrote Madison, "but the prerogative by which the crown stifles in the birth every Act of every part tending to discord or encroachment."[17] He later added, that "a constitutional negative on the

---

[14]Noah Webster, "An Oration on the Anniversary of the Declaration of Independence" (1802), in *American Political Writings during the Founding Era, 1760–1805*, 2 vols., ed. Charles S. Hyneman and Donald S. Lutz (Indianapolis, 1983), 2:1231–32. For a discussion of this question, see Gordon S. Wood, *The Creation of the American Republic, 1776–1787* (New York, 1969), p. 373.

[15]In Virginia, for example, Robert Dinkin found a 10-percent difference in voter turnout from one midcentury election to another. In New York, the difference was 15 percent; and in Pennsylvania there was as much as a 20-percent difference in turnout between controversial and noncontroversial contests (*Voting in Provincial America: A Study of Elections in the Thirteen Colonies, 1689–1776* [Westport, Conn., 1979], pp. 148, 151–52, 155; chap. 8 explores the motives for voter turnout).

[16]"A Democratic Federalist," *Independent Gazetteer,* Nov. 26, 1787, *Documentary History of Ratification*, 2:294.

[17]Madison speech, July 17, 1787, McClellan and Bradford, *Elliott's Debates*, 3:292. See also Daniel Howe's interpretation that the judiciary was the conscience of the body politic because it had the power to correct the operation of "unjust and partial laws" ("The Political Psychology of the Federalist," *William and Mary Quarterly*, 3d ser. 44 [1987]:500). John Adams may have had review in mind when he suggested that a

laws of the states seems necessary to secure individuals agst encroachment on their rights."[18] The volatility of the colonial electorate and the assemblies they returned was enough to give the Framers pause as they evaluated the successes of the parliamentary and congressional systems they knew.

As a second measure of legislative performance, consider the relations of Parliament and the American assemblies with their executives. Here, as with constituent relations, the success record of the two institutions was more mixed than might first appear.

First appearances on this issue would give Parliament a clear edge over the assemblies in its executive relations. The British legislature did, after all, consist of the "king in Parliament." It was the prime minister's job to serve as liaison between the king and the two houses with occasional exceptions; if he could not get a majority for policies the king approved, he was expected to resign. Kings could dismiss ministers they found personally objectionable, as George III, for example, dismissed George Grenville; but at the same time Parliament could make it hard for a king to hang on to a minister he personally liked. Henry Fox expressed a widely held feeling that "The House of Commons has a right, and sometimes exerted it, to accuse a Minister; and make it very unadvisable for a Prince to retain him in his favor."[19] At any one time the government's supporters in the House of Commons consisted of the minister's own followers and members of any groups who might have joined his coalition, along with varying numbers of MPs who supported the royal policies on general principle or because they were subject to royal influence. This influence was even greater in the House of Lords, where the king could create peers and generally controlled the bishop's bench. There was certainly good evidence for

---

scholar writing a history of the American Revolution must read "the records of the Board of Trade and plantations in Great Britain from its institution to its dissolution" (Adams, *Works of John Adams*, 5:appendix).

[18]Madison to Jefferson, Oct. 24, 1791, *Documentary History of Ratification*, vol. 13 (John P. Kaminski and Gaspare J. Saladino, eds.), p. 447. Some of the states had adopted judicial review during the Confederation period. See Burleigh Cushing Rodick, *American Constitutional Custom: A Forgotten Factor in the Founding* (New York, 1953), p. 91.

[19]Cited in Richard Pares, *King George III and the Politicians* (Oxford, 1954), p. 99. Fox's comment should be read in the context of Pares's whole chapter, "The Appointment and Dismissal of Ministers."

Franklin's argument that the king had not vetoed a law since 1707 simply because he didn't need to.[20] On the whole, however, the Framers did not think this kind of executive influence, if kept within limits, was particularly harmful. Many could see no way an executive could get along without the "attachments which the crown draws to itself and not merely from the force of its prerogative."[21] And they were at pains to explain that while separation of powers was a good thing, it need not be total.

The assemblies, by contrast, rarely learned how to work with the colonial governors through any means beyond the most primitive bargaining, in which the governor was expected to sacrifice some of his power in order to obtain favorable legislation from the assemblies. There had been noticeable improvements in assembly procedure over the eighteenth century, but these had generally been initiated by assemblymen to handle better their constituents' business — rather than to respond efficiently to a governor's proposals. Only infrequently were the assemblies able to see executive authority as other than something to be resisted, hence they never developed constructive ways of working with governors to develop policies of provincial benefit.

In part the difficulty stemmed from the fact that except for the

---

[20]June 4, McClellan and Bradford, *Elliott's Debates: Federal Convention,* pp. 61–62. The king's influence on the Lords through his appointment of Scottish peers and his ability to translate bishops and elevate peers even further is discussed in Pares, *George III and the Politicians,* pp. 41–42.

[21]June 2, McClellan and Bradford, *Elliott's Debates: Federal Convention,* p. 61. For Adams's views, see Correa Moylan Walsh, *The Political Science of John Adams: A Study in the Theory of Mixed Government and the Bicameral System* (New York, 1915), p. 111. Interestingly, late in the convention the Framers debated the virtues of making a two-thirds vote as opposed to a three-quarters vote of both houses necessary to override a presidential veto. They finally decided on two-thirds because it was unlikely a president could control one-third of the votes and hence protect his veto, but "if three-quarters be required, a few Senators having hopes from the nomination of the President to offices, will combine with him and impede laws" (Elbridge Gerry, Sept. 12, 1787, McClellan and Bradford, *Elliott's Debates,* p. 595). Their arguments suggest that while the president was expected to have substantial influence, it was less than that of the Crown over Parliament. An analysis of the House of Commons in 1788 listed 185 out of a possible 557 members of Parliament, exactly one-third, as "Party of the Crown . . . all those who would probably support his Majesty's Government under any Minister, not peculiarly unpopular" (Sir Lewis Namier, *Personalities and Powers* [London, 1955], pp. 31–32). See *Federalist* No. 47 for Madison's well-known explanation of Montesquieu's views on influence: "He did not mean that these departments ought to have no partial agency in, or no control over the acts of each other."

governors of Connecticut and Rhode Island, who were locally elected, the governors were viewed as representing alien authority and interest, "generally entire strangers to the people they are sent to govern, their interest is entirely distinct."[22] And, in part the problem stemmed, as Bernard Bailyn has told us, from the significant discrepancy between the governor's generous powers on paper and his actual powers to influence assembly votes: "An apparent excess of jurisdiction in the hands of the first—the executive or monarchical order . . . coupled incongruously with a severe reduction of the 'influence' available to the executive . . . and a social and economic order that blurred the expected distinctiveness of political leadership [resulted in] a political system which in any case would be troubled and contentious."[23] During the Revolution, both state and national leaders carried executive criticism to an extreme, reasoning that if colonial legislatures had worked efficiently on their own initiative, and not in response to gubernatorial pressure, there was no need to give executives independent power at all. The convention, of course, met partly in response to the failure of this approach.[24]

Could the Framers therefore conclude that Parliament worked better than the American legislatures in terms of its relations with the executive, so in this respect Parliament should be taken as the legislative model for the new nation? Not necessarily. Somehow British legislative-executive relations had become unbalanced before the American Revolution, and the disequilibrium that characterized the relations between George III and his Parliaments from 1763 to 1776 was in some measure the cause of Americans rebelling against it. No one was sure just how this disequilibrium had developed. Historians still debate whether responsibility for it belonged primarily to Parliament or the king—did Parliament encroach on colonial questions previously left to the king or did the monarch attempt to exert excessive influence over Parliament on these questions?—and certainly the Founding Fathers

---

[22]New York Assembly, 1749, cited in Richard L. Bushman, *King and People in Provincial Massachusetts* (Chapel Hill, 1985), pp. 81, 132.

[23]Bernard Bailyn, *The Origins of American Politics* (New York, 1968), pp. 104–5.

[24]See Willi Paul Adams, *The First American Constitutions: Republican Ideology and the Making of the State Constitutions in the Revolutionary Era* (Chapel Hill, 1980), chap. 12, esp. pp. 259–75.

were just as uncertain. They had read with sympathy Edmund Burke's charge that "the power of the crown was almost dead and rotten as Prerogative has grown up anew under the name of Influence,"[25] but with James Wilson they also suspected that "a more pure and unmixed tyranny sprang up in the parliament than had been exercised by the monarch."[26] Whichever the explanation, few members would have disagreed with Madison that government must be designed so "that its several constituent parts may, by their mutual relations, be the means of keeping each other in their proper places."[27]

In terms, therefore, of their compatibility with other essential features of government, their familiarity to the American public and their relations with other branches of government, the virtues of Parliament and the colonial assemblies were evenly matched in the eyes of the Framers. The defining characteristics of both types of legislatures were so loose that their functions could develop with considerable fluidity. We will have to look elsewhere for an explanation of the Founders' choice of a congress rather than a parliament.

We may get a clue if we move our attention away from legislative practice and look instead at the symbolic role the Framers saw for a legislature in political society. It may well have been here, in its symbolic associations, as opposed to its structure and function, that the drafters of the Constitution found a parliamentary system inappropriate for the new nation. There was little doubt among the Framers that the British government had functioned magnificently—for its time and place—but transferring a form of government specifically associated with the British people after their Glorious Revolution to Americans a century later had potential drawbacks.

As an initial model, parliamentary government was deservedly awesome. It was "one of the Governments in the world by which liberty and property are best secured,"[28] "the admiration and the envy of the

---

[25] "Thoughts on the Cause of the Present Discontent," *Works of Edmund Burke*, 1:160. See Bailyn, *Ideological Origins of the Revolution*, pp. 46–51, 85–93, 130–38. Hamilton concurred in *Federalist* No. 69.

[26] James Wilson, Aug. 16, 1787, McClellan and Bradford, *Elliott's Debates*, 3:440; Richard Johnson, "Parliamentary Egotisms: The Clash of Legislatures in the Making of the American Revolution," *Journal of American History* 74 (1987):338–62.

[27] *Federalist* No. 51.

[28] Speech of William Grayson, June 11, 1788, *Documentary History of Ratification*, vol. 9 (John P. Kaminski and Gaspare J. Saladino, eds.), p. 1169.

world."[29] "Where, among foreign nations, are the people who may boast like Britons?,"[30] whose government remained "the most stupendous fabric of human invention?"[31] It had worked so well, in fact, and it was such a tempting model that Elbridge Gerry, one of its few detractors, thought it was necessary to warn the Framers against using it as such.[32] Pierce Butler thought the Framers had actually copied much of it, "We, in many instances, took the Constitution of Britain, when in its purity, for a model and surely we could not have a better."[33]

Despite the obvious attractions of the British model, however, transporting it across the Atlantic had serious difficulties. The first, briefly explained, was that while the British government since 1688 had been extolled by Enlightenment writers such as Montesquieu as the finest of its time, the example to be emulated, there was always room for improving upon it, and the world looked to the United States to do so, to go it one better.[34] The settlement of 1688 had been a remarkable achievement, but it was managed only within the frame of British political tradition. The new nation could start afresh; the torch of the enlightened

---

[29]Benjamin Rush, "Address to the People of the United States," Feb. 1787, ibid., 8:46.

[30]Curtius, *Daily Advertiser* (New York), Sept. 29, 1787, *Documentary History of Ratification*, 13:269.

[31]Adams, *Works of John Adams*, 4:358. Adams and the others were writing, of course, around the time of the convention. M. E. Bradford finds a deep reverence for the British form of government among American leaders even during the Revolution. He argues that this reverence shaped the Revolutionary state constitutions and served as a check on advocates of radical change in the 1780s. "A revolution on these grounds," he writes, "could be revolutionary only up to a point; and once independence had been formalized . . . the same reverence for the English constitutional achievement surrounded, conditioned, and provided a language for reflection on their own legal necessities" (*Original Intentions: On the Making and Ratification of the United States Constitution* [Athens, Ga., 1993], pp. 22–24).

[32]Elbridge Gerry, May 31, 1787, McClellan and Bradford, *Elliott's Debates*, 3:41.

[33]Pierce Butler to Weeden Butler, Oct. 8, 1787, *Documentary History of Ratification*, 13:351. "An American Citizen I" was at pains to make clear that "the quarrel between the United States and the Parliament of Great Britain did not arise so much from objections to the form of government . . . as from a difference concerning certain important rights" (ibid., 2:139). The author of "Rudiments of Law and Government Deduced from the law of nature" (Charleston, 1783) had earlier lamented the tendency of Americans to revert to British customs for precedents and models whereby to build our political edifice (Hyneman and Lutz, *American Political Writings*, 1:566).

[34]Jack Greene refers to "the revolutionary hopes that the world might be changed for the better" (*Imperatives, Behaviors and Identities: Essays in Early American Cultural History* [Charlottesville, 1992], p. 366). These hopes were an important element in America's usefulness to the American as was the rejection of England implicit in her very existence. See Joyce Appleby, *Liberalism and Republicanism in the Historical Imagination* (Cambridge, Mass., 1992), p. 241.

world had been transferred from England to the United States, which would itself become the model for succeeding generations. We were "a new people, situated so advantageously to give the world the example of a constitution wherein man may enjoy all thoughts, exercise freely his whole faculties, and be governed only by nature, by reason, and by justice."[35] As Robert Porter said, the rest of the world would follow the laudable example of America in constructing governments. Ezra Stiles put it even better, "Mankind has tried all the forms of civil polity . . . except one . . . and that seems to have been reserved in Providence to be realized in America."[36] With such expectations at home and abroad, it would hardly do to re-create in the New World an institution whose greatest success, the Glorious Revolution, was a century in the past. If the U.S. government was to establish a new standard of excellence, it must be different.

A far more immediate drawback, in the Framers' eyes, was their assumption that government must be adapted to the character of a people. It both shaped that character and represented it; it must "fit," and parliamentary government was bound to be unsatisfactory because American character was beginning to be identified by the way it differed from the British: "The fixt genius of the people of America required a different form of Government."[37] "American character," as it was evolving over the eighteenth century, was the result of "two overlapping processes" — as Jack P. Greene describes it, "processes of Americanization and Anglicization." Anglicization occurred as metropolitan ties tightened and the standards of the metropolis more and more came to be the primary model for colonial behavior "especially among the upper ranks."[38] A common emulation of all things English gave colonial Americans, especially the elite, a unity of language and culture that transcended regional differences.

---

[35] Turgot to Dr. Richard Price, Mar. 22, 1778; the letter that inspired John Adams to compose his *Defence of the Constitutions of Government of the United States of America.* See Adams, *Works of John Adams,* 4:278–81.

[36] Ezra Stiles, "An Oration to Commemorate the Independence of the United States of America," *Columbian Magazine* (1791), cited in Jack P. Greene, *The Intellectual Construction of America: Exceptionalism and Identity* (Chapel Hill, 1993), p. 173.

[37] Edmund Randolph, June 1, 1787, McClellan and Bradford, *Elliott's Debates,* 3:46–47.

[38] Greene, *Imperatives, Behaviors and Identities,* p. 298.

At the same time, however, Americans were coming to define them-selves by the very un-Englishness of their character. In part this was simply because in the 1780s they were beginning to see themselves as acquisitive, aggressive, competitive for mastery of the abundant re-sources of an expanding countryside in a way the English, cramped up on their small island, could never be. But in part they saw themselves as un-English because the English had taught them to be so, starting back at the end of the seventeenth century, when ideas of national charac-ter were beginning to surface in the North Atlantic world. From 1680 to 1710, England received many thousands of refugees from the conti-nent, men and women driven out of their homelands by Louis XIV's domestic policies and foreign wars. The British government found itself questioning whether the hoards of new arrivals would make ac-ceptable citizens or not, and it developed its answer not on the basis of skills, religion, or even commercial organization, but on the qualities of character deemed necessary for assimilation into British society. It could hardly avoid falling into circular reasoning: the group character of the newcomers was compared for fit with slowly jelling ideas of English character, but English character itself was identified by the ways in which Englishmen differed from other people. Having inevita-bly concluded that most of the immigrants would not make good En-glishmen, the government shipped them over to America to become citizens of the colonies, and in 1740 Parliament provided a regular procedure for obtaining American citizenship.[39]

Americans picked up two lessons from this protracted experience. First, if the British refused their own citizenship to men they later deemed worthy of colonial citizenship, they were assuming that British character was different from the slowly evolving American character.[40] Second, Americans learned that a people defined their own character

---

[39] Alison G. Olson, "The Palatine Reception in England and America: Changing Ideas of Ethnicity at the Beginning of the Eighteenth Century," paper presented at the Massachusetts Historical Society, Nov. 1993; idem, "The Palatines and the Salzburgers: Two Eighteenth Century Groups of Refugees and Their Reception in England," paper presented at American Historical Association meeting, Dec. 1992.

[40] "While the bands of Union are so loose, we are no more entitled to the character of a nation than the hordes of vagabond traitors" was a lament reflecting the awareness that their national character was only beginning to jell (*American Recorder* [Charleston, S.C.], Mar. 16, 1787, *Documentary History of Ratification,* 13:75).

by their difference from other peoples, by what they were not, and in the 1780s what they were not was British.

How particularly was our political character assuming different features from the British by the 1780s? In the analysis of the Framers, contemporary British political society consisted of three orders, each with a different interest. The king represented the interest of the royal family, something separate from the rest of Englishmen. The House of Lords represented the titled, landed aristocracy;[41] the Commons was probably most often taken to represent the rest of the men of property. The Commons was the body whose breadth was least clear, but however inclusive it was assumed to be, it included a rank or ranks of people homogenized by the common need to balance deference to their superiors with assertiveness of an independent interest. Property owners from all geographical sections of England were assumed to share common outlooks arising from similarities of birth, status, and occupation; therefore, members of Parliament from one part of England could speak for commoners in all other parts.

Ironically, there is some evidence that the very decade in which the U.S. Constitution was drawn up was the one decade in the eighteenth century when the Framers' analysis of British political society was least applicable. In the 1780s there was arguably more thrust for change in British society than there had been since the Glorious Revolution or would be again before the 1830s. In this decade, immediately after the American colonies were lost, Englishmen questioned the very idea of a tripartite division of society into clearly distinguished units with long-running separate interests, and they questioned also the homogeneity of the propertied interest represented in the House of Commons. Nothing produces a questioning of political institutions more surely than losing a war.

One question Englishmen were beginning to sense concerned the roles of king, Lords, and Commons: were they really stable? George III even gave some signs of moving beyond his family interest and de-

---

[41] Wood, *Creation of the American Republic*, p. 241. Some members of the convention, such as John Dickinson of Delaware, saw the U.S. senators representing territory, with the Senate becoming "as near as may be to the House of Lords in England"; cited in Bradford, *Original Intentions*, p. 29.

veloping a popular constituency. Not long after the American war, the king turned out of office the ministerial team of Charles James Fox and Lord North, who proposed to remove considerable East India patronage from the monarch and give it to their followers. The king's resistance was not surprising, but what *was* surprising was his replacement of Fox and North by William Pitt, who came to the prime ministership advocating a broadening of the franchise and the disfranchisement of corrupt boroughs. It was a rare case — probably the only one of the century—where a monarch used the influence of the Crown to bring into office a man associated with parliamentary reform. Could George III be turning into the patriot king so ardently wished by opposition writers earlier in the century? Could he have been assuming a popular leadership, moving outside the exclusive defense of the interests of a hereditary monarchy? Not really likely, given the disposition of George III, but it is noticeable that by the end of the decade the king, formerly quite unpopular among his subjects, was beginning to be depicted in cartoons as Farmer George, the embodiment of solid English virtues.[42]

Another concern, more immediate to English leaders than to Americans, was a growing provincial revival in England that undermined the Framers' assumptions about Parliament representing the homogenized population of a tight little island. Newly self-conscious English provincial groups were becoming aware that great differences in geographical location were producing distinct regional interests for which representatives living in London could not necessarily speak. The Americans' earlier claim that Parliament could not speak for their own provincial interest was behind this new awareness. Political reform movements like the Yorkshire movement that sprang up during the American Revolution carried it further. Associations of manufacturers like that led by Sir Josiah Wedgwood went so far as to assume provincial rather than London leadership, and among such groups as the Dissenting Deputies there was pressure for more provincial representation. Growing demands from a variety of provincial segments in the

---

[42]See Vincent Carretta, *George III and the Satirists from Hogarth to Byron* (Athens, Ga., 1990), pp. 304–5, 312–13.

1780s brought into real question the supposed homogeneity of interests among England's electorate, on which rested the assumption that all people and regions were virtually represented in Parliament.[43]

It is easy to see these symptoms of change in retrospect, but less easy to assess how much the Americans were aware of them. The Framers did not acknowledge these changes, perhaps because they did not consider them strong enough, perhaps because discussing them did not suit the Framers' purposes, or most likely because they were not very conscious of them. Indeed, the Framers' detailed knowledge of English history before 1763 sometimes contrasts rather surprisingly with their apparent fuzziness on more recent events. Certainly the Framers read English newspapers, had English correspondents, even visited England themselves in the 1780s. But their accounts of contemporary English politics were sometimes so distorted as to raise questions about their ability to grasp them in detail. Charles Pinckney, for example, seems to have garbled some of the details on the king's dismissal of the Fox-North coalition in his July 24 speech to the convention.[44]

However accurate their impressions, the Framers saw Parliament as indissolubly connected with a three-tiered society, a society divided along social and economic, not geographical lines. To them, the House of Commons represented the socioeconomic interests of the lowest tier of electors throughout England. Plainly, this role would not do for an American legislature: a parliament would not fit either American political society or American character.

Two related differences between England and America seemed important for the Framers. First, they argued, the abundance of land throughout the continent meant that we were a people rapidly spreading over wide geographical areas, so we lacked the compact settle-

---

[43]On this, see for example, John Ehrman, *The Younger Pitt* (London, 1969), p. 253; John Money, *Experience and Identity: Birmingham and the West Midlands, 1760–1800* (Montreal, 1977), pp. 33–34; Witt Bowden, *Industrial Society in England toward the End of the Eighteenth Century* (New York, 1925), pp. 168, 177; Lord Manning Bernard, *The Protestant Dissenting Deputies,* ed. Omerod Greenwood (Cambridge, 1952), p. 31.

[44]Pinckney had the younger Pitt "cabal[ing] the Fox-North Coalition." Pitt forced himself into place this way; but "Fox was for pushing the matter still farther . . . he would have made the minister the king in form almost as well as in substance." It is hard to tell from this whether Pinckney was confused or unclear or Madison's notes were rushed (July 24, 1787, McClellan and Bradford, *Elliott's Debates,* 3:343).

ment that gave England "a sameness of interests throughout the kingdom."[45] A parliamentary system, James Wilson argued, was inadequate to such an extent of territory.[46] A parliament assumed to give virtual representation to all voters because of a supposed homogeneity of geographical interests could not provide representation, haggling, and compromise on issues that divided northern from the southern states.[47]

Second, the same ease of obtaining land prevented the development in the United States of a social system based on vast differences of landed wealth and fostering a culture of deference. As one speaker said, "The British government . . . is suited to an establishment of different orders of men";[48] or, as another speaker put it, "Great Britain contains three orders of people distinct in their situation . . . we have but one order."[49] "The natural differences among such groups are much greater in England."[50]

In short, the Framers concluded that they must not revert to "British customs, for precedents and models, whereby to build our political edifice."[51] Reluctantly, they had to share Charles Pinckney's lament: "Of the Constitution of Great Britain, I will confess that I believe it to be the best constitution in existence; but at the same time, I am confident it is one that will not or cannot be introduced into this country."[52] "We have no models for a similar one. Our manners, our laws,

---

[45]Hugh Williamson, July 24, 1787, ibid., 3:84.

[46]Debate in Pennsylvania Convention, Nov. 24, 1787, *Documentary History of Ratification*, 2:363.

[47]Note also that opponents of the Constitution were concerned that *no* republican government could handle problems of a country with the size and diversity of the United States. See Cecilia M. Kenyon, *The Anti-Federalists* (Indianapolis, 1966), pp. xxix–xlviii, and Jackson Turner Main, *The Anti-Federalists: Critics of the Constitution, 1781–88* (Chapel Hill, 1961), chaps. 6 and 7.

[48]Here it was not necessary to have an upper house useful for "checking the encroachments of the crown and the precipitation . . . of the people" ("A Democratic Federalist," *Independent Gazetteer*, Nov. 26, 1787, *Documentary History of Ratification*, 2:294). But note a dissent from William Burton: "A member of congress for Pennsylvania, stands in the same relation to the United States that a member of the British parliament for Yorkshire does to the whole realm" (13:53).

[49]Charles Pinckney, June 25, 1787, McClellan and Bradford, *Elliott's Debates*, 3:181.

[50]Louis Guillaume Otto to Count de Montmorin, Oct. 20, 1787, *Documentary History of Ratification*, 13:423.

[51]Greene, *Imperatives, Behaviors and Identities*, p. 184.

[52]Charles Pinckney, June 25, 1787, McClellan and Bradford, *Elliott's Debates*, 3:177.

the abolition of entails and of primogeniture, the whole genius of the people are opposed to it," echoed James Wilson.[53] In the end, the Framers decided that the symbolism of an old parliament with all its established associations would not be appropriate for a young nation seeking to be the example of a new political order.

If, then, the Framers were less concerned with the practices of the legislature than with its symbolism, less concerned with its function than its fiction, does this suggest that they approached the question of a legislature with more emotion than reason? Probably not.

The Framers faced a dilemma. Enlightenment thinkers, of whom they were certainly a part, and the Western world generally expected them to use their reason, their resources, and their new independence to create a political structure bold and innovative enough to serve as the most advanced model for Enlightenment politics and an appropriate government for a new people. "The novelty of the undertaking immediately strikes us," wrote Madison.[54] But their experience told them that the success of that government would be measured by its stability, and stability itself depends upon habits of obedience to institutions that are familiar, not novel.

They had to innovate, but not too much. In the end the Framers compromised on a legislature that functioned as a cross between the assemblies and the parliament people were used to. But they did not use either the label "assembly" or the label "parliament" for it: they changed the title to suggest a new symbolism. And what could be more reasonable than that?

---

[53]James Wilson, June 7, 1787, ibid., 3:84.
[54]*Federalist* No. 37.

Donald S. Lutz

The Colonial and Early State Legislative Process

THE LEGISLATURES to be discussed here, those that operated during the century and a half before the creation of the United States in 1789, are, together with the British Parliament, the direct antecedents of the U.S. Congress. The relationship between Congress and its Anglo-American ancestors is a profound one for the simple reason that the U.S. Congress more or less smoothly evolved from these earlier institutions. Those who sat down to organize the First Congress did not start de novo, but drew on their collective experience in the Continental Congresses and early state legislatures. Those who sat down in the First Continental Congress and newly independent state legislatures drew on their collective experience in colonial legislatures. The continuous, gradual replacement of legislators that defines Congress is, on average over the long run, about the same as that experienced by the move to independence and then nationhood. It is peculiarly true of an elective legislature that it is defined by the evolving rules carried in the heads of its constantly changing personnel. For this reason, we must begin where the evolution of relevant rules originated, and where the line of legislators began.

Limits of time and space will require that we omit a great deal of the complexity in the process leading up to the U.S. Congress. For example, there will be almost no discussion of the place of these earlier legislatures in the imperial political system and the effects of British politics on their operation.[1] What follows is not really history as much as it is a summary of colonial and early state legislative institutions that illuminates the origins of what came to be the standard rules defining the typical post-1789 state and national legislative process. Legislatures, like all political institutions, are not "things" in the way that, for example, a building is. They are, instead, human artifacts that consist of human behavior rather than human material production. If we are to understand the development of legislative institutions it is essential that we first understand what is meant by the term *institution.*

A political institution is a patterned process of decision making that endures over time. Both the pattern and the endurance over time result from a set of rules, accepted by the relevant political actors, that frame and direct the process. In effect, a political institution is defined by a set of accepted rules. These rules may be formal and written or informal and customary. Custom results from, and is based on, the institutional memory of the actors involved, and is usually preserved through rituals that encode the behavior implied by the customary rules. Invariably a political institution is defined by a combination of written rules and unwritten customs. The implications of the combination of rules defining an institution are revealed in the patterns of behavior that are observed. That is, when analyzing a political institution, one can begin with the written rules, compare the observed behavior with the patterns the rules would predict, and infer from the difference the informal rules that also are at work.

A central paradox of political institutions is that while they endure over time, they are constantly evolving. That is, while a political institution represents an attempt to introduce a significant element of order and predictability, it also is intended to provide for accountability to a society that itself is undergoing constant change. In a democratic system where political institutions are subservient to the needs of an organized community, the changing needs of that community take

---

[1] Those interested in the dynamics of the relationship between British metropolitan politics and that of her American colonies should consult Jack P. Greene, *Peripheries and Center: Constitutional Development in the Extended Politics of the British Empire and the United States, 1607–1788* (Athens, Ga., 1986); and Alison G. Olson, *Anglo-American Politics, 1660–1775: The Relationship between Parties in England and Colonial America* (Oxford, 1973).

precedence over institutional continuity. Still, as long as a political institution meets the general needs and expectations of the community, it will continue to be recognizable to political actors widely separated in time.

Since the working assumption of this volume is that our current national legislature is an extension of earlier American legislatures, including those of the colonial era, the task of this essay is to summarize the contributions of colonial and pre-1789 state legislatures to that enduring yet evolving institution, the U.S. Congress. Institutionally speaking, we are looking for the emergence of legislative processes that are recognizable to us today. Perhaps the best way to begin is by enumerating a number of propositions that together summarize the colonial legislative process.[2]

1. Colonial legislators in the middle and southern colonies consciously emulated rules and behavior that defined the English Parliament, in part because it was the most salient model for emulation and in part because they increasingly viewed their institution as equivalent to Parliament. New England legislatures did not attempt to emulate Parliament.

2. Even when there was conscious emulation, differences in the political reality found in America led to a drift away from parliamentary forms as they were evolving in England and toward a more recognizably American institution.

3. Overall, colonial contributions to the total legislative process that characterized the early U.S. Congress are important, but limited—

---

[2]These propositions summarize the consensus found in the literature, particularly Florence Cook, "Procedure in the North Carolina Assembly, 1731–1770," *North Carolina Historical Review* 8 (1931):258–83; John Pitts Corry, "Procedure in the Commons House of Assembly in Georgia," *Georgia Historical Quarterly* 13 (1929):110–27; Jack P. Greene, "Foundations of Political Power in the Virginia House of Burgesses, 1720–1776," *William and Mary Quarterly*, 3d ser. 10 (1959):485–506; idem, *The Quest for Power: The Lower Houses of Assembly in the Southern Royal Colonies, 1689–1776* (Chapel Hill, 1963); Lucille Griffith, *Virginia House of Burgesses, 1750–1774* (North Port, Ala., 1963); Ralph Volney Harlow, *The History of Legislative Methods in the Period before 1825* (New Haven, 1917); Sister Joan de Lourdes Leonard, "The Organization and Procedure of the Pennsylvania Assembly, 1682–1776," *Pennsylvania Magazine of History* 72 (1948):215–39; Elmer Isaiah Miller, *The Legislature of the Province of Virginia: Its Internal Development* (New York, 1907); Stanley M. Pargellis, "The Procedure of the Virginia House of Burgesses," *William and Mary Quarterly*, 2d ser. 8 (1927):73–86, 143–57; Elihu S. Riley, *A History of the General Assembly of Maryland, 1635–1904* (Baltimore, 1905); and Chester Raymond Young, "The Evolution of the Pennsylvania Assembly, 1682–1748," *Pennsylvania History* 35 (1968):147–68.

primarily because as locally oriented, non-national legislatures colonial lower houses had a different range of issues to deal with than Congress, or even the early state legislatures that evolved directly from them. Because of these factors, the early state legislatures were more important in evolving the distinctively American legislative process.

4. Regardless of the varying inclination to emulate Parliament, and despite any differences in their respective circumstances, there was considerable convergence in the legislative processes used in the colonies.[3] Space limitations prevent discussion of nonconverging processes, such as quorum requirements, but we can usefully summarize convergences as including the following:

A. In almost all instances there was de facto bicameralism consisting of an elective lower assembly and a council that functioned as an upper house — relations between these two bodies tended to be cooperative. Cooperation was strong enough that many important matters, such as taxation and accounting of expenditures, were often dealt with by joint committees — even in the initiation of legislation. In most colonies joint sessions and conference committees to work out differences on a bill were part of the normal process, whether they were used frequently or not.

B. There was a constant struggle between the legislature and the governor for political power — a struggle eventually won by the legislature, largely because of its control of the purse.

C. Lower houses were generally small (fifty members or fewer in most cases) compared to post-Revolutionary houses that would average twice as large.

D. The legislature generally had control of electing its officers, which consisted usually of a speaker, a clerk or clerks to take minutes and keep all legislative records, doorkeepers, and a sergeant at arms.

E. The Speaker of the lower house was often quite powerful. Typically, he presided over the House during deliberations, signed all bills after passage, acted as chief spokesman for the assembly in its dealings with the governor, and played a leading role in appointing committee members, assigning bills to committees, and agenda setting.

F. The lower house tended to be dominated by a small group of men who met in private virtually as a party caucus to guide, if not control, almost all major legislative matters.

---

[3]Greene, *Quest for Power,* pp. 3–4, 9–10.

G. The legislature used a few standing committees, but with one exception (Virginia) usually used select committees to write bills rather than standing committees.

H. Most legislatures developed a Committee of the Whole House, partly as a means of preserving secrecy vis-à-vis the governor, but primarily as the normal way to do its work.

I. Introduction of legislation by individual members was unusual. Select committees usually wrote the initial bill. However, much, if not most, of the work of the lower house was conducted while sitting as a committee of the whole. Standing committees outside of Virginia were not generally part of the actual lawmaking process, and even when they existed were subject to being ignored or bypassed.

J. Legislatures were heavily involved with responding to petitions from individuals in the population (such as requests for tax abatement) rather than with the writing of general legislation — consequently roll call votes or formal divisions were not large in number.[4]

K. The deliberative process was invariably organized around three readings of a proposal, with ample discussion before and/or after each reading. The calm, slow process that this produced was rarely circumvented.

L. There was a tendency for the legislature to collapse executive and judicial matters into the legislative process. Colonial legislatures, for example, were involved in the nomination and appointment of judges, revenue officers, military officers, and other public officials in the executive branch to a degree that often exceeded similar powers held by the English Parliament.

M. Formal rules defining legislative procedures were adopted or readopted at the beginning of each session. These rules, relatively few in number, were either read aloud so they could be copied by hand or posted for easy access by legislators.

N. By the 1770s colonial legislatures were experienced in the collec-

---

[4]In *History of Legislative Methods before 1825* Harlow provides a list of the kinds of petitions brought before the Virginia colonial assembly. They include requests for changes in the hunting laws, bounties for wolves, regulation of peddlers, control of stray animals, tobacco inspection, road repairs, establishing county boundary lines, salary increases for lighthouse keepers, and increased fees for printing public papers (p. 15). Despite the diversity of topics the legislature faced, it is interesting that a busy session would have perhaps sixty such petitions presented — a measure of the relatively light load carried by colonial legislatures, which is apropos proposition "O" listed below.

tion of information through public hearings and the summoning of witnesses.

O. There was a generally relaxed atmosphere that emphasized open debate and the lengthy consideration of matters rather than efficiency and maximum output. Any twentieth-century legislator observing a colonial legislature in operation would conclude that these men did not work very hard. Indeed they didn't, for the simple reason that by today's standards there wasn't very much to do.

P. The legislature had control over its own rules and proceedings, and had freedom of speech and freedom from arrest as the privileges normally granted to an English parliament.

One could cite other ways in which the colonial processes converged, but these suffice to indicate both the similarities and differences between colonial legislatures and the first U.S. Congress; and it is sufficient to show why we must look to the early state legislatures, as well as the Continental Congress — especially with respect to the committee system — to find the genesis of many of the rules and practices that came to define our national legislative institution.

Overall, these convergences describe a legislative process that is recognizable as a modified version of the parliamentary deliberative model, which emphasizes the seeking of common solutions for societywide problems through debates by legislators largely free from constituency pressures. The convergences do not describe the representative model, which emphasizes responding to the expressed needs and desires of specific subparts of the people to whom the legislators are closely tied. The former model is sometimes termed the *trustee theory of representation,* while the latter is sometimes termed the *delegate theory,* or the *mirror theory,* since it ideally seeks a legislature that resembles the population viewed in a concave mirror that reduces the population to an exact miniature, identical in every detail.[5]

If the typical colonial legislature tended to use the parliamentary deliberative model, the early state legislatures tended to use the mirror theory or representative model.[6] The shift in view between colo-

---

[5]The most comprehensive discussion of these and other aspects of representation theory is still found in Hannah Pitkin, *The Concept of Representation* (Berkeley, 1967).

[6]Representative essays on representation written by eighteenth-century Americans can be found in Charles S. Hyneman and Donald S. Lutz, eds., *American Political Writing during the Founding Era, 1760–1805,* 2 vols. (Indianapolis, 1983); particularly Carter

nial and early state theories of representation is perhaps summarized in the change in language used to describe messages from the electorate to the legislature. During the colonial era these were invariably termed *petitions,* which implied that the legislature could still do what it thought best. After 1776 these messages were more often than not termed *instructions,* which implied a close relationship between representative and electorate, in which the electorate was now in control.[7] Underlying the shift in the operational model of representation, and the change in language that reflected this shift, there lay the fundamental move from parliamentary sovereignty to popular sovereignty. The move to popular sovereignty was well underway during the colonial era but was not codified as the dominant perspective until after independence.[8]

It is of interest that the U.S. Congress seems to blend these two models by using the parliamentary deliberative model as the basis for the design of the Senate, and the mirror or representative model as the basis for designing the House of Representatives. One might conclude that the major contribution of colonial legislatures lay in developing processes typical of the Senate rather than the House, but this should not be pushed too far. One characteristic convergence among colonial legislatures was that they spent most of their time servicing individual petitions from the electorate, and they granted the overwhelming number of such particularistic petitions. This would seem to place them closer to the highly responsive theory supposedly underlying the House.

Also, it needs to be noted that the House of Representatives was constitutionally established (at least initially) to make the use of the mirror theory of representation quite difficult by creating a body too small (sixty-five members) to mirror much of anything. In sum, although it

---

Braxton, "A Native of This Colony," Virginia, 1776, pp. 328–39; [anon.], "The People the Best Governors," New Hampshire, 1776, pp. 390–400; John Adams, "Thoughts on Government," Boston, 1776, pp. 401–9; and Theophilus Parsons, "The Essex Result," Newburyport, Mass., 1778, pp. 480–531.

[7]Examples of this change can be found in Donald S. Lutz, *Popular Consent and Popular Control: Whig Political Theory in the Early State Constitutions* (Baton Rouge, 1980), esp. pp. 115–18.

[8]On this shift to popular sovereignty, see Edmund S. Morgan, *Inventing the People: The Rise of Popular Sovereignty in England and America* (New York, 1988).

is tempting to see colonial legislatures as using one model of representation and the state legislatures another, and to see each branch of Congress as utilizing one of these models to the exclusion of another, these temptations should be resisted. The element of truth that each contains masks the contributions made by colonial and early state legislatures to both houses of the U.S. Congress.

This can be illustrated by discussing in greater detail two developments in colonial legislative processes that are of interest for understanding later American legislatures — the use of standing committees and the importance of an unofficial "party" organization. A discussion of these two sets of legislative rules, one written and one unwritten, will illuminate the contributions of earlier American legislatures.

During the nineteenth century one obvious and fundamental difference between the legislative process in Britain's House of Commons and the American House of Representatives was the prominent use of a standing committee system in the United States. However, the practice of using standing committees began in the House of Commons at the end of the sixteenth century, and, ironically, American colonial legislatures adopted rules creating standing committees in imitation of the British at the very time the institution was disappearing in Britain.[9] A standing committee was used in Parliament as early as 1571, but the first modern standing committee that would be familiar to Americans was established in 1592. This committee, the Committee on Privileges and Elections, was appointed to examine and report on all cases and controversies involving elections returns. A decade later this committee was automatically included in the rules adopted at the beginning of each Parliament.

The use of standing committees took a peculiar turn in early-seventeenth-century Britain, when instead of comprising a few members they were established as committees of the whole that met on specified days. Thus, for example, in 1625 the House of Commons adopted a rule that on every Tuesday there would be a session of the whole House sitting as the Committee on Courts of Justice; on Wednesday and Friday as a committee of the whole on grievances; and on Thurs-

---

[9]This discussion is based on Harlow, *History of Legislative Methods before 1825*, pp. 3–5.

day as the Committee on Trade. By 1628 there were four such "grand committees," or committees of the whole House — on religion, courts of justice, grievances, and trade, plus a more modern standing committee on privileges. This was essentially the committee system in use in the House of Commons during the seventeenth and early eighteenth centuries — the very time when American colonial legislatures were taking shape. But, even as some of the nascent colonial legislatures were emulating Parliament's organization, the rise of cabinet government in Britain was rendering Parliament's committee system moribund and then irrelevant. The basis for cabinet government was also developing in the colonies in the form of an informal committee of legislative leaders that essentially controlled the institution, but this proto-cabinet system was based on organizing in opposition to the governor. With the onset of the Revolution the executive branch became too weak and/or too cooperative to generate a threat sufficient for the continued internal organization on such a simple oppositional basis. The break with Britain did more than eliminate Parliament as a model for emulation. It also overturned the psychological basis for colonial legislative organization — but more about that later.

The British model had a varying impact in America. New York virtually copied the House of Commons committee system, Virginia's committee system was heavily influenced, but Massachusetts organized itself as if the House of Commons did not exist.[10] In general, the New England colonies did not emulate Parliament very much. There were no standing committees in New Hampshire, Rhode Island, or Connecticut before the outbreak of the Revolution, and the few that operated briefly in Massachusetts resulted from local needs rather than from emulation of Parliament. New York's emulation was a case of copying form without substance. In 1737 New York adopted the British committee system, but these committees never carried forward the bulk of New York's legislative work. They served more as memorials of "ancient English usage" than as a functioning committee system.

In Virginia, however, the form was functional in a way that was not duplicated elsewhere in America. Rather than introduced all at once,

---

[10]Ibid., pp. 6–7.

as it had been in New York, the Virginia committee system evolved slowly in response to an increasing workload that required more efficient organization of the legislature. In this instance, the tendency to emulate Parliament was matched by a real need for such committees, as well as by a determination in Virginia not found elsewhere in the colonies to get the work done efficiently. By 1769 a developmental process that had begun in the 1680s had produced in Virginia a committee system comprising six standing committees, five of which duplicated in name and function those in Parliament. However, unlike Parliament, none of these were grand committees, or committees of the whole, although the Virginia committees sometimes approached this model. Typically, the Virginia committees began the session with about twenty to twenty-five members, but the legislature added members as the session went along until they ended up with between thirty and fifty members.[11] Furthermore, just before the Revolution, the Virginia House of Burgesses took the step of allowing anyone in the legislature who wanted to attend a committee meeting to also vote on the committee, although this privilege was extended with respect to only two of the standing committees. While the Virginia committee system thus had tendencies to imitate the British institution of the grand committee, it was in fact a very modern American-style committee system that most closely approximated the first U.S. Congress. Given the importance of the Virginians in American politics during the founding era, it is difficult not to see the Virginia colonial legislature as a seedbed of modern American legislative practices.

The use of functioning standing committees as the centerpiece of the legislative process was peculiar to Virginia, but outside of New England every colonial legislature had one or two standing committees. Except for Delaware, every colony from New York to Georgia had a committee on grievances, although there was some variation in name. In New York and New Jersey this was a grand committee, but elsewhere it was a standing committee of the modern type.[12] Another

---

[11]Ibid., p. 13.

[12]This committee not only considered complaints presented to it, but also formulated complaints itself that related to problems it perceived in the colony.

standing committee found in almost all the middle and southern colonies was the committee on privileges and elections—modeled after the very first House of Commons committee.[13]

Besides standing committees, a few select committees were regularly appointed in all of the colonies, and thus approached the status of standing committees. These select committees were a part of the committee system as a result of problems that needed to be addressed whenever the legislature met. For example, by the 1770s virtually every colonial legislature had a regularly recurring select committee to reply to the governor's speech, one to audit the public accounts, and one to report on temporary laws that needed to be renewed.[14]

This brief overview of the committee system allows us to partially summarize the influence of colonial legislatures in American legislative history. First, colonial experience introduced legislative politics to North America and placed legislatures at the center of politics. Second, they served as a conduit for English parliamentary forms and practices. Third, because of local colonial conditions or perspectives, parliamentary influence on American legislative history was both limited and altered. Fourth, by 1776, despite some diversity in colonial legislative institutions, there had been a convergence toward a distinctively American type of legislature. Fifth, the Revolution short-circuited any general tendency toward following parliamentary exam-

---

[13]This committee dealt with two diverse yet apparently unrelated sets of problems. The first was any matter relating from any election. The second was any question concerning "privileges." Under English common law, a privilege was an exemption from a standing law. Thus, for example, someone might ask for the privilege of exemption from a particular tax, or from a prohibition against hunting in a certain forest, or from a law that required citizens to be in their homes by a certain time in the evening. It would seem that since so many various questions could arise under either heading, this committee would be overwhelmed. However, the total number of petitions in these two categories, while constituting a major percentage of those addressed to the legislature, was not very large in a normal session. Creating a committee with these two charges was just a convenient way to organize for business.

[14]These committee titles are fairly clear. Every session had an opening speech from the governor, so it was to be expected that a reply had to be formulated, even though the speech and reply were often formalities. This committee had nothing else to do after formulating a reply. The auditing of public accounts was an important function, and one that would arise during every session. This arduous assignment indicates that some laws were either viewed as experimental and their effects had to be gauged, or else they dealt with matters that required frequent revision, such as the setting of prices.

ple. The Revolution also necessitated a revamping of legislative institutions such that the early state legislatures, although recognizable to its members who also had sat in colonial ones, nevertheless were set on a path of institutional development that more richly endowed the future national Congress than colonial legislative experience and rendered the colonial experience less and less relevant for these future developments. In order to understand more completely this last major conclusion, it is useful to consider another important aspect of colonial legislatures — the centrality of an informal party organization.[15]

A central feature of state legislative politics after 1776 was the presence of two major factions — one that supported the elected governor, and one that opposed him.[16] This bifactional party system differed from our contemporary one in that there was little if any connection between it and an organization in the more general electorate. The mass-based political parties with which we are now familiar were cre-

---

[15]Historians continue to be needlessly confused about the terms *party* and *faction*. A faction is a group of persons who form a cohesive, usually contentious, minority within a larger group. A political party is an established group organized to promote and support its principles and candidates *in an election*. Thus, for example, we can speak of a faction within a legislature that has no meaning outside of that body, whereas a political party, even though it is a faction within the legislature, is defined by its electoral activity outside of the legislature. The purpose or function of a party is to win elections. The purpose of a faction is to support a shared position in a dispute that affects more than those who share the position and requires the consent, support, or at least acquiescence of many in the larger group to achieve its ends. The terms *party* and *faction* are equivalent insofar as party derives from the Latin root *partire*, which means to divide, and factions always involve divisions; party also derives from the Middle English *partie*, which means "side," as in one side or the other. The confusion results when the word *party* is used not only to describe a legislative faction, but also to imply that it is a political party when there is no real organization outside of the legislature that solicits votes for an election. Therefore, the term *party* is put in quotes when it is used to describe a legislative faction — it is meant to imply in the context of this essay only an organized division, or one side, within that larger body, with no implication that there is an electoral organization outside of the legislature. One key aspect of a political party is that it has a name under which it publicly organizes, not some name supplied post hoc by a scholar.

[16]Bifactionalism refers to a strong bipolar split within a legislature such that either contending side could, in a given year, gain the ascendancy over the other in organizing and directing the legislative process. This switch would occur with some regularity at not-too-infrequent intervals. The tendency toward bifactionalism is discussed in Jackson Turner Main, *Political Parties before the Constitution* (Chapel Hill, 1973); but see also Van Beck Hall, *Politics without Parties: Massachusetts, 1780–1791* (Pittsburgh, 1972); Allan Nevins, *The American States during and after the Revolution, 1775–1789* (New York, 1924); and Lutz, *Popular Consent and Popular Control,* chap. 8.

ations of the nineteenth century.[17] If bifactional politics was characteristic of post-1776 American legislative politics, then dominant monofactional politics was more typical prior to 1776.[18] Although we can
identify a shifting kaleidoscope of factions in most colonial legislatures, these clusterings, with few exceptions, were issue specific, of
limited duration, and basically subordinate to the enduring dominant
faction formed to enhance legislative power vis-à-vis the governor and
Parliament.[19]

Those who have studied colonial legislatures typically refer to a
"junto" composed of legislative leaders who regularly met in what we
would recognize as a political caucus to map out strategy and decide
policy outcomes before matters were introduced in the legislature.
The basis for these "party" organizations was the attempt to carve out
as much local autonomy as possible within the British imperial system, which generally focused on the coordination of opposition to the
governor. The condition that made such centralized control of the

---

[17]A good entrée to the literature on party formation is Roy F. Nichols, *The Invention
of the American Political Parties* (New York, 1967), which discusses the evolution of factions into parties between 1601 and 1860. One might also consult Hall, *Politics without
Parties*, and Main, *Political Parties before the Constitution*, for more explicit discussion of
factional politics in the early state legislatures.

[18]"Dominant monofactional" means what it implies—the strong tendency for one
subpart of the legislature to organize successfully for domination of the legislative
process in the face of many other factions that organize in shifting coalitions to support
one side or another of a given issue. It also implies the tendency for this dominant
faction to endure as a coherent organizing force over long periods of time, despite
contention and challenges from other groups within the legislature to replace them.

[19]Our concern here is with legislative organization and practice, not factionalism in
the broader population. Marc Egnal and Alison Olson, for example, discuss the various
factions that arose over a variety of issues in colonial America, but Egnal's essay also
shows that in the Pennsylvania, New York, and Massachusetts legislatures an enduring
leadership group typically controlled the lower house for decades at a time, despite the
various other factional alignments that came and went. Jack Greene shows the same
thing for Virginia, North Carolina, South Carolina, and Georgia. In part, the stable
leadership group reflects the so-called "politics of deference" that was typical of colonial life, but it also reflects a commitment to the trustee version of representation
dominant at the time which, among other things, emphasized consensus in the face of
factional disputes. On the other hand, the delegate theory of representation more in
evidence after 1776 would make divided, competitive leadership factions more typical.
See Marc Egnal, "The Pattern of Factional Development in Pennsylvania, New York,
and Massachusetts, 1682–1776," and Alison G. Olson, "Empire and Faction: A Comment," in *Party and Political Opposition in Revolutionary America,* ed. Patricia U. Bonomi
(Tarrytown, N.Y., 1980), pp. 43–60, 61–69; as well as Greene, *Quest for Power,* esp. pp.
22–26, 34–35, 40–41.

legislature possible was the general consensus among legislators and their constituents that maximum control by local elected officials was preferable to control by distant bureaucrats. As a result, by the 1760s not only could the governor not muster a strong second faction in the legislature to support him, his council, which in theory was composed of the "better sort" who were supposedly inclined to support him and British policies, was in fact inclined to support the lower house in their attempts to maximize local control, or at the very least not inclined to support the governor in his struggle with the lower house.[20]

The mobilization of legislative support for local control masked a natural institutional tendency with which we are very familiar today — the inevitable attempt by members of an institution to accumulate as much power as possible. That is, even after the Revolution removed Crown-appointed executives, state legislatures continued to seek dominance over the executive branch. That this natural tendency for institutional aggrandizement was part of colonial politics is witnessed by the presence of a junto in each of the New England colonies where the governor was locally elected and thus not a threat to local political control. Connecticut had its "party caucus" that controlled the legislature just as North Carolina did. While the possibility of bifactional legislative politics was stronger in New England than elsewhere, it was difficult for even locally elected governors to compete with the legislature for power. The legislature controlled the purse and the executive did not have the large bureaucracy behind him that he does today, with its expertise and daily control of legislative implementation that permits selective enforcement.

The controlling caucus typically used appointment to the select and standing committees, and often the appointment of committee chairmen, as a primary tool of dominance. They also controlled the nominations for legislative leadership posts, such as the critical position of clerk, and could control which bills did or did not come to a vote, since legislation was invariably written by select committees whose member-

---

[20]For discussion on this particular point, see Gordon S. Wood, *The Creation of the American Republic, 1776–1787* (Chapel Hill, 1969), pp. 206–14; but see also Clarence L. Ver Steeg, *The Formative Years, 1607–1763* (New York, 1964), pp. 261–62. For a more general discussion of the development of the council into the Senate, see Jackson Turner Main, *The Upper House in Revolutionary America, 1763–1788* (Madison, 1967).

ship they controlled through their appointment power. Students of the phenomenon generally have rated New York and North Carolina as having the strongest dominant monofactional organization — to the point where the legislature transacted a lot of business that clearly belonged to the executive. But the largest colonies, Massachusetts and Virginia, had powerful leadership caucuses as well.[21]

While every colonial legislature had its version of this "junto," the deeper political structure that underlay this caucus differed somewhat from colony to colony. In Virginia, for example, it was the means whereby the tidewater region remained dominant in the legislature, particularly the large landowners. In Pennsylvania, it was Quaker dominated, which translated into preeminence for Philadelphia. In Massachusetts, the dominating faction was centered around the Boston delegation, and the Caucus Club, as it was actually named in public, ran Boston politics as much as legislative politics. John Adams colorfully described Caucus Club meetings: "This day, [I] learned that the Caucus club meets at certain times in the garret of Tom Dawes, the adjutant of the Boston regiment. He has a large house and he has a movable partition in the garret which he takes down and the whole club meets in one room. There they smoke tobacco until you cannot see from one end of the garret to the other. There they drink flip, I suppose, and they choose a moderator who puts questions to vote regularly; and selectmen, assessors, collectors, fire-wards, and representatives are regularly chosen before they are chosen in town."[22] The Caucus Club, the Boston town meeting, and the Massachusetts House of Representatives were all interlinked such that instructions from constituents to legislative representatives were sometimes manufactured by the legislative leaders themselves.

Some might recognize in this description the very essence of later American legislative politics, but the ease with which one faction dominated the legislature would not be typical later. Whether it evolved into a two-party system or a one-party multifactional system, later American legislatures would be characterized more by bitter internal factional

---

[21]See, for example, Harlow, *History of Legislative Methods before 1825,* p. 47.

[22]Charles Francis Adams, ed., *The Works of John Adams, Second President of the United States,* 10 vols. (Boston, 1850–56), 2:144; but in this instance taken from Harlow, *History of Legislative Methods before 1825,* p. 30.

struggles than by factional consensus. The highly centralized, dominant monofactional system of the colonial legislatures would not stand as a major contribution to later American legislative politics.

On the contrary, this dominant faction in colonial legislatures was closer to what we would now recognize as a cabinet in a parliamentary system in that it comprised the legislative leaders organized in opposition to the governor and English interference in local affairs. It differed from a cabinet in that these men did not have ministry appointments to head executive departments. Nor was it a faction in the sense in which the term is normally understood today. Although in some states the legislative "junto" was dominated by leaders from one economic or social group from the broader society, such as the dominance of tidewater planters in South Carolina, generally this informal controlling caucus comprised leaders from what otherwise might be considered opposed factions. The basis for unity among these legislative leaders lay in their mutual opposition to outside interference, a unifying force that would disappear with independence.

This informal colonial trend to emulate parliamentary politics was at variance with the colonial constitutions that did not provide for such centralized control. This is a good example of how an institution is a combination of formal written rules and informal rules that guide practices somewhat at variance with the formal ones. After independence, the absence of a common "enemy" generally led to the disappearance of these "juntos."[23] Their place was taken by a committee system that dispersed legislative power and made it more responsive to the conflicting demands being made by constituents. Not only

---

[23]The use of this word is restricted to literature from the early twentieth century before it came to imply rule by a small military clique, especially in Latin America. However, stripped of this historical baggage, the word is a good one for our purposes here. In Spanish and Portuguese speaking countries, a *junta* is a small council or legislative body in a government. Latin American constitutions will often describe and/or establish a junta as, for example, a body to nominate judges. Its root word connotes a "conference." However, the word *junto* refers to a small, usually secret group united for a common interest. The leadership caucus we are describing here was halfway between a junta and a junto. The term *caucus* is a more neutral word in today's lexicon, but a caucus is more in the nature of a meeting of like-minded people rather than a continuous body. Perhaps we could best characterize the small body we are discussing as "a recurring caucus or conference of like-minded men that is not secret but has attendance restricted to those with political influence, and whose purpose is to organize behavior for guiding the internal processes of a legislative body."

were legislatures now more open to representing the factional splits found in the general population, independence brought several other changes that would significantly affect their internal operation.

For one thing, whereas before legislatures had relatively few matters brought to them, independence meant that the full array of issues normally brought to a government was laid at legislative doors. The dislocations, property changes, and problems that resulted from the war for independence — especially with regard to economic matters — multiplied requests for legislative action. Also, the formal rules that assumed some distinction between legislative and executive functions were codified in state constitutions into a clearer separation of powers that somewhat recast the role of the legislature. In this regard the legislatures of newly independent states were the victims of their own politics during the colonial era. Colonial legislatures had pressed for an end to multiple officeholding, whereby the governor bought off members of the legislature by giving them paying positions in the executive branch at the same time. This policy in opposition to "place-men" was known as the "separation of powers" and was explicitly written into almost all of the first state constitutions.[24] However, separation of powers quickly took on the broader, more architectonic meaning with which we are familiar today. Even with the very weak governors that were characteristic of early post-independence governments, the expectation was that the legislature would not develop along parliamentary lines with all powers centered in the legislature. This constitutional development of the separation of powers, along with the dissolution of any basis for a junto, reinforced the move away from the parliamentary model.

All of these new tendencies were materially assisted by another major change in the formal rules found in the new constitutions — the legislatures were considerably increased in size. The lower houses in New Jersey, Connecticut, and North Carolina initially remained the same size, but New Hampshire's went from 30 to 75, Rhode Island's from 40 to 140, New York's from 30 to 60, Pennsylvania's from 36 to

---

[24]For further discussion, see Donald S. Lutz, *The Origins of American Constitutionalism* (Baton Rouge, 1988), pp. 156–57; for a complete discussion of the concept, see M. J. C. Vile, *Constitutionalism and the Separation of Powers* (Oxford, 1967).

70, Virginia's from 125 to 160, South Carolina's from 50 to 200, Georgia's from 15 to 66, and Massachusetts's lower house went from 100 to 200. By 1790 the state legislatures had together grown from the total of 497 members in 1776 to more than 1,100.

After independence we suddenly see legislatures that are much larger and thus more difficult for a small number of leaders to control, and the existing informal leadership structure has lost its rationale. The increased numbers of legislators make it not only possible but more likely that the legislature will represent more accurately the factional divisions within the population. The war and independence together have considerably increased the need for legislative action, and the people have been activated by these two events so that they are more willing to make their needs known to legislators. In short, there is much more to be done in the legislature, which means a much greater premium is now put on efficiency than during the colonial era; and a much larger, more divided legislature finds itself without the traditional leadership structure to guide it. The situation fairly pleaded for new forms of internal organization. The state legislatures began in 1776 to reorganize with an eye to providing coherence, efficiency, and accountability, but the development of new forms of internal organization was cautious and fitful.

The New American Legislature

The first major change was to make the upper house elective. This did more than formalize a bicameral legislature. It also reversed the role of the upper house. Whereas before it was viewed as a kind of privy council to the governor, and thus an instrument of his office, the Senate was now a watchdog over the executive. In certain respects the executive-Senate nexus looked the same. The upper house was to advise the governor on matters of war, foreign policy, appointments, and pardons; but now the upper house was an independent body with a will of its own and interests that were distinctly legislative rather than executive. To a certain extent this was a logical development on colonial trends. The upper house, which originally had been appointed to provide the royal governor a counterweight of local notables against the lower house, had in almost every colony consistently sided with the lower. The House of Lords model had never worked in America, and now the upper house was formalized as a part of the legislature that it had already in practice become. A residual of the House of Lords model was found in the general use of a much higher property requirement for Senate candidates, but this bow to distinguishing the two branches failed to produce any difference in the policies supported by the two branches. The main difference between the two branches was that because of its smaller size, and the "clubbier" atmosphere generated by the kind of men who could stand for election, its internal processes looked calmer, more deliberative, and less fractious than in the lower house. In a sense, they looked in their internal processes somewhat more like the colonial lower houses. However, they faced the same workload, the same electorate, and the same demands as the lower house. Despite a different feel to their proceedings, the state senates would move toward an organizational form developed first in the lower houses.

At first the lower houses did not look much different from their colonial predecessors either. The legislators brought with them a set of expectations and habits that made them conservative in the face of needed organizational change. However, the effect of the increased workload could not be denied. With the exception of New Hampshire, which continued to rely on select committees, lower houses moved to a small but growing number of standing committees to deal with the dramatically increasing number of petitions. Most legislatures had three or four committees to handle petitions, some had half a dozen, and Massachusetts had eight by 1788. Table 1 lists these standing state legislative committees as of 1789 and contrasts the situation with that at the end of the colonial period.

Equally important, it became customary to refer petitions to specific committees specializing in that area. Thus, for example, petitions regarding abatement of taxes would go to one committee, and petitions dealing with agricultural matters would go to another. This aspect of the developing committee system was driven by the need for efficiency.

The need for accountability led legislatures to focus more carefully on the disbursement of funds. A few colonial legislatures had developed a standing committee on accounts, but the state legislatures

Table 1. Standing committees in colonial and early state legislatures

1770	1789
New Hampshire None	None
Massachusetts (1) On petitions regarding the sale of land	(1) Finance (2) Encouragement of arts, agriculture, and manufactures (3) Incorporation of towns and town affairs (4) Accounts (5) New trials (6) Abatement of taxes (7) Petitions regarding the sale of real estate (8) Naturalization of aliens
Connecticut None	None
Rhode Island None	None
New York (1) Privileges and elections	(1) Privileges and elections (2) Ways and means (3) Grievances (4) Courts of justice
New Jersey (1) Grievances	(1) Accounts
Pennsylvania (1) Grievances	(1) Ways and means (2) Claims (3) Accounts
Maryland (1) Grievances and courts of justice (2) Accounts (3) Privileges and elections	(1) Grievances and courts of justice (2) Privileges and elections (3) Claims (4) Trade and manufactures
Virginia (1) Religion (2) Privileges and elections (3) Propositions and grievances (4) Courts of justice (5) Claims (6) Trade	(1) Religion (2) Privileges and elections (3) Propositions and grievances (4) Courts of justice (5) Claims (6) Commerce

Table 1. Continued

1770	1789
North Carolina	
(1) Accounts	(1) Public bills
(2) Claims	(2) Claims
(3) Propositions and grievances	(3) Propositions and grievances
(4) Privileges and elections	(4) Privileges and elections
	(5) Finance
	(6) Indian affairs
South Carolina	
(1) Grievances	(1) Grievances
(2) Privileges and elections	(2) Privileges and elections
	(3) Religion
	(4) Ways and means
	(5) Accounts
	(6) Public roads, bridges, causeways, and ferries
Georgia	
(1) Grievances	(1) Accounts
(2) Privileges and elections	(2) Privileges and elections
	(3) Committee on petitions no. 1
	(4) Committee on petitions no. 2
	(5) Committee on petitions no. 3

Source: Data from Ralph Volney Harlow, *The History of Legislative Methods in the Period before 1825* (New York, 1917), 259–61.

moved to a near universal use of such a committee. All bills presented to the state for payment were sent to a committee on accounts, whether it dealt with the purchase of supplies, public printing, caring for the poor, or transporting military supplies. This job, which today would go to the Treasury Department, was time consuming and kept the committee busy. That the job went initially to the legislature is a measure of the extent to which post-independence legislatures were carrying on in the tradition of colonial legislatures — only now the workload necessitated a standing committee.

Another standing committee that came into general use did not rest on colonial precedent and thus took longer and required more experimentation before taking final form. The absence of strong, independent governors in the new state governments to develop budgetary proposals, plus the inefficacious experience with simply printing money, combined to make legislators more sensitive to basing taxation on careful investigation. Committees were appointed to gather the information and make the estimates needed for fiscal planning. Initially, financial matters tended to be divided among several committees with no coordination or even personnel overlap between them, as had also been the general practice in colonial legislatures. One committee might be charged with preparing a tax bill, another with coming up with any means possible to raise money, and a third with restoring public credit. Although Virginia was the first state to appoint a ways and means committee that framed revenue bills (in 1779–80), Massachusetts was the first state to develop a coherent committee in response to fiscal matters. The Massachusetts ways and means committee was charged in 1780 with all aspects of finances, from monetary reform and taxation to preparing a budget and making appropriations. The committee developed a complete and coherent package that was not only presented to the legislature but to the people.

As effective as this committee was, Massachusetts did not keep it from year to year but returned to several select committees with divided charges until late in the decade, when a permanent finance committee was established. South Carolina in 1783 and North Carolina in 1784 moved to permanent ways and means committees that were used more consistently than in Massachusetts. These were also distinguished by having subcommittees that specialized in various aspects of the total financial picture. Pennsylvania had a well-developed and effective permanent finance committee in place by 1790, as did New York, although in the latter case many financial matters were still sent to select committees. None of the other states had by this date completed their respective experiments and established a permanent committee to deal with raising and/or spending money.

Aside from the standing committees for handling finances, accounts, and petitions, a number of committees were usually established that dealt with specific areas of general importance, such as commerce, agriculture, manufactures, and roads, although the areas were often blended. For example, Massachusetts had a committee charged with the encouragement of arts, agriculture, and manufactures. Maryland had a standing committee on manufactures, trade, and commerce. South Carolina had one on "Public Roads, Bridges,

Causeways, and Ferries." Perhaps equally important, whereas in colonial legislatures bills were usually written by select committees, except in Virginia, where they tended to be written by standing committees, legislation in the early state legislatures came primarily from standing committees with a certain amount of expertise in the area. Overall, developments in the committee system resulted in a greater amount of work being done more efficiently and with a higher level of expertise and accountability.

These developments were neither smooth nor inevitable. The confusion engendered by a suddenly much larger legislature with many inexperienced members taking on a greatly expanded workload without the old leadership mechanisms in place led to the simultaneous development in six states of a select committee whose job was to present to the House an outline of the work to be done during the session, including a list of bills that should be drawn up.[25] Part of its function was similar to today's steering committee, but in fact it raised for the last time the possibility of a move toward a parliamentary system.

North Carolina most clearly showed this possibility. It developed a committee on public bills, sometimes called the Grand Committee, which controlled the legislative agenda so completely that it became for a while the effective governing body of the state. Composed of the most powerful members of both houses, this joint standing committee by the late 1780s essentially formulated government policies and through its appointment powers directed the administration of these policies.[26] The key to its power lay in a governor who was elected by the assembly and thus its chosen creature, and in a constitution that granted considerable executive power to the legislature, and thus, by implication, to the committee on public bills.

Virginia provided a competitive model in which the legislative agenda was effectively set by the governor. Communications from the governor where distributed to the appropriate committees or presented to the Committee of the Whole House, which allowed him to have considerable effect on the legislative agenda, whereas in North

---

[25]These six states were New Hampshire, Massachusetts, Pennsylvania, North Carolina, South Carolina, and Georgia.

[26]The legislature was given power to appoint the attorney general, secretary of state, treasurer, members of the judiciary, and military officers, among others.

Carolina communications from the governor always went to the committee on public bills. By 1789 North Carolina had an internal power structure that could have allowed it to evolve toward a parliamentary system; but in the other states with a similar committee on public bills, there was no such trend. The gradual constitutional rebuilding of a more independent executive with real power partially explains why these other states moved to follow the Virginia model. Also, no other state provided so much executive power to the legislature in its constitution. Finally, the evolution of the committee system we have just described resulted in an effective way to organize legislative business that precluded the need for a central organizing committee. Bills and petitions introduced from the outside usually had a natural home, as did the recommendations from the governor. Agenda setting was more dispersed in North Carolina, but as the effectiveness of the committee system improved, agenda setting became more organized. It is perhaps no accident that as the committee system improved between 1776 and 1790 the various committees on public bills had less and less to do and simply faded away.

This brief discussion illuminates not only the road not taken but also the reasons for a historically recurring pattern in American legislative politics. Although we no longer are likely to develop a parliamentary system, whenever an executive is weak or from a different party than that which is in a majority in the legislature, we see a resurgence of the "North Carolina model" in the relevant legislature. Agenda setting seems to move from executive initiative to legislative initiative. One cannot help but be struck by how, in early 1995, Newt Gingrich was treated like a new president by the media, right down to frequent references to the "first hundred days," the "honeymoon period," and an agenda that looks like the Republican equivalent (in scope, not in content) to the New Deal. At the national level this legislative ascendancy in the face of a weakened executive is similar to the Johnson-Rayburn era during Eisenhower's presidency and the Joe Cannon era from 1903 to 1911.

This proto-parliamentary version in American legislative history will never become known as the "North Carolina model," at least in part because it does not describe any particular tendency in contemporary North Carolina legislative behavior. However, this periodically recurring pattern in American national and state legislative history first appeared in North Carolina's early state legislative history as the prominent and typical alternative to a legislature harnessed to a strong, effective executive; and as such it is one more indication of the importance of the early state legislatures for understanding post-1789 American legislative institutions.

Committee Procedures

There is very little direct, nonanecdotal information about how legislative committees carried on their work in the 1780s, and the literature on the topic is characterized by a good deal of speculation and inferential conclusions. However, a few interesting points about which we are certain bear repetition. Since standing committees were still a relatively new phenomenon after 1776, those who designed state houses usually did not take into account the need for committees to have a place to meet. In Massachusetts, committees met in what had been originally storage rooms on the third floor of the old State House, which does not imply a very high status for committee work. In New Jersey, they sometimes met in the old Meeting House, while in New York they might meet in the council chamber or Speaker's room. Since New York had four standing committees, at least half of them had to meet regularly somewhere else — usually in a private home. In Pennsylvania, there was a committee room at the east end of the State House, but once again since there were three standing committees this did not suffice and private homes were often used. In the other states, including Virginia, committees basically met in private homes, although in 1779 Virginia made state-owned committee rooms available.

Committee meetings were squeezed into times of the day when they did not conflict with normal legislative processes. Usually this meant they met in the evenings. Virginia also had morning committee meetings before the House assembled. However, standing committees in Massachusetts often met during the hours when the legislature was deliberating, unless committee members were needed on the floor to help provide a quorum. Membership on a standing committee therefore made for a very long day, and there were frequent complaints about fatigue and lack of time for normal living. It comes as no surprise, then, that outside of New England absences from committee meetings were a serious problem. Georgia resorted to fining absent committee members, but no evidence survives to support the effectiveness of this tactic. The New England states cleverly avoided the most severe manifestation of the problem by not having standing committees. While select committees in New England might still have attendance problems, a member of such a committee had a lighter workload for a much shorter period of time than did members of standing committees in other states, and they probably spent less time dodging committee meetings.

Conclusion

By 1789 Americans had evolved a legislative process guided by rules, both external and internal, considerably at variance with the parliamentary model. From a perspective of two centuries later, American legislative developments between 1619 and 1789 look relatively smooth and perhaps inevitable. In fact, the process was slow, guided by trial and error, somewhat fitful, and the outcome was not foreordained—it could have gone in a different direction. At the same time, despite the upheavals surrounding independence from Britain, the process was continuous, slowly cumulative, and had a logic guided by historical needs and circumstances, as well as by principles of self-government and English common law, that with hindsight does provide a kind of internal coherence for what finally did emerge.

Starting backward from 1789, we can trace, unambiguously, a line of descent from a relatively primitive early-seventeenth-century British Parliament. From this origin, even more primitive, local legislatures arise in North America from a transplanted parliamentary seed that was somewhat mutated by the presence of a stronger gene for popular government, a correspondingly weakened gene for aristocratic traits, and fewer obstacles to its independent growth. As these embryonic elements differentiated over time, a more complex, effective, efficient, and stable institution gradually arose. The primary contribution of colonial legislatures to the American institution of a national Congress, then, lay in their very existence and the deep experience they provided American politicians in the design and operation of legislatures. The first state constitutions were written by men steeped in colonial legislative politics. These same experienced legislators formed the core of those who operated the new state legislatures, served in the Continental Congresses, and wrote the three great American documents of foundation — the Declaration of Independence, the Articles of Confederation, and the U.S. Constitution. It is difficult to overestimate the importance of this long-term legislative experience during the colonial era. Those of us who have witnessed the attempts of Eastern Europeans to erect and operate political systems built around legislatures cannot help but be impressed by how much easier and more effective their efforts would be if they could draw upon more than a hundred years of continuous legislative experience as the Founders of America were able to do.

Table 1 is a simple and efficient exemplar of the process. Across the great divide of the Revolution we can see both continuity and development in legislative organization and process. Across the other great divide, represented by the writing and adoption of the U.S. Constitution, we will see similar continuity and development between the First Federal Congress and the early state legislatures. The continuous process will proceed so deliberately that the U.S. Congress of the 1860s will still look as much, if not more, like the early state legislatures as it will the present U.S. Congress. The evolving rules carried in the heads of overlapping legislators spanning almost four centuries on American soil constitutes one of the most enduring and successful political institutions in human history — an institution in which the current U.S. Congress is but a passing moment linking past and future.

R. B. Bernstein

Parliamentary Principles, American Realities

The Continental and Confederation Congresses, 1774–89

Introduction

ON MARCH 2, 1789, Charles Thomson, the secretary of the Confederation Congress, desperately searched the streets of New York City for a member of Congress. Thomson had served the Congress, in its several incarnations, since 1774; in some ways, and especially as the Confederation Congress had not secured a quorum since October 10, 1788, Thomson was the incarnation of American government under the Articles of Confederation. Now, two days before the Articles were to be supplanted by a Congress of the United States under the newly adopted Constitution, Thomson worried that the Confederation Congress might pass out of existence without even one official mourner at its funeral. Finally, Thomson found Philip Pell, a delegate from New York. Thomson recorded Pell's attendance

My sincerest thanks to Professors William E. Nelson and John Phillip Reid, New York University Law School; Ene Sirvet, editor, The Papers of John Jay, Columbia University; Kenneth R. Bowling, Charlene Bangs Bickford, and Helen E. Veit of the *Documentary History of the First Federal Congress;* John P. Kaminski, Gaspare J. Saladino, Richard Leffler, and Charles Schoenleber of the *Documentary History of the Ratification of the Constitution;* and my fellow panelists at the 1994 Capitol Historical Society conference. I want particularly to thank Joanne B. Freeman of the Department of History, University of Virginia, for our many spirited and stimulating discussions of "the guys" and this historical period.

This paper condenses parts of chapters 2 and 3 of R. B. Bernstein, *"Conven'd in Firm Debate": The First Congress as an Experiment in Government, 1789–1791* (forthcoming).

in the journal of the old Congress, and then the New Yorker was free to go.[1]

The ignominious end of the Articles of Confederation presaged the low historical reputation of the Continental and Confederation Congresses; the posthumous fame of those institutions has traced a weaving path paralleling the evolving historiography of American politics and government between 1774 and 1789.[2] Historians once dismissed the Continental and Confederation Congresses as symbols of a failed experiment in decentralized general government, thankfully abandoned with the adoption of the Constitution.[3] By contrast, in the last half-century, historians have begun to reevaluate the Articles of Confederation, the Continental Congress (which framed them), and the Confederation Congress (which held the union together under them and paved the way in 1787–89 for their—and its own—replacement).[4]

---

[1] Kenneth R. Bowling, "Goodbye 'Charle': The Lee-Adams Interest and the Political Demise of Charles Thomson, Secretary of Congress, 1774–1789," *Pennsylvania Magazine of History and Biography* 100 (1976):314–35; Edmund Cody Burnett, *The Continental Congress* (New York, 1941), p. 726.

[2] On the changing historiographical fortunes of the Confederation period, see Richard B. Morris, "The Confederation Period and the American Historian," *William and Mary Quarterly*, 3d ser. 13 (1956):139–56; idem, *The American Revolution Reconsidered* (New York, 1967), chaps. 3 and 4; and Richard B. Bernstein with Kym S. Rice, *Are We to Be a Nation?: The Making of the Constitution* (Cambridge, Mass., 1987), chap. 2.

Note that, unlike the conventional practice as described by Calvin C. Jillson and Rick K. Wilson in their admirable study, *Congressional Dynamics: Structure, Coordination, and Choice in the First American Congress, 1774–1789* (Stanford, Calif., 1994), p. 345 n. 1, I have preserved the distinction in nomenclature between the Continental and Confederation Congresses, even though the continuities between them far outweigh the sum of the differences. The at-best quasi-legitimate status of the Continental Congress in its various incarnations before 1781, and the institutional legitimacy accruing to the Confederation Congress from its roots in the Articles of Confederation, combine to justify the use of this terminology.

[3] The principal attacks on the Articles are John Fiske, *The Critical Period in American History, 1783–1789* (Boston, 1888), and Andrew C. McLaughlin, *The Confederation and the Constitution, 1783–1789* (New York, 1906). Fiske's book, written for a general audience by a historical popularizer without academic training, at best was obsolete within a decade of its first appearance; McLaughlin's book, a key volume in the original American Nation series, edited by Albert Bushnell Hart, is still valuable as historical scholarship.

[4] The principal scholarly defender of the Articles of Confederation was the late Merrill M. Jensen. His principal contributions to the historiography of the Confederation and the Confederation Congress include *The Articles of Confederation: An Interpretation of the Social-Constitutional History of the American Revolution, 1774–1781* (Madison,

As part of their reevaluation of government under the Articles of Confederation, historians have acknowledged that the Continental and Confederation Congresses played a prominent role in the thinking of those who devised the Congress authorized by the Constitution.

First, the Continental and Confederation Congresses comprised the only national legislature of which the Framers of the Constitution had firsthand experience. Nearly four-fifths of the delegates to the Federal Convention — forty-one of fifty-five — had been, or were then, delegates to Congress; even if we add the twenty-four delegates who were chosen but failed to attend, a clear majority — forty-eight of seventy-nine — had at least some experience of Congress.[5]

Second, the Confederation Congress was the first audience for the Framers' handiwork: it had authorized the convention and would be the first to evaluate that body's results. Therefore, congressional reactions to the convention's recommendations preoccupied convention delegates in Philadelphia and Congress in New York.[6]

Third, the Continental and Confederation Congresses were, in large part, the reasons for the convention and the roots of its ambiguous mandate; the convention's mere existence constituted a harsh critique of the Articles and of the Congress at their core.[7] And the

---

1940), *The New Nation: A History of the United States during the Confederation, 1781–1789* (New York, 1950), and *The American Revolution within America* (New York, 1974).

Leading studies of the Confederation period that have appeared since Jensen include H. James Henderson, *Party Politics in the Continental Congress* (New York, 1974); Jack N. Rakove, *The Beginnings of National Politics: An Interpretive History of the Continental Congress* (New York, 1979); and Richard B. Morris, *The Forging of the Union, 1781–1789* (New York, 1987). Jillson and Wilson, *Congressional Dynamics,* appeared after I delivered the original version of this paper; I am deeply indebted to this valuable study for its confirmation of the earlier paper's argument and findings, and for its suggestive and challenging approach to the history of the Continental Congress (and its successor, the Confederation Congress) as a political institution. See also, Jerrilyn Green Marston, *King and Congress: The Transfer of Political Legitimacy, 1774–1776* (Princeton, 1988).

[5]Compare the membership list in the Continental and Confederation Congresses presented in Jillson and Wilson, *Congressional Dynamics,* app. E at pp. 330–42, to that of the delegates to the Federal Convention provided in Charles C. Tansill, ed., *Documents Illustrative of the Formation of the Union of the American States* (Washington, D.C., 1927), pp. 85–86.

[6]See Bernstein with Rice, *Are We to Be a Nation?,* chap. 7.

[7]Ibid., chaps. 4, 6. See also the slashing critique of the Articles of Confederation — and thus of the Confederation Congress — in Hamilton's *Federalist* No. 15; for a discussion of Hamilton's critique of the Confederation as a core component of his argument in *The Federalist* for an energetic national government, see Richard B. Bernstein, "*The Federalist* on Energetic Government: *The Federalist* Nos. 15, 70, and 78," in *Roots of the*

convention delegates—indeed, every major figure in and observer of American politics—knew it. Two examples will suffice. In March of 1787 George Washington wrote to James Madison: "My wish is, that the Convention may adopt no temporizing expedients, but probe the defects of the Constitution"—that is, the structure of American government—"to the bottom, and provide radical cures, whether they are agreed to or not." By "defects" he meant the defects of Congress.[8] Nearly half a century later, in a letter written in 1832, Madison sought to instruct students of the history of the Federal Convention: "In expounding the Constitution and deducing the intention of its Framers, it should never be forgotten, that the great object of the Convention was to provide, by a new constitution, a remedy for the defects of the existing one."[9] Again, the "defects" Madison had in mind were the defects of the Continental and Confederation Congresses.

Most important, the Framers of the Constitution, like all Americans of the Revolutionary generation, confronted two linked issues that dominated American experiments in government throughout this period: what kind of polity the Americans were to have and what kind of politics that polity would support. The Framers embraced the prevalent assumption that the core of any form of government for an American republic had to be a legislature. They therefore focused their inquiries on the character of a legislature, its electorate, and its members. And, whether as models for emulation or for avoidance, the Continental and Confederation Congresses were the only exemplars of an American national legislative and representative body on a continental scale.

Context: Two Concepts of Legislatures

American ideas in the Revolutionary era about how legislatures do and should operate evolved within an intellectual context having roots on

---

Republic: American Founding Documents Interpreted, ed. Stephen L. Schechter (Madison, 1990), pp. 335–80.

[8]George Washington to James Madison, Mar. 31, 1787, in William T. Hutchinson et al., eds., *The Papers of James Madison,* 17 vols. (Chicago and Charlottesville, 1962–), 9:342–45 (quote on p. 344).

[9]James Madison to Professor Davis, Montpelier, 1832, reprinted in Max Farrand, ed., *The Records of the Federal Convention of 1787,* 4 vols. (1911; rev. ed., New Haven, 1937), 3:520.

both sides of the Atlantic Ocean. That context, which took generations to develop, shaped the Americans' knowledge of such institutions as Parliament, the colonial and state legislatures, and — most important for our purposes — the Continental and Confederation Congresses. In turn, it shaped the Americans' efforts to devise the institution that ultimately succeeded the Continental and Confederation Congresses — the Constitution of the United States.

American concepts of legislatures formed a spectrum framed by two opposed models: *deliberative* and *representational*. Both models delineated how their proponents believed legislatures *should* operate; each model's advocates caricatured the opposing model to depict how legislatures should *not* operate. As is so often the case with models, the legislatures that the Americans knew — specifically, the Continental and Confederation Congresses (and the Congress of the United States that was to replace them) — combined features of both models in varying proportions.

The Deliberative Model

For generations both Britons and British colonists in North America had aspired to realize the deliberative ideal in their political systems. In his 1774 address to the electors of Bristol, Edmund Burke summarized and extolled the deliberative model: Parliament is "a *deliberative* assembly of *one* nation, with *one* interest, that of the whole, where, not local purposes, not local prejudices ought to guide, but the general good, resulting from the general reason of the whole."[10]

The deliberative model required a special kind of legislator to make it work — one who considered only the general interest of the polity. Not his own interests, nor those of his friends, nor even the particular interests of those who elected him should deflect him from the pursuit of that goal. To that end, he should possess attributes vital to the exercise of sound judgment: talent, education, virtue, and, above all, economic and political independence. In short, the deliberative model incarnated the principles that Americans associated with Parliament at its best.

---

[10]Edmund Burke's speech to the electors of Bristol, Nov. 3, 1774, excerpted in Ross Hoffman and Paul Levack, eds., *Burke's Politics* (New York, 1949), pp. 114–17, quote on p. 116.

Deliberative legislators conducted their business within a matrix of rules and customs — *parliamentary* law — devised to foster reasoned and reasonable discussion. The hallmark of the deliberative legislator was his mastery of parliamentary law; thus, assemblies throughout the English-speaking world, especially in British North America, adopted parliamentary procedure, with only the most necessary accommodations to local conditions. They did so for three reasons. It was *convenient:* parliamentary procedure was the sole body of legislative procedure readily available to the colonists. It was *legitimate:* a colonial legislature using procedures developed by the Western world's greatest legislative body was claiming to be as legitimate as its model. And it was (they hoped) *aspirational:* parliamentary procedure would induce them to aspire to — perhaps to achieve — the high standards that they believed Parliament set.[11]

Those who rejected the deliberative model did not reject the goal it was supposed to achieve. Rather, they dismissed the ideal of the deliberative legislator at its core. As justification for spurning an ideal so generally shared throughout the Atlantic civilization, they invoked the equally prevalent assumption that the character of a political institution was determined by the character of its members; this postulate, they contended, made it impossible to base a legislature on a model deliberative legislator with no basis in reality. Nobody, they argued, could maintain the disinterested perspective necessary to define the general interest and to craft measures to give it effect. Either a legislator's apparent disinterestedness might be a pose cloaking his commitment to goals benefiting a faction, or it might be a delusion preventing the legislator from perceiving his own partisanship or biases. Indeed, these Americans feared, pretensions to enlarged views or disinterestedness might serve as a cloak for restoring the aristocracy with all its dangers.[12] Even if there were such a thing as a disinterested legislator,

---

[11]For an illustration of the importance that leading American politicians of this era attached to parliamentary procedure and parliamentary law, see Wilbur Samuel Howell, ed., *Jefferson's Parliamentary Writings* (Princeton, 1988) (vol. 2 of series 2 of Julian P. Boyd et al., eds., *The Papers of Thomas Jefferson*, 30 vols. [Princeton, 1950–]). See also Ralph V. Harlow, *The History of Legislative Methods to 1825* (New Haven, 1917); George Edward Frakes, *Laboratory of Liberty: The South Carolina Legislative Committee System, 1719–1776* (Columbia, S.C., 1970).

[12]Thus, in the 1788 New York ratifying convention, Melancton Smith warned of the

they concluded, there would be few of them in any legislative body; and those few would be overwhelmed by selfish, interested colleagues who would prevent them from fulfilling their responsibilities.[13]

The Representational Model

Those Americans who therefore rejected the deliberative ideal championed instead a legislature whose members would serve as faithful agents of the people, following their instructions and articulating their interests. Instead of seeking an idealized deliberative legislator as the basis for a sound republican legislature, they based their model legislature on the concept of actual representation; instead of relying on the individual legislator's judgment, they stressed his duty to be a devoted representative of his constituents.[14] The representational model gave the people control over the government by ensuring that their representatives in the legislature spoke for their constituents' interests; in the aggregate, these interests were supposed to amount to the interests of the whole — the only sound basis for informed public policy. Only the fullest airing of interests and grievances, the closest attention to the people's full range of needs and wants, could provide a sound foundation for governance. On June 16, 1787, William Paterson of New Jersey distilled the representational ideal into one sentence when he told the Federal Convention: "I came here not to speak my own sentiments, but the sentiments of those who sent me."[15]

Advocates of the representational model therefore sought to shape

---

dangers of a system of representation that would produce a government of "the natural aristocracy of the country": "The great easily form associations; the poor and middling class form them with difficulty. If the elections be by plurality, as probably will be the case in this state, it is almost certain, none but the great will be chosen — for they easily unite their interest — The common people will divide, and their divisions will be promoted by the others. . . . From these remarks it appears that the government will fall into the hands of the few and the great. This will be a government of oppression" (speech in the New York ratifying convention, June 20–21, 1788, reprinted in Philip Kurland and Ralph Lerner, eds., *The Founders' Constitution*, 5 vols. [Chicago, 1987], 1:410–11, quote on p. 411).

[13]Even so ardent an advocate of restoring the deliberative model as James Madison conceded, in *Federalist* No. 10: "Enlightened statesmen will not always be at the helm."

[14]On representation, see generally J. R. Pole, *Political Representation in England and the Origins of the American Republic* (London, 1966); John Phillip Reid, *The Concept of Representation in the Age of the American Revolution* (Chicago, 1989).

[15]William Paterson, speech of June 16, 1787, in Farrand, *Records of the Federal Convention*, 1:250.

the system of representation to produce a legislature whose members, taken together, would embody the whole electorate. This ideal acquired such persuasiveness in the 1770s in America that it could unite even such truculent antagonists as Thomas Paine and John Adams. In his influential 1776 pamphlet *Thoughts on Government,* John Adams addressed this paramount goal in framing new governments: "This representative assembly . . . should be in miniature an exact portrait of the people at large. It should think, feel, reason and act like them. That it may be the interest of this assembly to do strict justice at all times, it should be an equal representation, or, in other words, equal interests among the people should have equal interests in it. Great care should be taken to effect this, and to prevent unfair, partial, and corrupt elections."[16]

In *Four Letters on Interesting Subjects,* another influential pamphlet that appeared in Philadelphia at almost the same time as *Thoughts on Government,* Thomas Paine endorsed the representational legislature.[17] Ironically, although Paine agreed with Adams on the mode of representation, he rejected the argument that a bicameral legislature was needed as an internal check on power:

> The question is, whether such a mode would not produce more hurt than good. The more houses the more parties; and perhaps the ill consequence to this country would be, that the landed interest would get into one house, and the commercial interest into the other; and by that means a perpetual and dangerous opposition would be kept up, and no business be got through: Whereas, were there a large, equal and annual representation in one house *only,* the different parties, by being thus banded together, would hear each others arguments, which advantage they cannot have if they sit in different houses. To say, there ought to be two houses, because there are two sorts of interest, is the very reason why there ought to be but one, and *that one* to consist of

---

[16][John Adams], *Thoughts on Government* (Boston, 1776), reprinted in Charles S. Hyneman and Donald S. Lutz, eds., *American Political Writing during the Founding Era, 1760–1805,* 2 vols. (Indianapolis, 1983), 1:401–9, quote on p. 403.

[17]On the authorship of *Four Letters on Interesting Subjects,* see Gregory Claeys, *Thomas Paine: Social and Political Thought* (London and Boston, 1989), pp. 50, 61 n. 26, citing A. Owen Aldridge, *Thomas Paine's American Ideology* (Newark, Del., 1984), pp. 219–39; see also Jack Fruchtman, Jr., *Thomas Paine: Apostle of Freedom* (New York, 1994), pp. 86–88.

every sort. The lords and commons in England formerly made but one house; and it is evident, that by separating men you lessen the quantity of knowledge, and increase the difficulty of business.[18]

In addition to an exact method of representation, advocates of the representational model proposed three ways to bind legislators to the people's will: *annual elections,* which would compel the representative to explain and defend his conduct at brief, regular intervals to those whom he hoped to represent;[19] *rotation in office,* to prevent a representative from believing himself entitled to his office and forming interests different from those who elected him and to require him to experience, as a citizen, the effects of the laws and policies he had helped to shape;[20] and *instructions,* to enable the electorate to inform their representatives of their wishes and to require representatives to carry out those wishes.[21]

The prospect that a representative might differ from his constituents—a prospect that the deliberative model accepted—played no part in the representational model. If a representative diverged from his constituents, that difference proved the representative unfit to retain office. If the representatives did not reflect the character or composition of the society, then the mode of representation was radically

---

[18] [Thomas Paine], *Four Letters on Interesting Subjects* (Philadelphia, 1776), in Hyneman and Lutz, *American Political Writing,* 1:368–89, quote from "Letter IV," on pp. 385–86.

[19] Willi Paul Adams, *The First American Constitutions: Republican Ideology and the Making of the State Constitutions in the Revolutionary Era,* ed. and trans. Rita and Robert Kimber (Chapel Hill, 1980), pp. 243–45. See, for example, Adams, *Thoughts on Government,* in Hyneman and Lutz, *American Political Writing,* 1:406: "And these and all other elections, especially of representatives and counsellors, should be annual, there not being in the whole circle of the sciences a maxim more infallible than this, 'where annual elections end, there slavery begins.' "

[20] Adams, *Thoughts on Government,* in Hyneman and Lutz, *American Political Writing,* 1:406: "This will teach them the great political virtues of humility, patience, and moderation, without which every man in power becomes a ravenous beast of prey."

[21] "The inhabitants of every District . . . had an unquestionable right to instruct their respective Delegates on that or any other subject. It is to be presumed that no member of either house would have thought himself at liberty to disregard the instruction of a majority of his constituents" ("Philodemus" [Thomas Tudor Tucker], *Conciliatory Hints, Attempting, by a Fair State of Matters, to Remove Party Prejudice* [Charleston, 1784], reprinted in Hyneman and Lutz, *American Political Documents,* 1:606–30, quote on 607–8). On this subject, see Adams, *First American Constitutions,* pp. 246–49. For an interesting reflection on instructions, see Pole, *Political Representation,* pp. 541–42.

defective, to the extent of the difference between representatives and constituents.[22]

Those who rejected the representational model lampooned the legislature it envisioned as a rowdy gathering of proxies of special interests, seeking only to gain advantages for their supporters—usually at the expense of other interests, almost always at the expense of the general good. They also derided representational legislators as crude, ignorant, and incapable of forming disinterested views—and thus of identifying and giving effect to the general good.

For example, on May 25, 1766, the young Thomas Jefferson observed a sitting of the lower house of the Maryland legislature in Annapolis. As part of his legal training,[23] Jefferson had immersed himself in parliamentary law; he had attended legislative sessions in Virginia, and his mentor, George Wythe, had introduced him to the highest circles of Virginia politics and society. Jefferson's high-minded and thorough preparation for the bar and public life did not prepare him for the Marylanders' raucous politicking, however. Stunned by the experience, he unburdened himself in a letter to his boyhood friend John Page. Though he wrote with the labored facetiousness that characterized his youthful letters, Jefferson was clearly dismayed by what he saw.[24]

Jefferson began with satiric comments on the assembly's physical setting: "I went into the lower [house], sitting in an old courthouse, which, judging from it's form and appearance, was built in the year one."[25] He

---

[22]This is a constant theme of the pamphlet literature of the Revolutionary era. See, for example, Adams, *Thoughts on Government,* in Hyneman and Lutz, *American Political Documents,* 1:403; [Theophilus Parsons], *The Essex Result* (Newburyport, Mass., 1788), reprinted in Hyneman and Lutz, *American Political Documents,* 1:480–522, quote on p. 497. See also Adams, *First American Constitutions,* pp. 234–35.

[23]Edward Dumbauld, *Thomas Jefferson and the Law* (Norman, Okla., 1978), pp. 3–17; Frank Dewey, *Thomas Jefferson, Lawyer* (Charlottesville, 1986), pp. 9–17; David N. Mayer, *The Constitutional Thought of Thomas Jefferson* (Charlottesville, 1994), pp. 3–11; on his study of parliamentary law, see Howell, *Jefferson's Parliamentary Writings,* pp. 3–4.

[24]Thomas Jefferson to John Page, May 25, 1766, in Boyd, *Jefferson Papers,* 1:18–20. An extract from this letter appears in Howell, *Jefferson's Parliamentary Writings,* pp. 3–4; the editor of this volume misstates the recipient's name as John Gage.

[25]Boyd, *Jefferson Papers,* 1:19. Jefferson's criticism of the appearance of the meeting place of the Maryland assembly may be rooted as much in his architectural tastes as in his assessment of the legislature itself; his aversion to colonial architecture is well known. See generally Jack McLaughlin, *Jefferson and Monticello: The Biography of a Builder* (New York, 1991).

also disapproved of the noise enveloping the courthouse: "I was surprised on approaching it to hear as great a noise and hubbub as you will usually observe at a publick meeting of the planters in Virginia."[26] He continued with cutting sketches of the assembly's speaker and clerk:

> The first object which struck me after my entrance was the figure of a little old man dressed but indifferently, with a yellow queue wig on, and mounted in the judge's chair. This the gentleman who walked with me informed me was the speaker, a man of very fair character, but who by the bye has very little the air of a speaker. At one end of the justices' bench stood a man whom in another place I should from his dress and phis have taken for Goodall the lawyer in Williamsburgh, reading a bill then before the house with a schoolboy tone and an abrupt pause at every half dozen words. This I found to be the clerk of the assembly.[27]

Jefferson reserved greater derision for the assembly's members: "The mob (for such was their appearance) sat covered on the justices' and lawyers' benches, and were divided into little clubs amusing themselves in the common chit chat way. I was surprised to see them address the speaker without rising from their seats, and three, four, and five at a time without being checked."[28] Not only did the legislators diverge radically from what Jefferson thought they should be — their methods of doing business appalled the young enthusiast for parliamentary law: "When [a motion was] made, the speaker instead of putting the question in the usual form only asked the gentlemen whether they chose that such or such a thing should be done, and was answered by a yes sir, or no sir; and tho' the voices appeared frequently to be divided, they never would go to the trouble of dividing the house, but the clerk entered the resolutions, I supposed, as he thought proper. In short every thing seems to be carried without the house in general's knowing what was proposed."[29]

Jefferson's letter opens a window for us onto the range of opinions and expectations that Americans of the Revolutionary generation held of what legislatures and legislators should be. The letter describes how a colonial legislature behaved — and (in Jefferson's view) how it should not behave; further, it suggests a constellation of assumptions

---

[26] Boyd, *Jefferson Papers*, 1:19.
[27] Ibid.
[28] Ibid., 1:19–20.
[29] Ibid., 1:20.

as to what a legislature should and should not be and how its members should and should not act. Finally, that Jefferson expected John Page to find his derisive miniature portrait of the Maryland assembly both amusing and reasonable suggests that Jefferson's assumptions were not unique to him. Indeed, these assumptions were integral to the Americans' understanding of legislatures and legislative political culture; their complex evolution and interaction formed the intellectual mulch from which the Continental and Confederation Congresses, and ultimately the First Congress, grew.

Models in Conflict

In 1776, basking in the first glow of Revolutionary fervor, many Americans accepted without a second thought the representational model and the ideal it epitomized. They had experienced the dangers that resulted when a distant legislature (Parliament) that denied direct representation to all members of the polity lacked familiarity with the interests of those whom it sought to govern.[30] These Americans valued the representational model precisely because, they hoped, it would force American legislatures to conform to American realities. Even so, principally in their reliance on parliamentary procedure and in their continuing appeals to the ideal of the general good, they remained loyal to isolated elements of the deliberative model. They argued, however, that a legislature on the representational model could achieve the general good at least as easily as a legislature on the deliberative model could do.

A Digression on State Constitution Making

In 1775–76 Americans scrambled to respond to the crisis of legitimacy caused by the collapse of British colonial government. They embraced the challenge with greatest enthusiasm and creativity in devising new state governments, in part because of the urgings of the

---

[30]The most thorough and convincing discussion of the Americans' constitutional arguments against Great Britain is John Phillip Reid, *Constitutional History of the American Revolution*, 4 vols. (Madison, 1986–93; one vol. abridged ed., 1995); see also idem, "Another Origin of Judicial Review: The Constitutional Crisis of 1776 and the Need for a Dernier Judge," *New York University Law Review* 64 (1989):963–89.

Second Continental Congress (responding, in turn, to the badgering and pleas of John Adams).[31] Beginning in 1776, the states adopted new constitutions, most of them built around a strong legislature on the representational model.[32] The Americans' state legislatures tended to be large, and every state constitution provided for annual legislative elections. Because of the Americans' distrust of those branches of government — the executive and the judiciary — that they associated with the oppressive excesses of colonial politics and British rule, they tended to give their legislatures dominance within state constitutional frameworks. In Pennsylvania — a model followed by Georgia and the "independent republic of Vermont" — the constitution even did away with an independent executive; it provided instead for a supreme executive council to be chosen by the legislature and be responsible to it.[33] In most other states, the governor was to be chosen by and responsible to the legislature; he lacked power to veto legislation or make executive and judicial appointments or had to share such powers with a council.[34] The only state constitution before 1780 to buck this tide was New York, whose 1777 constitution authorized an independent

---

[31]See Richard B. Bernstein, "John Adams's *Thoughts on Government,* 1776," in Schechter, *Roots of the Republic,* pp. 118–37 (including texts of *Thoughts on Government* and the Second Continental Congress's resolution of May 10–15, 1776, calling on the states to form new, republican governments).

[32]The leading studies of state constitution making in the Revolutionary era are Adams, *First American Constitutions;* Donald S. Lutz, *Popular Consent and Popular Control: Whig Political Theory in the Early State Constitutions* (Baton Rouge, 1980); and idem, *The Origins of American Constitutionalism* (Baton Rouge, 1988). See also Bernstein with Rice, *Are We to Be a Nation?,* chap. 3.

[33]On Pennsylvania, see J. Paul Selsam, *The Pennsylvania Constitution of 1776: A Study in Revolutionary Democracy* (Philadelphia, 1936); Robert M. Brunhouse, *The Counter-Revolution in Pennsylvania, 1776–1790* (Harrisburg, Penn., 1942); Paul Doutrich, "From Revolution to Constitution: Pennsylvania's Path to Federalism," in *The Constitution and the States,* ed. Patrick Conley and John P. Kaminski (Madison, 1988), pp. 37–53; and Pole, *Political Representation,* pp. 250–80. On Georgia, see Kenneth Coleman, *The American Revolution in Georgia, 1763–1789* (Athens, Ga., 1958); Albert B. Saye, "Georgia: Security through Union," in Conley and Kaminski, *The Constitution and the States,* pp. 77–92. On Vermont, see Michael Bellesiles, *Revolutionary Outlaws: Ethan Allen and the Struggle for Independence on the Early American Frontier* (Charlottesville, 1993); and Michael Sherman, ed., *A More Perfect Union: Vermont Becomes a State, 1777–1816* (Montpelier, Vt., 1991).

[34]See, for example, Gordon S. Wood, *The Creation of the American Republic, 1776–1787* (Chapel Hill, 1969), pp. 132–43 (esp. pp. 138–39). For a discussion of one such constitution, the Virginia Constitution of 1776, see Pole, *Political Representation,* pp. 281–338.

governor elected directly by the people but who shared his appointment and veto powers with a Council of Appointment and a Council of Revision, respectively.[35] Not until 1780 did Massachusetts adopt a new constitution, drawing extensively on New York's model, that decisively rejected the concept of legislative supremacy and provided the basis for most states' later reworkings of their Revolutionary constitutions.[36]

The Challenge of Confederation

At the same time that they labored to provide new, legitimate state constitutions for themselves to supplant colonial systems of government, Americans began, more hesitantly and with greater difficulty, to construct an independent American government. The Continental Congress and its institutional successor, the Confederation Congresses, were testing grounds for the Americans' expectations of how an American legislature and its members should function, reflecting the struggle between the deliberative and representational models. Just as important, they epitomized the American effort to balance the principles they wished to salvage from the heritage of Parliament with the realities of American public life.[37]

By contrast to the considered process of forming new state constitutions, the Continental Congress just grew. The First and Second Continental Congresses based themselves on patterns defined by such intercolonial conferences as the Stamp Act Congress of 1765 and the Albany Congress of 1754.[38] These patterns mixed deliberative fea-

---

[35]See William A. Polf, *1777: The Political Revolution and New York's First Constitution* (Albany, N.Y., 1977); Bernard Mason, *Prologue to Independence: The Revolution in New York, 1773–1777* (Lexington, Ky., 1975); Stephen L. Schechter, "The New York State Constitution, 1777," in Schechter, *Roots of the Republic,* pp. 166–87 (including the text of the constitution); and John P. Kaminski, "Adjusting to Circumstance: New York's Relationship with the Federal Government," in Conley and Kaminski, *The Constitution and the States,* pp. 225–49.

[36]See Ronald M. Peters, Jr., *The Massachusetts Constitution of 1780: A Social Compact* (Amherst, Mass., 1978); Richard B. Bernstein, "The Massachusetts Constitution, 1780," in Schechter, *Roots of the Republic,* pp. 188–226 (with the annotated text of the constitution); and Pole, *Political Representation,* pp. 172–249.

[37]The discussion in these paragraphs draws on the leading studies of the Continental and Confederation Congresses; see note 4 above.

[38]On the Albany Congress, see Robert Newbold, *The Albany Congress and Plan of Union of 1754* (New York, 1955); on the Stamp Act Congress, see Edmund S. Morgan and Helen M. Morgan, *The Stamp Act Congress* (1955; 3d rev. ed., Chapel Hill, 1995).

tures, such as parliamentary procedure, with representational features, such as equal representation for the colonies.

The First Continental Congress was a simple body, a collection of delegates from twelve of the thirteen colonies. It met for a limited period with little expectation of institutional continuity. And it had a well-defined set of goals: to identify and publicize the dangers of British colonial policy, to define the methods and targets of an intercolonial response to that policy, and to adopt a method for deciding what to do next. It met all those goals. At the same time, the First Continental Congress propelled colonial politicians into a long and difficult process of learning to think of themselves as having common interests and being coequal participants in a common enterprise: American politicians shaping American politics.[39]

At the close of the First Continental Congress, the delegates resolved, among other things, to call a second such congress to meet in Philadelphia in May 1775. Circumstances, however, transformed the Second Continental Congress into a de facto American government, known by 1776 as the Continental Congress. War between British forces and colonial militias had erupted in Massachusetts the month before the delegates met. The colonial governments, already pervaded with a sense of impending crisis, had begun to crumble under the stress of the worsening controversy between the mother country and the colonies of British North America. As a result, the Second Continental Congress had to stay in existence long beyond its delegates' expectations to monitor and respond to the evolving crisis. As the colonies moved toward independence, the Second Continental Congress assumed not only the legislative powers of the disintegrating colonial legislatures and the estranged Parliament, but also executive powers formerly associated with royal governors and the Crown.[40]

Almost against its will, Congress authorized a revolution for American independence. Within a year of its convening, it had begun to oversee the founding of legitimate state governments, to consider the opening of relations with foreign powers, and to direct the waging of a war with Britain by an army that it had organized and sent into the field. All that was wanting was for Congress to cross the Rubicon — to

---

[39]This point is the core of the argument in Rakove, *Beginnings of National Politics*.
[40]Ibid., pp. 63–132; Marston, *King and Congress*.

reconstitute itself as a legitimate institution of government for an independent America. On June 12, 1776, as it prepared to declare American independence and to seek foreign assistance in the war with Great Britain, Congress named a committee to begin drafting a new form of American government.[41]

The process of drafting took well over a year, as Congress wrestled with the delicate task of striking a balance between creating an American government and preserving the legitimate sovereignty of the new states. Though delegates as opposed in their views as Benjamin Franklin (who favored independence) and John Dickinson (who opposed it) agreed that an American Congress required a generous allotment of power, protests from jealous defenders of state sovereignty whittled down their proposals. The result, which the Continental Congress proposed to the states on November 15, 1777, was the Articles of Confederation.

Congress and the American people waited anxiously for nearly four years for all thirteen states to ratify the Articles. Between November 15, 1777, when Congress proposed the Articles to the states, and March 1, 1781, when the last state, Maryland, adopted them, Congress voluntarily operated by reference to the Articles. This long delay had three effects, one benefiting the Articles and two damaging them. First, it gave Congress a head start on getting used to conducting business under the Articles. Second, it weakened the authority of the Articles and of Congress in the public mind. Third, by providing a showcase for the weakness of the framework the Articles had envisioned, it sparked movements to revise the Articles even before they were adopted.[42]

Anatomy of an Institution

The Congress authorized by the Articles blended aspects of the deliberative and representational models. Founded "for the more conve-

---

[41]Jensen, *Articles of Confederation*, pp. 107–245, 249–53; Rakove, *Beginnings of National Politics,* 135–239; and Donald S. Lutz, "The Articles of Confederation, 1781," in Schechter, *Roots of the Republic,* pp. 227–48 (with annotated text of the Articles).

[42]More than a year before Maryland put the Articles into effect, the young Alexander Hamilton urged the necessity of sweeping constitutional reform. See Alexander Hamilton to [?], [Dec. 1779–Mar. 1780?], in Harold C. Syrett and Jacob E. Cooke, eds., *The Papers of Alexander Hamilton,* 27 vols. (New York, 1961–87), 2:236–51 (and consult editorial note on the possible date and possible recipient of this letter on pp. 234–36); Alexander Hamilton to James Duane, Sept. 3, 1780, in ibid., 2:400–418.

nient management of the general interests of the several states,"[43] it was supposed to draw on parliamentary principles of reasoned and reasonable deliberation while taking account of the representational constraints of American politics.

Like all other American legislative and representative assemblies, Congress based its procedures on parliamentary law. Thomas Jefferson, who learned his parliamentary law from George Wythe, the greatest American parliamentarian, helped frame the first procedures of Congress, which were solidly based on the procedures of Parliament and which later Congresses tinkered with only as needed.[44] The procedures were useful, even admirable — but they were not enough. For the most part, the representational constraints on Congress predominated.

First, Congress had only one house, in which each state — large or small, rich or poor — had one vote. Rooted in the intercolonial conferences of the seventeenth century, the rule of equal representation was an uneasy compromise. Politicians from large states agitated for a "more equitable" rule based on population, the value of property, or the payment of taxes to Congress. Despite all efforts to secure that "more equitable" rule, state equality was the only system on which any intercolonial and interstate body could agree. And yet that rule reinforced the character of Congress as a council of representatives of states on the representational model rather than an American legislature on the deliberative model.[45]

Second, state legislatures had an array of powers over their delegates to Congress. They had the power to decide how to choose delegates. Most legislatures retained this power for themselves; only two states — Connecticut and Rhode Island — elected delegates by popular vote. Delegates served one-year terms, but not more than three of any

---

[43] Articles of Confederation, art. 5, reprinted in Tansill, *Documents*, pp. 27–37 (quote on p. 28).

[44] See Jillson and Wilson, *Congressional Dynamics*, app. B, pp. 307–12, for the texts of rules adopted by the Continental and Confederation Congresses on Sept. 6, 1774 (p. 307), July 16, 1776 (pp. 307–8), May 26, 1778 (pp. 308–9), and May 4, 1781 (pp. 309–12). These rules are reprinted from Worthington C. Ford et al., eds., *Journals of the Continental Congress, 1774–1789*, 36 vols. (Washington, D.C., 1904–37), 1:25–26 (1774), 5:573–74 (1776), 11:534–35 (1778), and 20:476–82 (1781).

[45] On the quarrel over state equality in the framing of the Articles, see Jensen, *Articles of Confederation*, pp. 140–45; Rakove, *Beginnings of National Politics*, pp. 140–44, 146, 151, 157–59, 173–75, 179; and Pole, *Political Representation*, pp. 344–53.

six years; Congress thereby lost the benefit of experience among its members. State legislatures also could instruct and recall their delegates. And, each state paid its own delegates' salaries. These methods of selection, removal, and compensation further emphasized the representational features of Congress. They also left delegates hostage to the actions of state legislatures; delegates often complained about states' failures to pay them, and presidents of Congress regularly beseeched state governments to send delegates so that Congress could muster a quorum to do its business.[46]

Third, the Articles established super-majority limits on key powers of Congress. Every treaty, declaration of war, measure for coining or printing or borrowing money, measure for maintaining an army or navy, or admission of a new state required the backing of nine of the thirteen states—as did any action of Congress's "executive committee," the Committee of the States. Also, no amendment to the Articles could succeed without the support of all thirteen states. These limits were intended, first, to prevent the Confederation from becoming a powerful, distant central government and, second, to ensure that Congress could adopt only measures commanding the support of a general consensus—but they enabled minority interests to protect themselves at the expense of the general good, and to cripple any attempt to get Congress even a small grant of added powers.[47]

Fourth, the Articles withheld other vital powers from Congress—including powers to impose taxes and to regulate interstate or foreign commerce. Again, these decisions reflected the American bias against centralized government—yet they left Congress at the mercy of state governments' willingness to comply with congressional requisitions, the only means that Congress had to raise revenue. And many states did not comply.[48]

Finally, the Confederation's lack of an independent executive and

---

[46]On absenteeism, see Jillson and Wilson, *Congressional Dynamics*, pp. 155–62, and Rakove, *Beginnings of National Politics*, pp. 168, 198–99, 216, 345, 355–57, 371.

[47]Articles of Confederation, art. 9 (on treaties, declarations of war, money, and maintaining army and navy), art. 10 (on Committee of the States), art. 11 (on admission of new states), and art. 13 (on amending procedure), in Tansill, *Documents*, pp. 34–35.

[48]See generally Roger H. Brown, *Redeeming the Republic: Federalists, Taxation, and the Origins of the Constitution* (Baltimore, 1993); E. James Ferguson, *The Power of the Purse: A History of American Public Finance, 1776–1790* (Chapel Hill, 1961).

judiciary accentuated Congress's character as a council of states. Congress had only those executive functions that the states were willing to entrust to it. Even its ramshackle executive departments—Foreign Affairs, War, and Finance—had no formal warrant; Congress never sought any, fearing that any proposed amendment to the Articles on this subject would fail, depriving it even of ad hoc executive bodies.[49] The court that Congress created—the Court of Appeals in Cases of Capture—existed in a similar jurisprudential limbo.[50] The one court the Articles authorized was only a procedure for naming congressional committees to arbitrate interstate disputes, which proved only as effective as the states' willingness to accept its decisions.[51] And yet the burden of executive and judicial business prevented Congress from shouldering whatever legislative duties were entrusted to it.[52] No wonder that when, in January 1787, George Washington asked John Jay for advice as to what the Federal Convention ought to do, Jay counseled, "Let Congress legislate—let others execute—let others judge."[53]

Thus, the closest thing the Americans had developed to a national legislature oscillated between the deliberative and the representational models, between parliamentary principles and American realities. Congress under the Articles had all the drawbacks built into the Articles with few, if any, of the advantages that the Second Continental

---

[49] On these departments, see generally Jennings B. Sanders, *Evolution of the Executive Departments of the Continental Congress, 1774–1789* (Chapel Hill, 1935), and the discussion in Morris, *Forging of the Union*, pp. 95–97. On the Continental and Confederation Congresses' various forms of administration for treasury and public finance, see Ferguson, *Power of the Purse*. On the War Department, see Harry M. Ward, *The Department of War, 1781–1795* (Pittsburgh, 1962). On the presidency of the Continental Congress, the leading study is still Jennings B. Sanders, *The Presidency of the Continental Congress, 1775–1789: A Study in American Institutional History* (Chicago, 1930). See also the suggestive discussion in Morris, *Forging of the Union*, pp. 99–108, and the comments in Jillson and Wilson, *Congressional Dynamics*, pp. 71–90.

[50] On this court, see generally Henry J. Bourguignon, *The First Federal Court: The Federal Appellate Prize Court of the American Revolution, 1775–1787* (Philadelphia, 1977).

[51] Articles of Confederation, art. 9, in Tansill, *Documents*, pp. 33–35. The leading study is Peter S. Onuf, *Origins of the Federal Republic: Jurisdictional Controversies in the United States, 1776–1787* (Philadelphia, 1983).

[52] For a generally cogent analysis that gives perhaps too much weight to the presentist concept of a nascent but stillborn committee system in the Continental and Confederation Congresses, see Jillson and Wilson, *Congressional Dynamics*, pp. 91–131.

[53] John Jay to George Washington, Jan. 7, 1787, in Henry P. Johnston, ed., *The Correspondence and Public Papers of John Jay, 1763–1826*, 4 vols. (New York, 1890–93), 3:226–29, quote on p. 227.

Congress possessed. The political factors that enabled the Second Continental Congress to act for the general interest—the urgency of the Revolution and its attendant patriotic fervor[54]—could not supply the Confederation's want of real power, for those factors were gone, save in some delegates' mournful remembrances of lost American glories. Conceived as the core of the Revolutionary American government and therefore as an agency to determine and to achieve the general good, Congress became a council of representatives of the states. It expended at least as much energy hearing and attempting to resolve interstate controversies as it did attempting to solve American problems. Congress's lack of authority to enforce its decisions sapped its ability to perform even its representational functions.[55]

As Congress was torn by the conflicting influences of the representational and deliberative models, individual delegates faced comparable clashes of roles and responsibilities. Jack Rakove ably describes the congressman's subjection "to the tug of competing loyalties":

> As a *delegate* from Virginia, Madison was obliged to protect its immediate interests. When members from other states argued that Virginia should yield its territorial claims, he had to defend the terms upon which the assembly insisted its concessions would be made. Yet on other occasions, Madison had to address his constituents as a *member* of Congress. If they complained that the northern states had failed to relieve the South from the British offensive, he had to explain why they should still support the union that Congress embodied. Within Congress, too, he learned that one could lose influence by being too faithful to constituents' interests.[56]

Delegates found that service in Congress posed as many frustrations as challenges. The Articles established institutional and structural conditions that simultaneously augmented and constricted the importance of the individual delegate within the Confederation Congress.

---

[54] For a study that ably presents and analyzes some remarkable initiatives of the Second Continental Congress to foster republican virtue, see Ann Withington, *Toward a More Perfect Union: Virtue and the Formation of American Republics* (New York, 1991).

[55] See, for example, Joseph L. Davis, *Sectionalism in American Politics, 1774–1787* (Madison, 1977) and Onuf, *Origins of the American Republic.*

[56] Jack N. Rakove, *James Madison and the Creation of the American Republic* (Glenview, Ill., 1990), pp. 20–21.

Because, as noted earlier, the Articles did not create any separate American executive or judicial institutions, the Confederation Congress had all powers and responsibilities vested in the United States; the delegates to the Confederation Congress thus were the principal formal actors in national politics.

And yet the Articles — specifically, Article 5 — hobbled the delegates' ability to shoulder those responsibilities.[57] Article 5 forbade a member from serving more than three years in every term of six years and barred any delegate from the presidency of Congress longer than one year in any three-year period; this provision precluded the development of either incumbency or seniority as a measure of authority and power within the Confederation Congress, and thus prevented the development of any formal internal structure or hierarchy. As each delegate joined or left Congress, therefore, the character of the institution changed to a greater extent than otherwise would be the case. Moreover, Article 5 also specified that the Confederation Congress vote by state delegations. This requirement both preserved the practice that had characterized every previous intercolonial and interstate assembly and kept the states at the core of congressional business. The procedure of voting by states minimized the formal power of the individual delegate; nonetheless, it put a premium on a delegate's ability to persuade his colleagues, both within his state's delegation and in other states' delegations, to build consensus behind a given policy.[58]

Finally, the conditions of American politics under the Articles rendered debate in the Confederation Congress the principal method of formulating national public policy — unless American politicians who thought in national terms sought to explore extraconstitutional means to reform American government.[59] The weaknesses of the Confederation as a form of government combined with the power of the states, and the states' willingness to use that power aggressively to pursue their own interests, to compel American politicians to pay heed to local and regional problems. The consequent need to define shared and competing interests and to identify common ground on which to build

---

[57] Articles of Confederation, art. 5, in Tansill, *Documents*, pp. 28–29.

[58] Jillson and Wilson, *Congressional Dynamics*, pp. 132–63.

[59] Of course, this is precisely what happened. See, for example, Bernstein with Rice, *Are We to Be a Nation?*, chap. 4 and sources cited.

congressional consensus augmented the value and importance of debate in the congressional process.

In the years between the end of the Revolutionary War and the supplanting of the Articles by the Constitution, the Confederation Congress confronted — or evaded — such issues as the appeals by New York and other states for aid in suppressing secessionist movements; the states' inconsistent records of payment of or delinquency on Confederation requisitions; the apportionment of federal war debts among the states; and the Mississippi controversy of 1786. These controversies reminded all who concerned themselves with national questions that American politics was a problem of shifting fields and influences. Delegates to Congress had to keep in mind the need to maintain an atmosphere within the Confederation Congress of collegiality, mutual respect, and the shared interests of the American people despite their residence in different states.

The prevalence of representational politics at the national level before the Constitution may have been an inevitable result of American federalism. Even those who urged the forging of an American union realized the obstacles facing them grounded in the realities of federalism — some at the time, others with the advantage of hindsight. In 1786, George Washington explained to his nephew his belief that conflicts of national and state loyalties were a major source of the troubles affecting the Confederation: "That representatives ought to be the mouth of their Constituents, I do not deny; nor do I mean to call into question the right of the latter to instruct them. It is to the embarrassment, into which they may be thrown by these instructions in *national* matters that my objections lie."[60]

More than forty years later, in 1818, the aged John Adams tried to explain this state of affairs to Hezekiah Niles, a noted journalist who had not lived through the Revolutionary period:

> The colonies had grown up under constitutions of government so different, there was so great a variety of religions, they were composed of so many different nations, their customs, manners, and habits had so little resemblance, and their intercourse had been so rare, and their

---

[60]George Washington to Bushrod Washington, Nov. 15, 1786, reprinted in Kurland and Lerner, *Founders' Constitution*, 1:399.

knowledge of each other so imperfect, that to unite them in the same principles in theory and the same system of action, was certainly a very difficult enterprise. The complete accomplishment of it, in so short a time and by such simple means, was perhaps a singular example in the history of Mankind. Thirteen clocks were made to strike together. A perfection of mechanism, which no artist had ever before effected.[61]

As Adams had reason to remember, those politicians who sought to derail measures in the Continental and Confederation Congresses found it useful to invoke the staggering heterogeneity and range of interests of the people of the thirteen states. This tendency manifested itself as early as the First Continental Congress. When, on September 6, 1774, Thomas Cushing of Massachusetts moved that its sessions begin with prayer, John Jay of New York and John Rutledge of South Carolina objected that the motion was impracticable because delegates professed such a variety of religious beliefs. By this diversionary tactic they intended to split the advocates of independence along religious lines — but Samuel Adams's expressed willingness to "hear a prayer from a man of piety and virtue, who is at the same time a friend of his country" defused their ploy. That is, Jay and Rutledge used a representational stratagem to short-circuit Congress, which Adams foiled by invoking the broadness of mind characteristic of the deliberative legislator.[62]

The "prayer precedent" of 1774 foretold the course of American politics before the Constitution. Throughout the fifteen years from the convening of the First Continental Congress in 1774 to the expiration of the Confederation Congress in 1789, problems of diversity of interests and manipulations of that diversity plagued American politics. As the war continued, and the glow of Revolutionary fervor and cooperation diminished, rivalries between states and regions resurfaced within Congress and without, further complicating the delicate balancing act of holding together a revolution and a nation without creating that fearful monster, a centralized American government.[63] These prob-

---

[61]John Adams to Hezekiah Niles, Feb. 13, 1818, quoted in Richard E. Ellis, *The Union at Risk* (New York, 1987), p. 2.

[62]Edward Humphrey, *Nationalism and Religion in America, 1774–1789* (1924; reprint ed., New York, 1965), pp. 411–12.

[63]Rakove, *Beginnings of National Politics*, is especially good on this point.

lems only worsened after the winning of independence in 1783; with the great impetus for Revolutionary unity gone, the representational tendencies inherent in the Confederation grew explosively.[64]

Even politicians who believed themselves friends of the national interest risked destroying any hope of achieving the general interest by misreading the clashing interests within Congress. The Jay-Gardoqui controversy of 1786 illustrates this problem. John Jay, the Confederation's secretary for foreign affairs, hoped to secure American navigation rights to the Mississippi River by beginning negotiations with Don Diego de Gardoqui, the Spanish envoy to the Confederation; the Spanish had denied Americans access to the Mississippi and to New Orleans unless they swore allegiance to Spain. Gardoqui refused but offered instead an advantageous commercial treaty with the United States — if Jay ceded American claims to those navigation rights. Jay proposed to pursue the offer, reasoning that the southern states would grow so quickly that the Spanish would have to acknowledge American navigation rights. The infuriated delegates from the five southern states charged that Jay was sacrificing their states' interests to those of the commercial states of New England and the Middle Atlantic. They demonstrated that their states' five votes could prevent any treaty negotiated on the basis Jay proposed from receiving the needed nine votes in Congress. There was thus no treaty between Spain and America until 1795.[65]

The Confederation's faults were not the only problem plaguing American politics in the 1780s; the states became arenas for factional dispute even more intense, if possible, than in the colonial period. Alarmed for the success of the Revolution, those politicians who thought in national terms linked the factionalism of state politics with the excessive powers granted to legislatures by most state constitutions *and* the inability of the Confederation to force states to comply with federal policies to achieve the general good. Nationalist politicians with theoretical inclinations took the logical next steps; they reasoned,

---

[64]Ibid.

[65]Frederick Marks III, *Independence on Trial: Foreign Affairs and the Making of the Constitution* (Baton Rouge, 1973), pp. 21–32, 105–6; Richard B. Morris, *Witnesses at the Creation* (New York, 1985), pp. 152–59; Davis, *Sectionalism in American Politics*, pp. 109–26; Rakove, *Beginnings of National Politics*, pp. 349–50; Jensen, *New Nation*, pp. 170–73.

first, that the strength of the state legislatures under the representational model exacerbated the problems flowing from their excessive constitutional powers and, second, that the weakness of Congress under that model prevented any general solution to American problems. These ills had begun to pervade the whole system and, in consequence, to jeopardize the health of the American body politic.[66]

Toward Constitutional Reform

To be sure, the Continental and Confederation Congresses had amassed a significant record of achievement in the years between 1774 and 1787. They had coordinated the colonists' intellectual, political, and military resistance to Britain; they had declared American independence and fostered a creative explosion of state constitution making; they had launched an American diplomatic corps and secured a place for the fragile new nation in world politics; they had somehow helped General Washington hold together the Continental Army until the final victory in 1783; they had helped secure a remarkably advantageous treaty of peace from Britain that recognized American independence and doubled the new nation's size without compromising its sovereignty; and, most creative of all, they had devised a series of territorial ordinances that promised to foster the development of an expanded United States without the threat of colonialism.[67] But the

---

[66]Patrick T. Conley, *Democracy in Decline: Rhode Island's Constitutional Development, 1776–1841* (Providence, 1976); Irwin H. Polishook, *Rhode Island and the Union, 1774–1791* (Evanston, Ill., 1969); Brunhouse, *Counter-Revolution in Pennsylvania;* Edward Countryman, *A People in Revolution: New York, 1760–1790* (Baltimore, 1981); Rhys Isaac, *The Transformation of Virginia, 1740–1790* (Chapel Hill, 1982); Thomas J. Buckley, S.J., *Church and State Struggle in Revolutionary Virginia, 1776–1787* (Charlottesville, 1977); Van Beck Hall, *Politics without Parties: Massachusetts, 1780–1791* (Pittsburgh, 1975); William E. Nelson, *Americanization of the Common Law: The Impact of Legal Change on Massachusetts Society, 1760–1830* (Cambridge, Mass., 1975); Robert A. Gross, ed., *In Debt to Shays: The Bicentennial of an Agrarian Rebellion* (Charlottesville, 1993); and David Szatmary, *Shays's Rebellion: The Making of an Agrarian Insurrection* (Amherst, Mass., 1980). See generally Conley and Kaminski, *The Constitution and the States;* Patrick T. Conley and John P. Kaminski, eds., *The Bill of Rights and the States* (Madison, 1992); Michael Allen Gillespie and Michael Lienesch, eds., *Ratifying the Constitution* (Lawrence, Kans., 1989); Morris, *Forging of the Union;* idem, *The American Revolution Reconsidered.*

[67]On these achievements, see Burnett, *Continental Congress;* Rakove, *Beginnings of National Politics;* Morris, *Forging of the Union;* Onuf, *Origins of the Federal Republic;* Bernstein with Rice, *Are We to Be a Nation?,* chaps. 2, 4; Richard H. Kohn, *Eagle and Sword: The Federalists and the Creation of the American Military Establishment, 1783–1802* (New York,

looming threat to the Confederation from its own weaknesses and from the seeming decline of state politics into bitter factionalism overshadowed these achievements — both for politicians who thought in national terms in the 1780s and for generations of later historians.[68]

Assessing the Confederation's problems, James Madison built a powerful critique of the representational model as the core of his case for constitutional reform. His April 1787 memorandum "Vices of the Political System of the U[nited] States" stressed dangers flowing from the representational model's versions of politics and lawmaking.[69] Although he derived most of his evidence from the state legislatures (explaining that "those [evils] which are found within the States individually, . . . have an indirect influence on the general malady and must not be overlooked in forming a compleat remedy"),[70] he also took aim at Congress, tracing causal connections between politics in the states and the defects of the general government. Denouncing the Confederation's "want of sanction to the laws, and of coercion," Madison pointed out the consequences of Congress's lack of power to compel the state governments to abide by the general interest (as defined by Congress).[71] Drawing on his congressional experience, Madison explained why states resisted congressional definitions of the general good:

> In the first place, Every general act of the Union must necessarily bear unequally hard on some particular member or members of it, secondly the partiality of the members to their own interests and rights, a partiality which will be fostered by the courtiers of popularity, will naturally exaggerate the inequality where it exists, and even suspect it

---

1971); Charles Royster, *A Revolutionary People at War: The Continental Army and American Character, 1775–1783* (Chapel Hill, 1979); E. Wayne Carp, *To Starve the Army at Pleasure: Continental Army Administration and American Political Culture, 1775–1783* (Chapel Hill, 1984); Peter S. Onuf, *Statehood and Union: A History of the Northwest Ordinance* (Bloomington, Ind., 1987); Peter S. Onuf, "The Northwest Ordinance, 1787," in Schechter, *Roots of the Republic,* pp. 249–65 (with annotated text of the ordinance).

[68]See notes 4 and 5 above.

[69]James Madison, "Vices of the Political System of the U[nited] States," [Apr. 1787], Hutchinson, *Madison Papers,* 9:345–58. Madison later drew on and reworked material from the "Vices" memorandum in his convention speeches of June 6 and 19, 1787; see Farrand, *Records of the Federal Convention,* 1:134–36, 314–22; and, most famously, in *Federalist* No. 10.

[70]Madison, "Vices," in Hutchinson, *Madison Papers,* 9:353–57, quote on p. 353.

[71]Ibid., 9:351.

where it has no existence, thirdly a distrust of the voluntary compliance of each other may prevent the compliance of any, although it should be the latent disposition of all.[72]

Madison declared these to be "causes & pretexts which will never fail to render federal measures abortive."[73]

In Madison's view, the state legislatures' inability to achieve the general good, combined with their tendency to pursue their own interests at the expense of the whole, required national constitutional reform. A reconstituted American polity would be able to identify and secure the general interest by restraining the states' excesses as well as formulating and enforcing national policy. He therefore sought to devise an American constitutional solution for those defects. His analysis of Congress, in effect, noted that that institution combined deliberative and representational features and responsibilities with no clear way of holding the two in balance. In fact, he maintained, the representational traits of Congress crippled its efforts to secure the national interest. Further, its structure was defective precisely because it impeded whatever deliberative capabilities Congress possessed. Finally, its want of power prevented its effective use of those capabilities to identify national goals and to articulate and enforce national policies.

Devising a National Legislature

Thus, as nationally minded politicians prepared for the Federal Convention, they coalesced around a reform agenda shaped by a resurgence of the deliberative model and a growing critique of the representational model. The deliberative model drove many delegates' plans to reinvent Congress; the representational model, as incarnated in the state legislatures and the Confederation Congress, became the focus of their alarm and the principal target of their efforts to redesign the American political system.

They did not, of course, get their way. First, ironically, the interstate

---

[72]Ibid., 9:351–52.
[73]Ibid.

conferences that led to the Federal Convention, and the convention itself, resembled the Confederation Congress and the political evolution that gave rise to it—a blend of deliberative and representational features. The convention's procedures, again, were parliamentary, a bow to the deliberative ideal; its grudging adoption of the rule of equal state representation, and its repeated tussles with state interests, reflected the enduring representational realities of American politics.[74]

The only solution that a majority of the convention could accept— that embodied in the Constitution—again blended the two models, although with a significant increase in federal power that made it possible for the new Congress to hold both the deliberative and the representational models in a more stable balance. Delegates from the small states retained equality of representation in one branch of Congress, the Senate, and then happily vested added grants of power in Congress. Other features of the Constitution rejected specific aspects of the Articles, seeking to ensure that the members of the new Congress would conform more to the deliberative than the representational model: senators and representatives were to serve fixed terms, without either term limits or the risk of recall by the states; the general government (not the states) would pay their salaries. Perhaps most important, each representative and senator had one vote; this abandonment of the state-unit rule for voting indicated the Framers' faith and expectation that members of Congress would consult with one another as deliberative legislators seeking the general good. With executive powers spun off into the presidency and such executive departments as Congress might create, and judicial powers reassigned to a Supreme Court and such lower federal courts as Congress might create, the new

---

[74]For the first set of the convention's rules, adopted May 28, 1787, see Farrand, *Records of the Federal Convention,* 1:8–10 (Journal), 10–12 (Madison); for the supplemental rules adopted May 29, 1787, see 1:15–16 (Journal), 17 (Madison). These rules echo the rules of the Continental and Confederation Congresses and parallel the central principles of Anglo-American parliamentary law, adapted to the tasks confronting the convention. Pennsylvania's delegates, seconded by Virginia's, at first planned to challenge the rule of state equality but abandoned their effort, especially after the Delaware delegates informed their colleagues that they were forbidden to consent to abandonment of the rule of state equality. For Madison's account of the tussle, circa May 28, 1787, see 1:10–11 n. 4.

national legislature would be freed of many of the burdens that had crippled the Confederation Congress. And yet the Senate would share the key executive powers over appointments and foreign affairs; would have sole authority to try all impeachments voted by the House of Representatives; and would share with the House an indirect means of control over the federal courts, reshaping the judiciary's structure, powers, and jurisdiction. Viewing the Confederation Congress in light of the Constitution yields an unexpected conclusion — that it was not discarded along with the rest of the Articles of Confederation but persisted in revised and more functional form as the Senate of the United States.

In sum, the successes *and* the failures of the Continental and Confederation Congresses influenced the Federal Convention's design of Congress. Although the convention largely reacted *against* these precedents, that reaction took the form of institutional salvage and reconstructive surgery to preserve the benefits and advantages those precedents also carried with them. The most important example of this unacknowledged set of benefits derived from the Continental and Confederation Congresses was the continuation, in the First Congress, of parliamentary procedure as the matrix within which Congress conducted debate, formulated policy, and enacted laws. The reasons to emphasize reasoned debate, which prevailed in the Continental and Confederation Congresses, continued to be important in a national legislature, most of whose members were veterans of those earlier bodies. Thus, the constraints of political reality, as well as institutional models and precedents, contributed to the primacy of debate in American legislative politics.

Though the Framers of the Constitution rejected the Articles, they did not discard the Congress at the Articles' core.[75] The Continental and Confederation Congresses taught the Framers valuable lessons

---

[75] But see Jillson and Wilson, *Congressional Dynamics,* p. 300: "These delegates had among them a cumulative total of 99 years of experience in the Continental Congress. This experience made them anything but protective of that institution. Almost as soon as the convention achieved a quorum, the members closed the doors, swore one another to secrecy, and killed the Continental Congress. . . . Though several members are recorded as expressing doubts that the convention had the authority to [destroy] . . . the old order of the Articles, no member is recorded as having pleaded that the old Congress might be a useful part of the new order."

about the conflict between Parliamentary principles and American realities, between the deliberative and representational models of legislatures; they shaped the Congress of the United States by reference to those lessons. The Congress authorized by Article I of the Constitution is a transformed but still recognizable descendant of the Continental and Confederation Congresses.

II: Establishment of the First Federal Congress

R. B. Bernstein

A New Matrix for National Politics

The First Federal Elections, 1788–90

THE STORY OF the first federal elections under the Constitution is one of hopes thwarted, of expectations shattered, of fine and high-sounding theories of politics and government that blew up in the faces of those who had devised them. It is a story of a group of politicians who devised a document that, they maintained, would provide a new basis for solving the nation's problems and who used that docu-

This article presents material and arguments that I will treat at greater length and depth in R. B. Bernstein, *"Conven'd in Firm Debate": The First Congress as an Experiment in Government, 1789–1791* (forthcoming), chap. 5. I thank those friends and colleagues who have encouraged me and advised my work, in particular Joanne B. Freeman, John Phillip Reid, William E. Nelson, Ene Sirvet, Martin Flaherty, Bill Braverman, Phillip Haultcoeur, Deborah Paulus, and Dennis Graham Combs. I presented a much earlier version of this article to the New York University Law School Colloquium on Legal History, whose comments both encouraged me to persevere and focused my lines of inquiry. I also gratefully acknowledge the friendship and support of Kenneth R. Bowling, Charlene Bangs Bickford, and Helen E. Veit, who preside over the *Documentary History of the First Federal Congress,* one of the premier scholarly projects in American historiography, and who have been unfailingly encouraging of a project I am taking entirely too long to finish; Dr. Gaspare J. Saladino of the *Documentary History of the Ratification of the Constitution and the Bill of Rights,* who for more than a decade has exemplified scholarly collegiality; and Dean Harry H. Wellington and the faculty, staff, and students of New York Law School (in particular, the students in my spring 1995 course, "Law and Literature"). Finally, I am grateful to Kenneth R. Bowling and to Donald R. Kennon and Rebecca Rogers of the Capitol Historical Society for giving me the opportunity to present the paper that was the seed of this article at the April 1995 conference on the First Federal Congress.

I dedicate this article to the memory of Michael Psareas (1955–95).

ment as the basis for their effort to win control of Congress, put their agenda into law, and transform the nature of American politics.[1] And it is, finally, a story of how the new nation's politics did not work out the way that these politicians hoped, predicted, and promised it would.

The first federal elections took place in late 1788 and 1789 (with an aftershock in Rhode Island in 1790).[2] The Constitution's architects and supporters hoped to establish a new matrix for national politics, and a special kind of politics within that matrix. They sought to foster one kind of national politics, *deliberative politics* — reasoned and reasonable deliberation about the general good. And they sought to foreclose a diametrically opposed kind of politics, *representational politics* — the deliberate, self-conscious advocacy of local or special interests. They associated representational politics with the excesses and turbulence of state governments, and with the imbecility (that is, want of power) of the Confederation. They hoped that deliberative politics would be the essence of the Constitution and that the government authorized by the Constitution would be insulated against the dangers of representational politics. They failed, and that failure boded ill for the new constitutional system and for the new U.S. Congress at that system's core.

The First Omen: Congress, Elections, and the Capital

In the summer and fall of 1788, though Federalists celebrated the Constitution's ratification with parades and dinners, their public celebrations masked equally strong private anxieties.[3] Though Antifeder-

---

[1] Captious critics might draw comparisons between the Constitution, the aegis of the Federalists of 1788–89, and the "Contract with America," the aegis of the Republicans who took control of the House of Representatives in the 104th Congress after sweeping the 1994 congressional elections. See generally Louis Fisher, "The 'Contract with America': What It Really Means," *The New York Review of Books,* June 22, 1995, pp. 20–24, discussing Ed Gillespie and Bob Schellhas, eds., *Contract with America: The Bold Plan by Rep. Newt Gingrich, Rep. Dick Armey and the House Republicans to Change America* (New York, 1994).

[2] The principal source for this paper is the innovative Merrill Jensen, Robert A. Becker, and Gordon DenBoer, eds., *The Documentary History of the First Federal Elections, 1788–1790,* 4 vols. (Madison, 1976–89), cited hereafter as *DHFFE.*

[3] See, for example, Whitfield J. Bell, Jr., "The Federal Processions of 1788," *New-York*

alists pledged their support for the Constitution once the Constitution had prevailed, they too nursed private doubts and convictions. Therefore, politicians at national and state levels struggled to control the transition to the Constitution, the core of which was the first federal elections.

All who took part in those elections recognized that by adopting the Constitution the American people had established a new matrix for American politics — to adapt the phrase coined by Jürgen Habermas, a new national public sphere.[4] Resolving to pursue their goals within that matrix, they focused on the elections for the Senate and House of Representatives. Contrary to modern expectations, congressional elections loomed larger in the eyes of the Revolutionary generation than the first election for president and vice president — in large part because they knew who would be chosen the first president. George Washington had a "lock" on the office — if he wanted it. By contrast, nobody had a clear or certain "lock" on the new Senate and House of Representatives. Americans knew that Congress would play the pivotal role in determining how the government authorized by the Constitution would be set in motion, what powers it would claim, what institutions (besides those specified in the Constitution) it would possess, and how those institutions would wield the powers granted to them. Thus, as for the first time they chose members of a national legislature, Americans continued to refine their expectations of Congress, of those who would be part of it, and of its place in the nation's new political system.

At first, despite the task's novelty and complexity and the residual bitterness of the ratification controversy, the transition to the Constitution was smooth and orderly. However, a development as ominous as it was unforeseen — the dispute over what city would host the new government — threatened to derail the first federal elections and thus reduce the Federalists' victory to ashes.

Historical Society Quarterly 46 (1962):5–39; Richard B. Bernstein with Kym S. Rice, *Are We to Be a Nation? The Making of the Constitution* (Cambridge, Mass., 1987), pp. 213, 216–17.

[4] See Jürgen Habermas, *The Structural Transformation of the Public Sphere: An Inquiry into a Category of Bourgeois Society,* trans. Thomas Burger (1962; reprint ed., Cambridge, Mass., 1989); Craig T. Calhoun, ed., *Habermas and the Public Sphere* (Cambridge, Mass., 1992).

Federalists and Antifederalists had given comparatively little thought to the capital question; they had been far more concerned with whether the Constitution would be put into effect at all. Even the needed ninth ratification of the Constitution — by the New Hampshire convention in June 1788 — did not abate the contentiousness of American politics. In the Confederation Congress, for example, Abraham Yates, Jr., of New York, an ardent Antifederalist, remained defiant as long as he could. Yates described to his relation and political ally Abraham Lansing his defiant reaction to the news of New Hampshire's ratification: "I was addressed by several of the members: what would the state of New York do now? I tell them the same they would have done if New Hampshire had not adopted it. They will adopt but I hoped not without previous amendments, that my mind was made up that if all the twelve states were to come in that New York would not, and I trusted they would not."[5] Yates was not unique. Throughout the ratification controversy Antifederalists had hinted that they and their allies would resist the Constitution even if it went into effect.

Worried Federalists collected rumors of Antifederal plots against the Constitution's effectuation, exchanged news of their researches by letter, and implored one another to send the most accurate intelligence available.[6] Their letters demonstrate their awareness that victory in the ratification campaign was only one stage of a continuing struggle with the Constitution's opponents over the American future. For example, on July 27, 1788, James McHenry of Maryland, a signer of the Constitution who had been an aide to George Washington during the Revolutionary War, reported a disturbing rumor to his old commander: "It is whispered here that some leading characters among you have by no means dropped their resentment to the new constitution, but have determined on some secret plan to suspend the proper organization of the government or to defeat it altogether."[7] Still reeling

---

[5] Abraham Yates, Jr., to Abraham G. Lansing, June 25, 1788, in *DHFFE*, 1:24.

[6] On American politicians' reliance on the "collection" of political intelligence and evidence of public opinion, see the important and valuable study by Joanne B. Freeman, "Slander, Poison, Whispers, and Fame: Jefferson's 'Anas' and Political Gossip in the Early Republic," *Journal of the Early Republic* 15 (1995):25–57. Freeman's article informs the various levels of investigation and analysis presented in this article and the larger study from which it is drawn.

[7] McHenry to Washington, July 27, 1788, in *DHFFE*, 2:109.

from Maryland's tumultuous and bitter ratification contest,[8] McHenry found the rumored secret plan "so serious and alarming a circumstance that it is necessary to be apprised of its truth, and extent that we may be on our guard against attempts of the antifederals to get into our assembly, as in all probability the next legislature will meet before the time for commencing proceedings by the new Congress."[9] Noting that in Maryland "every means is made use of to do away with all distinction between federal and antifederal and I suspect with no very friendly design to the federal course," McHenry begged Washington for news: "If such a plan has been hatched I think you must have heard of it. I shall therefore be much obliged to you to give me a hint of it as soon as possible."[10]

McHenry's letter makes explicit the Federalists' implicit assumption that their victory in the ratification campaign was only one stage of a continuing struggle with the Constitution's opponents. It also illustrates the emergence of a national public sphere in which citizens of different states shared political intelligence and coordinated political activities across state lines.[11] Here, for example, a Marylander and a Virginian could exchange gossip about Virginian political machinations that in turn could affect national interests. Though Antifederalists were slow to appreciate the possibilities of and devise strategies for coordinated national action, the specter of a national Antifederalist movement lurked in the rumors that so exercised McHenry.[12]

---

[8]See Gregory Stiverson, "Necessity, the Mother of Union: Maryland and the Constitution, 1785–1789," in *The Constitution and the States: The Role of the Original Thirteen States in the Framing and Adoption of the Federal Constitution,* ed. Patrick T. Conley and John P. Kaminski (Madison, Wis., 1988), pp. 131–52, and sources cited on pp. 151–52; Peter S. Onuf, "Maryland: The Small Republic in the New Nation," in *Ratifying the Constitution,* ed. Michael Allen Gillespie and Michael Lienesch (Lawrence, Kans., 1989), pp. 171–200, and sources cited on pp. 199–200.

[9]McHenry to Washington, July 27, 1788, in *DHFFE,* 2:109.

[10]Ibid.

[11]See, for example, John T. Alexander, *The Selling of the Constitutional Convention: A History of News Coverage* (Madison, Wis., 1990); Gaspare J. Saladino, "The Federalist Express," in *New York and the Union: Contributions to the American Constitutional Experience* ed. Stephen L. Schechter and Richard B. Bernstein (Albany, N.Y., 1990), pp. 326–41.

[12]For example, in late June 1788, as the New York and Virginia ratifying conventions deliberated the Constitution, Robert Yates, a leading New York Antifederalist, wrote to George Mason, a principal Virginia Antifederalist, seeking to build political alliances across state lines to impede the Constitution's adoption. Yates's effort was too little, too late. See Robert Yates to George Mason, June 21, 1788, Emmet Collection No. 9528,

As soon as he received McHenry's letter, Washington penned a reply imbued with his habitual caution: "I am less likely than almost any person to have been informed of the circumstances to which you allude."[13] Washington had a point; had there been an Antifederal conspiracy to prevent the Constitution from taking effect, the president of the Convention that had drafted the Constitution would have been the last man in the nation to learn of the plot. Moreover, the high feelings sparked by the ratification contest had disrupted ties between Washington and such former allies as George Mason, who otherwise would have remained among Washington's principal allies and informants.[14] In retrospect, however, Washington's caution takes on a larger significance, as he intended it to do; rather than expressing tact and reserve, it suggested Washington's doubts about the substance of McHenry's letter. Though such Federalists as McHenry were right that the struggle would continue, they were wrong about what form it would take. Later historians have confirmed Washington's suspicion that Federalist alarm at Antifederalist schemes to block the launch of the new government far outweighs evidence that such plans existed.[15]

Once both Virginia and New York ratified the Constitution in the

---

Rare Books and Manuscripts Division, New York Public Library, quoted and discussed in Bernstein with Rice, *Are We to Be a Nation?* pp. 208–9.

[13] Washington to McHenry, July 31, 1788, reprinted in *DHFFE*, 1:55.

[14] On Washington's friendship with George Mason and its disruption by the ratification controversy, see James Thomas Flexner, *George Washington and the New Nation, 1783–1793* (Boston, 1970), pp. 135–37; "Editorial Note: The Virginia Ratifying Convention of 1788," in *The Papers of George Mason*, 3 vols., ed. Robert A. Rutland (Chapel Hill, 1970), 3:1047–48.

[15] On the abortive attempts to organize a second convention to rewrite the Constitution before its effectuation, see Kenneth R. Bowling, "Politics in the First Congress, 1789–1791," Ph.D. diss., University of Wisconsin, 1968, pp. 6–13, 121–28; Linda Grant DePauw, "The Anticlimax of Antifederalism: The Abortive Second Convention Movement, 1788–89," *Prologue* 2 (1970):98–114; Richard E. Ellis, "The Persistence of Antifederalism after 1789," in *Beyond Confederation: Dimensions of the Constitution and American National Identity*, ed. Richard R. Beeman, Stephen Botein, and Edward C. Carter II (Chapel Hill, 1987), pp. 295–314; and Edward P. Smith, "The Movement toward a Second Constitutional Convention in 1788," in *Essays in the Constitutional History of the United States in the Formative Period, 1776–1789*, ed. J. Franklin Jameson (Boston, 1889), pp. 46–115. But see Steven R. Boyd, *The Politics of Opposition: Antifederalists and the Acceptance of the Constitution* (Millwood, N.Y., 1979), chap. 6, asserting — though without adducing evidence — that some Antifederalists did threaten violent resistance to the establishment of the Constitution.

summer of 1788, even such die-hard Antifederalists as Yates gave up active resistance.[16] On August 8, 1788, Yates signaled his surrender by joining the other New York delegates to the Confederation Congress in an agreement pledging all the signatories, whenever those New Yorkers favoring the Constitution were absent from Congress on official business, to vote to support the inauguration of the new government and to secure the capital for New York City. Yates won only one concession: he made sure the document provided that such votes would be contrary to his private views, and that its language would permit him to vote in conformity with his own views in circumstances where he could do so without serious consequences to New York.[17]

Thereafter, both Federalists and Antifederalists turned with relief to organizing and conducting the first federal elections. As recommended by the Federal Convention in its resolutions of September 17, 1787, that process had three phases. First, the Confederation Congress was to adopt an electoral schedule; second, the state governments were to establish electoral procedures; third, the elections would take place under state supervision.[18] Each phase was equally

---

[16]The Virginia convention's narrow margin (89–79) provided little reassurance for the Federalists, even though the state's Antifederalists grudgingly accepted the Constitution's triumph. See generally John P. Kaminski et al., eds., *The Documentary History of the Ratification of the Constitution and the Bill of Rights, 1787–1791*, 17 vols. to date (Madison, Wis., 1976–), vols. 8–10; for secondary sources, see 8:xlvi–xlvii.

As with Virginia, the New York convention's narrow margin (30–27) and the suspicious tone of the convention's instrument of ratification did nothing to reassure the Federalists or to reconcile the Antifederalists to the Constitution's triumph; on the contrary, the New York convention included in its resolutions language dangerously approaching a conditional ratification of the Constitution. See generally Linda Grant DePauw, *The Eleventh Pillar: New York State and the Constitution* (Ithaca, N.Y., 1966); Stephen L. Schechter, *The Reluctant Pillar: New York and the Adoption of the Constitution* (Troy, N.Y., 1985); John P. Kaminski, "Adjusting to Circumstances: New York's Relationship with the Federal Government, 1776–1788," in *The Constitution and the States,* ed. Patrick T. Conley and John P. Kaminski (Madison, Wis., 1988), pp. 225–49; and Cecil L. Eubanks, "New York: Federalism and the Political Economy of Union," in Gillespie and Lienesch, *Ratifying the Constitution,* pp. 300–340. For the text of New York's instrument of ratification, see Charles C. Tansill, ed., *Documents Illustrative of the Formation of the Union of the American States* (Washington, D.C., 1927), pp. 1034–44.

[17]Agreement between Abraham Yates, Jr., and the Other New York Delegates, Aug. 8, 1788, in *DHFFE,* 1:81–82.

[18]Resolutions of the [Federal] Convention submitting the Constitution to the Confederation Congress, Sept. 17, 1787, in *DHFFE,* 1:6–7.

important to the launching of the new government—but the third stage was most challenging, for never before had Americans attempted popular elections for a national political institution on such a scale.

On July 2, 1788, the Confederation Congress began planning the transition. With only Yates of New York opposed and the North Carolina and Rhode Island delegates not voting (because of their states' failure to ratify the Constitution), Congress named a committee to "report an act to Congress for putting the said Constitution into operation in pursuance of the resolutions of the late Federal Convention."[19] Within a week, the committee brought in its report; the schedule it proposed provoked virtually no disagreement.

The committee reported, however, that it could not fix one detail of its mandate — "the place for commencing proceedings under the said Constitution." The committee's failure proved a troubling omen. That issue soon eclipsed every other aspect of the transition. For the next two months an increasingly frantic and bitter Confederation Congress disputed the relative merits of cities from New York to Baltimore.

Once the capital became the grail of American politics, the controversy over its site threatened to derail the implementation of the Constitution.[20] The stakes in the capital dispute were clear and significant, blending questions of interest and principle — but, in the view of observers and participants alike, interest predominated. The long, contentious struggle to resolve the capital issue became a textbook illustration of the ways that questions of representational politics could interfere even in so clear a measure for the general good, so paradigmatic an instance of deliberative politics, as the establishment of a form of government that the people's representatives had duly approved.

The cities vying for the honor, the states where they were situated, and the delegates in Congress who represented them saw direct, immediate benefits in capturing the prize. Increased public revenues and private profits would result from a shift of many different kinds of business to the new seat of government, from the need to accommodate the

---

[19]Journals of Congress, July 2, 1788, in *DHFFE*, 1:28–29, esp. p. 29.

[20]The leading study is Kenneth R. Bowling, *The Creation of Washington, D.C.: The Idea and Location of the National Capital* (Fairfax, Va., 1991). See also idem, *Creating the Federal City: Potomac Fever* (Washington, D.C., 1988).

government's personnel and from the enhancement of prestige for the city, state, and region where the government would have its home.

Considerations of convenience and efficiency influenced the delegates almost as much as interest did. The capital's site had to expedite the workings of the new government; a central location with extensive resources of transportation and communication would ease officials' travels between their home states and the capital and expedite the promulgation and enforcement of federal laws and policies.[21]

Finally, the capital's location would shape the character of the new government. A capital in the rural South would feel the influence of farming interests, thus pushing the new government in the direction of agrarian democracy; one based in an established northern city would feel the influences of commercial, manufacturing, and speculating interests, impelling the government in the direction of a commercial republic. At times, politicians blended these various considerations to produce surprising results. For example, Theodore Sedgwick of Massachusetts, a Federalist ordinarily friendly to commercial and manufacturing interests, protested: "I consider [Philadelphia] as the most improper of any great town on the continent because it is the greatest commercial place in America, and because it is generally believed that there exists in that town an undue influence inimical to the general good."[22] Sedgwick's hostility to Philadelphia was founded not on his hostility to commercial interests, however, but on his suspicion of Philadelphians and Pennsylvanians. As is so often the case in American history, a foreign observer put his finger on the true issue. In the wake of the adoption of the election ordinance, Antoine R. C. M. de la Forest, the French consul general in New York, reported to the Comte de la Luzerne, the foreign minister, that "each side fears that the [state] which has Congress nearest it will have too much influence on national affairs."[23]

---

[21]On the importance of a central location for American state capitals in this period, see Rosemarie Zagarri, *The Politics of Size: Representation in the United States, 1776–1850* (Ithaca, N.Y., 1987), pp. 8–35.

[22]Theodore Sedgwick to Benjamin Lincoln, Aug. 1, 1788, in *DHFFE*, 1:57. Sedgwick eventually became a Massachusetts Representative in the First Congress; see the sources cited in note 47.

[23]Antoine R. C. M. de la Forest, French consul general in New York, to Comte de la Luzerne, Sept. 14, 1788, in *DHFFE*, 1:139–40, quote on p. 139.

The arguments over the capital issue repeatedly delayed the Confederation Congress's adoption of an election ordinance. As some cities saw their prospects dwindle, their advocates became despondent. When, in mid-August 1788, it appeared that Philadelphia would not be selected as the home of the new government, the noted Philadelphia printer Mathew Carey wrote: "Politics are as dull here as with you. We have, for a long time, chameleon-like, fed ourselves on air; and counted the vast fortunes we were all most assuredly to make, by the return of Congress. Some of us, I believe, had fixed on the places where our estates were to be purchased, and settled on the number of years we were to remain in business, favoring the public with our services; but we have awoke, and found it all a dream. 'Blessed are they that expect nothing, for they shall never be disappointed.' "[24]

More important, the contests between special interests impeding the effectuation of the general interest alarmed friends of the Constitution, who feared that the spirit of faction would cripple the new government at its birth. For example, even so politic a national figure as George Washington — who had more experience than most with the dilatoriness of the Continental and Confederation Congresses — could not contain his annoyance at the delegates' failure to resolve the capital issue. "The present Congress, by its great indecision in fixing on a place at which the new Congress is to convene, have hung the expectations, and patience of the Union on tenter hooks, and thereby (if further evidence had been necessary) given a fresh instance of the unfitness of a body so constituted to regulate with energy and precision the affairs of such an extensive empire."[25] Abandoning the claims of his native city, a writer in the *Pennsylvania Mercury* expostulated: "Let the place of meeting be New York, Philadelphia, or Baltimore, nay, the banks of the Potomac, Ohio, or Mississippi, let it be anywhere;

---

[24]Mathew Carey to Ebenezer Hazard, Aug. 14, 1788 (excerpt), in *DHFFE*, 1:89.

[25]George Washington to Samuel Powel, Sept. 15, 1788, quoted in *DHFFE*, 1:91 n. 3 (emphasis in original). (Although Congress acted on September 13, Washington had not yet received the news when he wrote to Powel.) Accord, Robert Morris to Samuel Meredith, Aug. 20, 1788: "I don't care much how this question is determined but I think it ought to be soon determined"(*DHFFE* 1:95); and *Massachusetts Centinel*, Aug. 20, 1788: "The delay does not give satisfaction to the masters of Congress, The People, who scruple not to attribute it to motives, which it is to be hoped do not exist" (*DHFFE* 1:95).

but for Heaven's sake, let the *vox populi* prevail, let the government be put in motion."[26] In a more jovial tone, newspaper publisher Thomas B. Wait wrote from Portland, Maine (then part of Massachusetts), to George Thatcher, a Massachusetts delegate in Congress who later represented the Maine district in the First Congress:

> Why, my friend, do you contend so warmly for New York, as the seat of government? Do you, in this, act the part of a true Federal Philosopher? We should remember the question is not, what will be most convenient or best suit the interest of New England, but what does the interest of the Union require? How shall that be accommodated? But this last I suppose would be an odd question in Congress. There, it is the Southern interest, or the Northern; and every man of them ranges himself upon one side or the other, and contends with as much earnestness and warmth as if at an Olympic game.[27]

The increasingly thorny dispute even attracted the attention of foreign governments. For example, on July 30, 1788, the Comte de Moustier, the French minister plenipotentiary to the United States, recorded in his journal information from the supposedly secret debates of the Confederation Congress: "Mr. [Alexander] Hamilton alleged that the delegates from New York were going to lose their popularity if the new Congress did not remain in that state because they had solemnly promised it at the [New York ratifying] Convention if the new Constitution were ratified there. Mr. [James] D[uane], one of its delegates, has declared that his reputation was lost if Congress changed its residence. It is astonishing that the personal interest of each delegate is so active in attracting Congress to his own state."[28]

Exhaustion and frustration finally derailed Congress's quest for a definitive solution to the capital issue. On September 13, 1788, it adopted without dissent an election ordinance providing "that the present Seat of Congress [be] the place for commencing Proceedings under the said Constitution."[29] The resolution was silent on the reasons for the delay, for all attempts to add explanatory language had

---

[26] *Pennsylvania Mercury,* Sept. 9, 1788, in *DHFFE,* 1:126.

[27] Thomas B. Wait to George Thatcher, Aug. 21, 1788 (excerpt), in *DHFFE,* 1:95–96 (emphasis in original).

[28] Journal of Comte de Moustier, July 30, 1788, in *DHFFE,* 1:55.

[29] Election ordinance, Sept. 13, 1788, in *DHFFE,* 1:132–33, quote on p. 133.

gone down to defeat. Most delegates kept their feelings to themselves, expressing only relief that the debate was ended and the machinery for establishing government set in motion. Nathan Dane, an Anti-federal Massachusetts delegate to Congress, was one of the few delegates willing to record his views. He reported to Gov. John Hancock that the "long and somewhat disagreeable discussion" had ended; he noted another element of the compromise, linked to the selection of New York, underlying the election ordinance: "The delegates of Massachusetts and most of the Eastern delegates wished the new government to meet at a much earlier period, but the Southern members said it was impracticable for them in their extensive states to make their elections and meet sooner, and as the Eastern members had their choice as to the place of meeting, and the Southern gentlemen were many of them disappointed in this, it was thought advisable not to press them very hard as to the time of meeting."[30] But other politicians expressed their disgust with special interests even though, in the capital controversy, they had campaigned hard for their own region. Rep. James Madison of Virginia penned a disgruntled letter to Washington that is replete with unconscious irony: "It has, indeed, been too apparent that local and state considerations have very improperly predominated in this question, and that something more is aimed at than merely the first session of the government at this place."[31] These politicians' failures to admit, or even to see, the contradiction between their denunciations of "local and state considerations" and their own vigorous pursuit of such goals presaged further such difficulties.

The States Devise Political Technology[32]

The adoption of the election ordinance passed the baton to the state governments, which were to devise electoral procedures, as the Consti-

---

[30]Nathan Dane to Gov. John Hancock, Sept. 14, 1788 (excerpt), in *DHFFE*, 1:137.

[31]James Madison to George Washington, Sept. 14, 1788, in *DHFFE*, 1:138–39, quote on p. 138.

[32]The phrase "political technology" comes from Morton White, *Philosophy, The Federalist, and the Constitution* (New York, 1987), pp. 13, 199–203. On the relationship between scientific and technological thought and the making of the Constitution, see

tution required.[33] They thus had remarkable power over the operations of the new general government — but, as they tried to figure out how to wield this power, the states operated in a vacuum. It was not clear what would happen if states chose not to hold elections. Under the Confederation, if a state legislature did not choose delegates to Congress, the state went unrepresented until its legislature acted. Such gaps in representation did not endanger the legitimacy of the Confederation Congress, though the lack of a quorum (often because of a state's failure to send delegates) at times disrupted its institutional continuity.[34] But state failure to conduct elections for a new national legislature might cripple the new system in its cradle. Many politicians who thought in national terms therefore kept an anxious watch as the state governments set the electoral process in motion.

Only three states — New York, North Carolina, and Rhode Island — did not hold elections during the time set by the election ordinance. North Carolina and Rhode Island still had not ratified the Constitution; once they did ratify, in November 1789 and May 1790, respectively, they held elections as promptly as the vagaries of eighteenth-century transportation and communications allowed.[35] By contrast, New York's delays grew out of factional strife. The state assembly (dominated by Antifederalists) and the state senate (controlled by

---

generally Michael Foley, *Law, Men and Machines: Modern American Government and the Appeal of Newtonian Mechanics* (London, 1990), passim; and I. Bernard Cohen, *Science and the Founding Fathers: Science in the Political Thought of Franklin, Adams, Jefferson, and Madison* (New York, 1995), esp. pp. 237–80. Note, however, that there is a profound distinction between science and technology. See generally Lewis Wolpert, *The Unnatural Nature of Science* (1992; Cambridge, Mass., 1993), pp. 25–34.

[33] "The Times, Places and Manner of holding Elections for Senators and Representatives, shall be prescribed in each State by the Legislature thereof; but the Congress may at any time by Law make or alter such Regulations, except as to the Places of chusing Senators." U. S. Constitution, art. I, sec. 4, cl. 1.

[34] On absenteeism and its effects on the Continental and Confederation Congresses, see Calvin Jillson and Rick K. Wilson, *Congressional Dynamics: Structure, Coordination, and Choice in the First American Congress, 1774–1789* (Stanford, Calif., 1994), pp. 155–62, and Jack N. Rakove, *The Beginnings of National Politics: An Interpretive History of the Continental Congress* (New York, 1979), pp. 168, 198–99, 216, 345, 355–57, 371. Volume 1 of the *DHFFE* contains numerous appeals to state legislatures to ensure that the states had a full representation in Congress for the critical business of adopting transition legislation; on those occasions when all thirteen states were represented, the circumstance was widely discussed as the first instance of full representation of the states since 1776.

[35] See *DHFFE*, 4:301–73 (North Carolina), and 4:375–449 (Rhode Island).

Federalists) deadlocked for months over issues of electoral procedure, but state issues, the fallout of ratification, and personal animosities complicated their wrangles. New York eventually did establish procedures for electing representatives and chose a Senate delegation, but the deadlock cost the state its voice in the first election of a president and vice president.[36] (By pursuing their agenda so aggressively, New York's Antifederalists ironically failed to secure their state's electoral votes for Gov. George Clinton, the Antifederalists' choice for vice president, thus sabotaging Antifederal hopes to capture a key position in the new government.)[37]

The state legislatures had an easier time working out their methods for selecting senators than in devising election procedures for the House of Representatives; most states reworked for the choice of senators the mechanisms they had used to select delegates to the Confederation Congress.[38] Even here, however, conflicts arose over whether, in those states with bicameral legislatures, upper and lower houses should vote together or separately; once again, partisan divisions exacerbated these conflicts.[39]

In devising elections for representatives, each state had to decide whether to divide itself into districts or to elect all its representatives at large. As in so many other cases, this procedural issue had both constitutional and political implications. Many Antifederalists had charged that Federalists, whom they condemned as foes of popular govern-

---

[36]See ibid., 3:191–564; Tadahisa Kuroda, "New York and the First Presidential Election," *New York History* (1988):19–51; idem, "The Electoral College in the Early Republic, 1787–1804: The New York Experience," in Schechter and Bernstein, *New York and the Union*, pp. 618–29. See generally the new monograph, idem, *The Origins of the Twelfth Amendment: The Electoral College in the Early Republic, 1787–1804* (Westport, Conn., 1994).

[37]See, for example, Edward Carrington to James Madison, Nov. 9–10, 1788 (excerpt): "Mr. H[enry] is putting in agitation the name of Clinton for Vice Presidt." (*DHFFE*, 4:88); New York City Federal Republican Committee to Antifederalists in Other States, circa Nov. 13, 1788, in *DHFFE*, 4:91 (circular letter, apparently in Melancton Smith's handwriting, urging all Antifederalists to rally behind Clinton for vice president); and other documents scattered through volume four of *DHFFE*. For an excellent, well-documented discussion of Clinton's short-lived candidacy, see John P. Kaminski, *George Clinton: Yeoman Statesman in the New Republic* (Madison, Wis., 1993), pp. 169–78 (chap. 31, "An Antifederalist Vice President").

[38]The following five paragraphs are based on the four volumes of *DHFFE*.

[39]As noted above, this was one of the key issues that delayed the selection of New York's senators (*DHFFE*, 3:513–44).

ment, favored at-large electoral systems to ensure the election of those with "general reputations." Though such men might seem best quali-fied to represent the people in the House, Antifederalists maintained that men of enlarged reputations and general views would not — could not — be familiar with the range of interests, problems, and conditions within their state.[40]

Politics more than principle, however, was the driving force behind the choice of at-large or district systems. In each state, Federalists and Antifederalists fought for at-large or district systems based on their sense of which would give them a better chance of representation in the new House. Five states — Pennsylvania, New Hampshire, Connecti-cut, Delaware, and New Jersey — adopted at-large systems. Federalist legislative majorities in Pennsylvania and New Jersey approved at-large systems to ensure Federalist majorities; Connecticut (where Antifeder-alism was negligible) retained the system by which it had elected dele-gates to Congress since 1779. Delaware and Rhode Island had no choice; because the Constitution had assigned them only one repre-sentative, their House elections were necessarily at-large.[41] New Hamp-shire's Federalists made a brief and ineffective plea for district elec-tions, but the state adopted an at-large system, with a second election scheduled to fill vacancies left over by the first election; this election proved necessary, as nobody received enough votes to win any of the state's three seats in the first election. Maryland and Georgia adopted a hybrid system, in which candidates for each of the state's House seats were nominated from districts but had to stand for election statewide.[42]

The five states that chose district systems — South Carolina, Mas-

---

[40]For example, "Letters of Brutus, No. IV (Nov. 29, 1787)," in *The Complete Anti-Federalist*, 7 vols., ed. Herbert J. Storing (Chicago, 1981), 2:382–87, quote on p. 387: "Provision should have been made for marking out the states into districts, and for choosing, by a majority of votes, a person out of each of them of permanent property and residence in the district which he was to represent." Accord, "Letters from the Federal Farmer to the Republican," No. III (Oct. 10, 1787), in *The Complete Anti-Federalist*, 2:234–45, esp. pp. 235–36.

[41]See the documents collected in *DHFFE*, 2:81–85. In 1789 North Carolina elected by district; Rhode Island in 1790 conducted an at-large House election for the same reasons of necessity that had imposed the choice on Delaware. See the sources col-lected in ibid., 4:375–449.

[42]Two tickets, one Federalist and the other Antifederalist, competed to represent the state in the House, and the Federalists prevailed. See the documents collected in ibid., 2:98–245.

sachusetts, North Carolina, Virginia, and New York — then tackled another vexatious issue: whether to use existing county or state legislative districts to delimit House districts or to define new districts of relatively equal population. Yet again, in devising political technology to serve the new national public sphere, representational politics contaminated what the Federalists had hoped would be a reliable system of political filtration to elect only men of "general reputation" and "elevated views" — deliberative legislators — to the House. Some states engaged in what we would call "gerrymanders," though the term did not yet exist.[43] For example, Massachusetts drew district lines favoring its more conservative eastern counties, as opposed to the Maine district and the more radical (and Antifederalist) western counties.[44]

Charges and countercharges of boundary manipulation plagued all the states that conducted their House elections by a district system. Virginia provided the most famous example of pre-1812 gerrymandering. Led by the vengeful Patrick Henry, still smarting from his defeat at James Madison's hands in the state's 1788 ratifying convention, the legislature's Antifederal majority devised a House district for Madison that saddled him with a solid Antifederal majority and enabled the popular Antifederalist James Monroe to run against him, thwarting Federalist efforts to draw the district to comprise a Federalist majority.[45]

---

[43]The term *gerrymander* is rooted in the Massachusetts state elections of 1812 and was named for the state's Republican governor, Elbridge Gerry. Gerry's modern biographer presents a convincing case that Gerry was not responsible for the partisan system of distorted district boundaries associated with him, and thus the term *gerrymander* is an unfair coinage. See the discussion in George A. Billias, *Elbridge Gerry: Founding Father and Republican Statesman* (New York, 1976), pp. 316–17.

[44]See the sources collected in *DHFFE*, 1:431–763; Van Beck Hall, *Politics Without Parties: Massachusetts, 1780–1791* (Pittsburgh, 1971), pp. 304–16; Billias, *Gerry*, pp. 215–17.

[45]See *DHFFE*, 2:317–49 (the documents for Virginia's Fifth Congressional District); "Editorial Note: Madison's Election to the First Federal Congress, October 1788–February 1789," in *The Papers of James Madison*, 17 vols. to date (Chicago and Charlottesville, 1962–), vol. 11 (Robert A. Rutland, William M. E. Rachal, Charles F. Hobson, Jeanne K. Sisson, eds.), pp. 301–4. Madison's failed candidacy for the Senate and his arduous but successful campaign for the House forms a major theme of the balance of volume 11 of the *Madison Papers*. Secondary sources include Richard R. Beeman, *The Old Dominion and the New Nation, 1788–1801* (Lexington, Ky., 1972), pp. 23–27; Irving N. Brant, *James Madison: Father of the Constitution, 1787–1800* (Indianapolis, 1950), pp. 235–44; Ralph Ketcham, *James Madison* (New York, 1971), pp. 275–77; Jack N. Rakove, *James Madison and the Creation of the American Republic* (Glenview, Ill.,

The problem confronting Madison was only one example of a recurring phenomenon distressingly familiar from colonial and state politics.[46] Here, as in so many other aspects of the first federal elections, preexisting configurations of state and local politics interacted with the new demands of setting the Constitution in motion to shape the federal electoral process and define its results. The campaigns for the House presented curious and often internally inconsistent political agendas, as candidates at once promised to safeguard their constituents' interests and to work for the new Constitution's success and the general good.[47]

Testing Assumptions

As the first federal elections unfolded across the nation, their purposes expanded beyond selecting the first legislators under the new Constitution. The candidates who vied for office, their supporters and opponents, journalists, and the people inaugurated a new chapter of the shared conversation about what the government created by the

---

1990), pp. 78–79; Henry Mayer, *A Son of Thunder: Patrick Henry and the American Revolution* (New York, 1987), pp. 446–52; and Harry Ammon, *James Monroe: The Quest for National Identity* (New York, 1971), pp. 75–77.

[46]For influential studies of apportionment in early American politics, see Orin Grant Libby, "The Geographical Distribution of the Vote of the Thirteen States on the Federal Constitution, 1787–8," *Bulletin of the University of Wisconsin* 1 (1894); and Charles W. Roll, "We, Some of the People: Apportionment in the Thirteen State Conventions Ratifying the Constitution," *Journal of American History* 56 (1969):21–40. See also Robert J. Dinkin, *Voting in Provincial America: A Study of Elections in the Thirteen Colonies, 1689–1776* (Westport, Conn., 1977).

[47]In Massachusetts, for example, Fisher Ames ran in the House election for the seat representing Boston and its environs and defeated the Antifederalist leader Samuel Adams on twin bases: Ames's loyalty to the new Constitution and his sensitivity to issues of trade and commerce. Theodore Sedgwick, running for the House in a western district comprising Hampshire and Berkshire counties, had to endure five separate elections before winning his seat; while asserting his sincere attachment to the newly ratified federal Constitution as a major justification for his candidacy, he had to contend with divisions between Hampshire and Berkshire politicians, and charges of deism designed to sap his strength among voters of conservative religious beliefs. In addition to the documents collected in *DHFFE*, 1:431–763, see Winfred E. A. Bernhard, *Fisher Ames: Federalist and Statesman, 1758–1808* (Chapel Hill, 1965), pp. 68–75; Richard E. Welch, Jr., *Theodore Sedgwick, Federalist: A Political Portrait* (Middletown, Conn., 1985), pp. 66–70.

Constitution would be, what place it would occupy in the new nation's public life, what powers and responsibilities it would assume, and how it would exercise those powers and fulfill those responsibilities.[48] In sum, the first federal elections became the focus of renewed political and constitutional controversy, the successor in logic and chronology to the struggle for ratification.

Still, even as they contended over issues of substantive constitutional interpretation, both Federalists and Antifederalists emphasized the overriding importance of putting the right men in the right offices, so that the right interpretations of the Constitution and the right administration of the government that document authorized would prevail. The election of the vice president, who would preside over the Senate, illustrates this central aspect of the first federal elections' constitutional and political importance. As noted above, it was a foregone conclusion that George Washington would be elected the first president, though it was not certain until the last minute that he would accept the office. But there was no comparable clear candidate for the vice presidency. Antifederalists saw the election of a vice president as a chance to recover ground lost in the ratification contest; they hoped to elect a vice president (most backed New York's Gov. George Clinton or Massachusetts's Gov. John Hancock) who would exert Antifederal influence on the Constitution's effectuation, the Senate's administration, and the enactment of the first federal laws. By contrast, Federalists worked to prevent Antifederal success and to ensure that the eventual vice president (John Adams of Massachusetts) would not emerge as a competitor for prestige and influence with President Washington.[49] In another, more famous example of the significance of the elections of 1788–89 for the future of the new constitutional system, Antifederalists made their demand for a federal declaration of rights a vital issue

---

[48]Chapter 5 of R. B. Bernstein, *"Conven'd in Firm Debate,"* presents a detailed analysis of this pivotal though neglected chapter of the shared conversation of American constitutional discourse.

[49]According to his most recent scholarly biographer, John Adams did not learn at the time that Federalists were seeking simultaneously to elect him but also to hold down his electoral votes so as to deprive him of independent political authority. John Ferling, *John Adams: A Life* (Knoxville, 1992), pp. 298–99. On Adams's unhappy and frustrating vice presidency, see generally Linda Dudik Guerrero, *John Adams's Vice Presidency, 1789–1797: The Neglected Man in the Forgotten Office* (New York, 1982).

during James Madison's contest with James Monroe to represent Vir-ginia's Fifth District in the first U.S. House of Representatives.[50]

National political and constitutional questions were not alone in defining the first federal electoral agendas — nor did these issues oper-ate in a vacuum. Again, as in the ratification controversy of 1787–88, preexisting partisan divisions in each state profoundly influenced the federal elections of 1788–90. Groups already at each other's throats simply shifted their contests to a new arena; they competed for new and potentially valuable prizes of office and sought to safeguard state and local interests in the new federal government. The exact nature of these influences varied from state to state, sometimes within each state from one House district to the next. A few examples suffice.

In South Carolina the contest to choose the representative for the district including the state capital, Charleston, was determined by a controversy over the federal government's power to injure a vital local interest — slavery. In that district, the historian David Ramsay, already suspected as an outsider because he had been born in New Jersey, was a strong contender in a three-way contest with a suspected Loyalist, Wil-liam [Loughton] Smith, and a local Revolutionary War hero, Com-modore Alexander Gillon.[51] In the last days before the election, anti-

---

[50]See the sources cited in note 40. For the Virginia disestablishment struggle that provided the background and context of this election, see also Thomas E. Buckley, S.J., *Church and State in Revolutionary Virginia, 1776–1787* (Charlottesville, 1977); Merrill D. Peterson and Robert D. Vaughan, eds., *The Virginia Statute for Religious Freedom: Its Evolu-tion and Consequences in American History* (Cambridge, 1986).

[51]"Editorial Note: The David Ramsay-William Smith Controversy in the Charleston District, 22–25 November 1788," *DHFFE*, 1:173–74, and documents collected in pp. 174–98. On the lives and records of the principal candidates, see George C. Rogers, Jr., *Evolution of a Federalist: William Loughton Smith of South Carolina (1758–1812)* (Columbia, S.C., 1962), esp. pp. 162–71; and Arthur Shaffer, *To Be an American: David Ramsay and the Making of the American Consciousness* (Columbia, S.C., 1991), esp. pp. 167–87.

Alexander Gillon's candidacy in this election is a puzzle; both Smith and Ramsay ignored him, and he played a little role in the election; that he received twice as many votes as Ramsay is rather an indication of the catastrophic failure of Ramsay's candidacy than of Gillon's strength at the polls. A noted merchant and landowner beset in the last decade of his life by financial difficulties, Gillon had served during the Revolutionary War as a privateer, with the grandiloquent title "Commodore of the South Carolina Navy." Gillon, a fervent advocate of the Revolutionary War, vigorously opposed the return of former Loyalists to the state and was an ardent supporter of the interests of the South Carolina backcountry. At the same time that he was a candidate for the U.S. House of Representatives, he also ran for and won election to the South Carolina House of Representatives from the backcountry Saxe Gotha district. The editors of the

Ramsay rumors apparently began to circulate through Charleston. Our first concrete evidence of those rumors is an anonymous newspaper article that appeared in Charleston's *City Gazette* on Saturday, November 22, 1788, two days before the South Carolina elections were to begin. This article denied widespread rumors that Ramsay "would if elected, use his endeavors to promote an emancipation of the Negroes in this state."[52] Attributing the rumors to Smith's supporters, Ramsay launched a flanking counterattack with a pseudonymous article charging that Smith did not meet the citizenship and residence requirements set forth in Article I, Section 2 of the federal Constitution.[53] As the broadside and newspaper war between Smith and Ramsay continued, the issue of emancipation continued to haunt Ramsay and sap his strength at the polls, while the counterissue that Ramsay sought to raise proved too legalistic and abstract to make headway with the electorate.[54] The anti-Ramsay polemicists kept the focus on Ramsay. The writer of one broadside (whom historians have identified as Ralph Izard, Smith's father-in-law, who became one of South Carolina's two senators) challenged Ramsay directly: "Will the letter writer say, that he has never declared that he thought slavery ought to be abolished, or that he never distributed pamphlets which were intended to render the inhabitants of this state odious in the eyes of the world. If he should have the effrontery to do so, proofs of this fact, upon oath, shall be given to the public."[55] After mounting a vigor-

---

DHFFE note that "his opponents tried repeatedly to remove him from the legislature by electing him to other offices" (*DHFFE*, 1:220–21), and perhaps his candidacy in the first federal elections exemplified this tactic.

[52] *City Gazette* (Charleston, S.C.), Nov. 22, 1788, in *DHFFE*, 1:174.

[53] [David Ramsay], "An Elector for Charleston District to the Public," in *City Gazette*, Nov. 22, 1788, in ibid., 1:174–76. Smith responded vigorously that same day — apparently, with success. See "William Smith to the Citizens of Charleston District," broadside dated Nov. 22, 1788, in ibid., 1:176–81, and see the additional contributions to the controversy cited in note 47.

[54] See "An Enemy to Quibblers," *City Gazette*, Nov. 24, 1788, in ibid., 1:184 (disputing Ramsay's charges against Smith); [David Ramsay?], "A Short Reply to a Long Piece Signed William Smith," broadside dated Nov. 24, 1788, in ibid., 1:185–87; [David Ramsay], "A Calm Reply," broadside dated Nov. 24, 1788, in ibid., 1:187–88; William Smith, "A Dose for the Doctor," broadside dated Nov. 25, 1788, in ibid., 1:193–94.

[55] [Ralph Izard?], "Another Elector for Charleston District," broadside dated Nov. 22, 1788, in ibid., 1:182–83, quote on p. 183. Ramsay answered with another broadside: "A Calm Reply," dated Nov. 24, 1788, in ibid., 1:187–88: "I declare, that I never approved of the emancipation of the Negroes of this country, and I hold, that the

ous defense of Smith's satisfaction of the Constitution's qualifications clause, another anonymous writer observed: "I beg leave to submit to the serious consideration of my countrymen . . . that they should be very cautious to elect such persons only as have a fellow feeling with themselves, in all matters which touch the happiness and welfare of their country. Who can be so likely to answer this description as men united to them by the tie which binds countrymen together."[56] Having thus indirectly but deftly raised the twin specters of Ramsay's birth in New Jersey and his lack of enthusiasm for slavery, this writer then evoked the fear that united all Americans contemplating the launching of the new national government: "The history of the proceedings of the federal government it has been truly said, will be a narrative of the conflicts of local prejudices. Should they elect men cold in their interests — whose minds have received from foreign causes a bent unfavorable to their good — feeble must be their exertions in the general struggle, and hurled along in a vortex of irresistible force, this country will soon have to lament its folly, and imprudence."[57]

Ramsay and others blamed these attacks for his third-place finish, far behind Smith and Gillon.[58] As Ramsay observed with rueful bitterness in a letter to his friend John Eliot, pastor of the New North Church in Boston, Massachusetts, "Such is the temper of our people here that it is unpopular to be unfriendly to the further importation of slaves. That would be certainly wrong on every principle."[59] That Ramsay in

---

adoption of such a measure would be ruinous both to masters and slaves. Experience proves, that those who have grown up in the habits of slavery are incapable of enjoying the blessings of freedom." Ramsay next answered the charge of disseminating antislavery pamphlets by claiming that "a number of packets" containing antislavery pamphlets by Thomas Clarkson, a British abolitionist, had been left at his house, sealed and already addressed "to particular gentlemen." Ramsay concluded, "I forwarded them as letters, without knowing their contents till after they were opened. My own copy I never read nor circulated." Ramsay's biographer suggests that Ramsay's residence in South Carolina induced him to modify the vigor and candor of his views on slavery (Shaffer, *To Be an American*, pp. 167–87).

[56] "A Native of South Carolina to the Public," *City Gazette*, Nov. 25, 1788, in *DHFFE*, 1:190–93, quote on p. 193.

[57] Ibid. See also "Epaminondas to the Public," *City Gazette*, Nov. 25, 1788, in ibid., 1:188–90: "Nothing less than the dearest and most important interests of this country may be agitated and concluded upon on Congress."

[58] "Election Returns for the Charleston District," *State Gazette*, Dec. 1, 1788, in ibid., 1:196.

[59] David Ramsay to John Eliot, Nov. 26, 1788 (excerpt), in ibid., 1:195.

1789 brought a challenge to Smith's right to serve in the First Congress indicates the extent and persistence of his resentment.[60]

In Virginia, James Madison, pitted against James Monroe in a House district gerrymandered by the state's Antifederal legislature under the direction of Patrick Henry, discovered that his foes were circulating charges that Madison would not support amending the Constitution to include a declaration of rights. As his friend Edward Carrington reported to him in an anxious letter on November 15, 1788, "It is busily circulated that you declared in Convention that the Constitution required no alteration whatever."[61] Hardin Burnley, another political ally (who represented Madison's home county in the Virginia House of Delegates), similarly reported to Madison on the machinations of the Antifederalists: "Every Subject which has been introduced into the Legislature & which has had the most distant relation to the new Constitution has before its determination been made a federal & antefederal question. Great endeavours are making to give the Elections the same turn and to propagate an idea that you are wholly opposed to any alteration in the Govt. having declared that you did not think that a single letter in it would admit of a change."[62]

Madison's foes had two objectives in mind, one national and the other local. First, they hoped to discredit Madison in the new theater of national politics; second, they sought to separate him from the core of his political operations — his usually reliable Baptist supporters, who strongly favored adding a guarantee of religious liberty to the new Constitution. Madison therefore bowed to necessity and, to rally the Baptists once more behind his candidacy, made public commitments

---

[60]See the discussion in ibid., 1:195–96 n. 2; Chester Harvey Rowell, *A Historical and Legal Digest of All the Contested Election Cases in the House of Representatives of the United States from the First to the Fifty-sixth Congress, 1789–1901* (1901; reprint ed., Westport, Conn., 1976), pp. 37–38.

[61]Edward Carrington to James Madison, Nov. 15, 1788, in *DHFFE*, 2:317–18, quote on p. 318. Carrington repeated the report in his letter to Madison dated Nov. 26, 1788, excerpted in ibid., 2:321. On the complex relationships between national politicians (such as James Madison) and their local friends and supporters (such as Edward Carrington, Hardin Burnley, and George Lee Turberville), and these politicians' use of gossip as the currency of political alliance and loyalties, see Freeman, "Slanders, Poison, Whispers, and Fame."

[62]Hardin Burnley to James Madison, Dec. 16, 1788, in *DHFFE*, 2:328–29, quote on p. 328.

to work for constitutional amendments — in particular, for guarantees of religious liberty. To carry out this aim, he penned a letter to George Eve, a Baptist minister. In this missive Madison first explained his previous opposition to constitutional amendments — on the grounds that "I have never seen in the Constitution as it now stands those serious dangers which have alarmed many respectable citizens" and that advocates of amendments urged such measures solely to prevent the Constitution's adoption. However, he explained, the success of the Constitution changed the circumstances forming the context for deciding on amendments:

> Amendments, if pursued with a proper moderation and in a proper mode, will be not only safe, but may serve the double purpose of satisfying the minds of well meaning opponents, and of providing additional guards in favour of liberty. Under this change of circumstances, it is my sincere opinion that the Constitution ought to be revised, and that the first Congress meeting under it, ought to prepare and recommend to the States for ratification, the most satisfactory provisions for all essential rights, particularly the rights of Conscience in the fullest latitude, the freedom of the press, trials by jury, security against general warrants &c.[63]

Eve promptly circulated the text of this letter among the Baptists of Orange County. Madison further spread word of his position on amendments through the placement of newspaper articles containing carefully crafted leaks from his "private" correspondence.[64] He thus succeeded in mobilizing his Baptist supporters behind his candidacy; their acknowledgment of his loyalty both to "those essential rights, which have been thought in danger" and to their interest in protecting their own religious liberties was vital to his success at the polls.[65] Not only Madison but his constituents recognized these facts. Both to acknowledge Madison's support for a cherished position and to remind

---

[63]James Madison to George Eve, Jan. 2, 1789, in ibid., 2:330–31.

[64]See, for example, "A Republican Federalist and James Madison," *Virginia Independent Chronicle* (Richmond), Jan. 28, 1789, in *DHFFE*, 2:338–40; "Extract of a letter from the Hon. JAMES MADISON, jun. to his friend in this county," *Virginia Herald* (Fredericksburg), Jan. 29, 1789, in ibid., 2:340–41; James Madison to George Thompson, Jan. 29, 1789, in ibid., 2:341–44.

[65]James Madison to Thomas Mann Randolph, Sr., Jan. 13, 1789, printed in *Virginia Independent Chronicle,* Jan. 28, 1789, *DHFFE*, 2:338–40, quote on p. 339.

him that the voters would monitor the newly elected representative's future conduct, the Baptist minister John Leland wrote to Madison in early 1789: "I congratulate you in your Appointment, as a Representative to Congress, and if my Undertaking in the Cause conduced Nothing else towards it, it certainly gave Mr. Madison one Vote.... If I could see all the Laws I should be glad, altho' in Person, I have little use for them. — One Thing I shall expect; that if religious Liberty is anywise threatened, that I shall receive the earliest Intelligence."[66]

Finally, in most states' Senate contests, the legislature sought to balance geographical, political, and economic divisions reflected in state politics. Thus, for example, in Pennsylvania the great merchant Robert Morris of Philadelphia balanced the wealthy landowner William Maclay from the central part of the state.[67] As George Thatcher of the Maine district of Massachusetts wrote to his wife, "[Maclay] is a member of Council in that state and highly respected by the landed interest, as Morris is by the mercantile."[68] Similarly, after a tussle over the Antifederalists' attempts to elect Dr. Charles Jarvis to a Senate seat, Massachusetts chose two Federalists, Caleb Strong from western Northampton County and Tristram Dalton from eastern Essex County. Maryland elected one senator from the eastern and one from its western shore; New Jersey elected one from the northern part of the state and one from the southern.[69] Bicameral state legislatures sometimes faced pro-

---

[66]John Leland to James Madison, ca. Feb. 15, 1789, in *DHFFE*, 2:346–47. The date is conjectural, supplied by the editors of *DHFFE*.

[67]On the election of Pennsylvania's senators, see *DHFFE*, 1:232 and the documents collected on pp. 293–96; see also the introduction and appendix E, "Biography of William Maclay," to Kenneth R. Bowling and Helen E. Veit, eds., *The Diary of William Maclay and Other Notes of Senate Debates* (Baltimore, 1988), pp. xii–xiii, 431–41, esp. pp. 438–39. This edition is volume 9 of *The Documentary History of the First Federal Congress*, 14 vols. to date (Baltimore, 1972–), cited hereafter as *DHFFC*.

[68]George Thatcher to Mrs. George (Sarah) Thatcher, Oct. 1, 1788 (excerpt), in *DHFFC*, vol. 1 (Linda Grant DePauw, Charlene Bangs Bickford, and LaVonne Marlene Siegel, eds.), p. 294 (emphasis in original). Similarly, the Philadelphia polemicist and Federalist Tench Coxe reported to James Madison that Maclay was "our agricultural Senator [and] a decided Federalist, of a neat clean landed property. . . . My own opinion is that he is properest character for the agricultural member in the state" (Tench Coxe to James Madison, Oct. 22, 1788 [excerpt], in ibid., 1:296).

[69]See the editors' summation in ibid., 1:438, and the documents collected on pp. 521–25.

tracted Senate elections because Federalists controlled one house and Antifederalists the other; New York did not make a choice until three months after the Senate met.[70]

That local partisan splits and regional interests influenced the first federal elections — either directly or by giving local coloration to national issues — seems self-evident to modern eyes. To appreciate the importance of this point for the character of the new government, however, recall that such Federalists as Madison had sought to design a national government that would be insulated from influence by local or regional interests. They had built into that grand design — or so they hoped — safeguards to ensure that those likely to be candidates for office under the Constitution would be immune from local factional pressure. They found, to their horror, that precisely the reverse was the case; many new senators and representatives were all too aware of the interests of "the folks back home" and of the necessity to protect those interests as the new government adopted legislation to secure the general good. Madison's hope that the Congress of the United States, the central institution of the government limned in the Constitution, could function free of local interests and factional pressures was thus doomed even before the First Congress convened.

Indeed, even so ardent a nationalist, so vigorous a critic of local and partial interests as Alexander Hamilton could not resist the temptation to invoke such interests when they served his goals. In March 1789, *The New-York Packet* reported a speech that Hamilton delivered at a public meeting held in New York City on February 27, 1789, to electioneer for Federalist John Laurance, a candidate to represent the city in the U.S. House of Representatives. As he had done the previous summer in the debates of the New York ratifying convention and the Confederation Congress, Hamilton stressed an issue dear to the hearts of his fellow New Yorkers — keeping the federal capital in New York City: "That as the residence of Congress would doubtless be esteemed a matter of some import to the city of New-York, and as it would certainly be contended for — Our representative should be a man well qualified in oratory to prove, that this city is the best station for that

---

[70]See the documents collected in ibid., 3:513–56.

honorable body. That Mr. Lawrence was well acquainted with the mercantile laws, and closely attached to the real interest of his commercial
fellow citizens — Therefore a very proper person to represent us."[71]

In sum, in the era of the first federal elections state and national
politics were not sharply distinct arenas, nor did one clearly dominate
or determine the other; rather, the first federal elections unfolded on
two levels of public life at the same time — within state and local political contexts and within the new national public sphere. The tensions
between these two levels helped to shape the elections' results.

Conclusion: "The Actual Forces of Politics"

Throughout 1788 and early 1789, besides coping with the demands of
his law practice, Alexander Hamilton maintained an extensive correspondence monitoring the first federal elections. Though he focused
his attention on the presidential election, he still kept an eye on contests for the House and the Senate. In November 1788 he learned
from James Madison that Patrick Henry had blocked his election to
the Senate and was working to construct a House district that would
dash Madison's hopes for election to that body. Worried lest Madison
be excluded from national legislative politics, Hamilton scribbled a
letter to his friend and ally: "I could console myself for what you mention respecting yourself, from a desire to see you in one of the Executive departments did I not perceive that the representation will be
wanting in characters of a certain description. . . . If you are not in one
of the branches, the Government may severely feel the want of men
who unite to zeal all the requisite qualifications for parrying the machinations of its enemies."[72] Hamilton concluded by indulging his habit
of giving brusque advice: "Might I advise it would be [best] that you
bent your course to Virginia."[73]

Three months later, in March 1789, James Madison was a tired

---

[71]Alexander Hamilton, [Speech at a Political Meeting, Feb. 27, 1789], reported by
"A Spectator," *The New-York Packet,* Mar. 3, 1789, in Harold C. Syrett and Jacob E.
Cooke, eds., *The Papers of Alexander Hamilton,* 27 vols. (New York, 1961–87), 5:276–77.

[72]Alexander Hamilton to James Madison, Nov. 23, 1788, in ibid., 5:235–37, quote
on p. 236.

[73]Ibid.

and disillusioned man. Having won his hard-fought campaign for the House of Representatives, he was preparing to travel to New York City to take his seat in that body. As he reviewed a newspaper list of the representatives elected to the First Congress, doubt overtook him. Madison confided his worries to Edmund Randolph, "I see on the lists of Representatives a very scanty proportion who will share in the drudgery of business."[74]

Madison's pessimism, in part congenital, also had roots in the defeat of his hopes for the first federal elections. During the Federal Convention and in *The Federalist,* he had predicted and promised that the electoral process limned in the proposed Constitution would refine the pool of prospective candidates to produce a House of Representatives filled with distinguished statesmen devoted to achieving the general good through reasoned and reasonable deliberation:

> The aim of every political Constitution is or ought to be first to obtain for rulers, men who possess most wisdom to discern, and most virtue to pursue the common good of the society; and in the next place, to take the most effectual precautions for keeping them virtuous, whilst they continue to hold their public trust. . . .
>
> Let me now ask what circumstance there is in the Constitution of the House of Representatives, that violates the principles of republican government; or favors the elevation of the few on the ruins of the many? Let me ask, whether every circumstance is not, on the contrary, strictly conformable to these principles; and scrupulously impartial to the rights and pretensions of every class and description of citizens?[75]

Madison's anxious review of the list of his colleagues in the first House of Representatives persuaded him that the results of the first federal elections, however, belied his confident prophecies. Rather than effectuating a filtration of talent to produce an assembly of deliberative legislators, the first federal elections offered ominous evidence that representational politics — the kind of politics that Madison and his allies had sought to bar from the national level — had penetrated

---

[74]James Madison to Edmund Randolph, Mar. 1, 1789, in *Madison Papers,* 11:453.

[75]*Federalist* No. 57 (Madison), in Alexander Hamilton, James Madison, and John Jay, *The Federalist,* ed. Jacob E. Cooke (Middletown, Conn., 1961), pp. 384–90, quote on pp. 384–85.

the Constitution's electoral system and was poised to taint the work of the First Congress.

Throughout *The Federalist,* Madison and Hamilton had conceded that because each senator would represent his state in the Senate and would owe his election to his state's legislature, he thus would be more likely to speak for and seek to effectuate his state's interests.[76] Even so, speaking through the convenient mask of "Publius," they had insisted that senators also would have distinguished characters, superior abilities, and exalted public spirit—qualities essential to discharging their roles and responsibilities under the Constitution. Senators, Madison had hoped, would constitute a "temperate and respectable body of citizens" who would speak for "the cool and deliberate sense of the community," which "ought in all governments, and actually will in all free governments ultimately prevail."[77] And yet the states' choices of senators boded similarly ill for the Framers' hopes. This realization exacerbated the apprehension that oppressed the Revolutionary generation as they prepared to launch their new experiment in government. None went so far as the aristocratic South Carolina politician Charles Pinckney, who chided his former colleague from the Federal Convention, James Madison:

> When you write, answer me candidly as I am sure you will the following Queries, without suffering any little disappointment to yourself to warp your Opinion.
>
> Are you not, to use a full expression, abundantly convinced that the theoretical nonsense of an election of the members of Congress by the people in the first instance, is clearly and practically wrong. That it will in the end be the means of bringing our councils into contempt & that the legislature are the only proper judges of who ought to be elected?[78]

Aware, perhaps, of the alarming tenor of his questions, Pinckney tried to reassure Madison:

> Do not suffer these and other queries I may hereafter put to you, to startle your Opinion with respect to my principles. I am more than ever

---

[76]See, for example, *Federalist* No. 39 (Madison), in ibid., pp. 250–57, esp. p. 255; *Federalist* No. 9 (Hamilton), in ibid., pp. 50–56, esp. p. 55.

[77]*Federalist* No. 63 (Madison), in ibid., pp. 422–31, quotes on p. 425.

[78]Charles Pinckney to James Madison, Mar. 28, 1789, in *Madison Papers*, vol. 12 (Robert A. Rutland et al., eds.), pp. 33–36, quote on p. 33.

a friend to the federal constitution, not I trust from that fondness which men sometimes feel for a performance in which they have been concerned but from a conviction of it's intrinsic worth. From a conviction that on it's efficacy our political welfare depends. My wish is to see it divested of those improprieties which I am sure will sooner or later subvert, or what is worse bring it into contempt.[79]

Madison never answered Pinckney's questions, with their odd mixture of well-born arrogance and philosophical curiosity about political building. Still, the feelings that actuated Pinckney's letter differed in degree, not in kind, from those perplexing his Federalist allies in early 1789.

A third, unrecognized stage of the making of the Constitution, the first federal elections were as plagued with risks and uncertainties as the Federal Convention of 1787 or the ratification struggles of 1787–88 had been. Both in the Confederation Congress and in each state, Federalists and Antifederalists competed to control the process by which the new federal government would go into effect. Contests within each state between local interests and factions influenced the elections' planning, conduct, and results. In sum, the first federal elections posed a set of critical challenges to the success of the untried constitutional system; the responses of the evolving electoral system to these challenges both shaped the character of politics under the new Constitution and indicated that the federal government would not function as its designers had hoped. Or, as James Bryce wrote more than a century ago in *The American Commonwealth,* "So hard is it to keep even a written and rigid constitution from warping and bending under the actual forces of politics."[80]

---

[79]Ibid., 12:35.
[80]James Bryce, *The American Commonwealth,* 3d ed., 2 vols. (New York, 1893), 1:101.

Charlene Bangs Bickford

"Public Attention Is Very Much Fixed on the Proceedings of the New Congress"

The First Federal Congress Organizes Itself

> We are in a wilderness without a single footstep to guide us. It is consequently necessary to explore the way with great labour and caution. Those who may follow will have an easier task.
>
> — REP. JAMES MADISON OF VIRGINIA TO
> JAMES MADISON SR., JULY 5, 1789

ALL NEW GOVERNMENTS and administrations take certain actions at their inception that effectively set the tone of government and provide the people with a sense of the philosophy and intentions of their governors. Frequently, such first actions could be characterized as symbolic. Many organizational and protocol decisions set a certain tone while also establishing precedents that survive for decades, or even centuries, afterward. Although the rules, procedures, and organization of a legislative body can seem mundane, they are central to the operation of that body; those who understand and know how to use these tools have an advantage.

Attendance

Members of the First Federal Congress immediately found themselves in the position of having to shore up the image of the new government because of problems with obtaining a quorum. The Confederation Congress had been too often paralyzed by the nonattendance of its members. Consequently, the members of the First Federal Congress who were on hand in New York on the appointed first day of the session were anxious to avoid any image of impotence caused by the lack of a quorum. They hoped that the new government could begin its work promptly, conveying a just impression of the seriousness of their attention to duty to the expectant public. But on March 4 only eight senators and thirteen representatives appeared and took their seats. Although the attendance of four more senators and seventeen additional representatives was necessary to constitute a quorum in each body, those members in New York at first evinced optimism: Sen. Robert Morris, for example, predicted that the quorum needed to count the votes for president and vice president would be in attendance in a day or two.[1]

One week later no additional senators had arrived, and those present grew concerned and decided to take action. They took their first officially recorded action and wrote their absent colleagues imploring them to hasten to New York: "We apprehend that no Arguments are necessary to evince to you the indispensable necessity of putting the Government into immediate operation, and therefore earnestly request, that you will be so obliging as to attend as soon as possible."[2] By this action and the follow-up letter sent to eight of the missing senators on March 18, the senators present clearly demonstrated their belief that the nation's business was too important to be delayed.

House members also grew impatient to proceed with business, particularly the establishment of a revenue system for collecting impost and tonnage duties. Election delays in New Jersey and New York accounted for some of the missing members, but on March 5 only Connecticut was fully represented and five of the states that had ratified the Constitution were unrepresented. While there is no record of

---

[1] Robert Morris to Gouverneur Morris, Mar. 4, 1789, Rare Book Room, Cornell University Library, Ithaca, New York.

[2] Senators Langdon, Wingate, Strong, Johnson, Ellsworth, Morris, Maclay, and Few to Senators Dalton, Paterson, Elmer, Read, Bassett, Carroll, Henry, Lee, Grayson, Izard, Butler, and Gunn, Mar. 11, 1789, *Documentary History of the First Federal Congress, 1789–1791,* 14 vols. to date (Baltimore, 1972–), vol. 1 (Linda Grant DePauw, Charlene Bangs Bickford, and LaVonne M. Siegel, eds.), p. 4 (hereafter *DHFFC*).

united action by the attending representatives to urge the other members to hasten to New York, Rep. Abraham Baldwin wrote on March 23 that "letters have been sent to the absent members and there is reason to believe there will be a congress this week."[3]

As March passed, those in New York grew more concerned about the image of powerlessness that was being conveyed. "I am inclined to believe that the languor of the old Confederation is transfused into the members of the New Congress," Rep. Fisher Ames confided to a friend.[4] Sen. William Maclay expressed his irritation: "It is greatly to be lamented, That Men should pay so little regard to the important appointments that have evolved on them."[5] Others counted the days and realized that it would be impossible to put a revenue system into place in time to take benefit from the spring and early summer importations.

Members of Congress feared the loss of public confidence and the respect of foreign nations because of Congress's inability to act. The following letter from Connecticut Gov. Samuel Huntington to that state's senators demonstrates that some were receiving communications that served to validate these fears:

> Public attention is very much fixed on the proceedings of the new Congress: I am frequently obliged to give one general answer to satisfy enquiries, which is, that Congress are not yet competent in numbers to proceed to business. I know not but that particular embarrassments in some States may be sufficient excuse for delay to this time; but did those States duly consider the consequences: that at this important Crisis earnest expectation may grow into impatience & finally change to loss of Confidence, & distrust by long disappointment, I am sure procrastination must create anxiety in the friends to the Constitution.[6]

Eventually the attention of senators and others focused upon George Read of Delaware as the senator who should be further

---

[3]Baldwin to Tench Coxe, Mar. 23, 1789, Box 3, Coxe-Incoming, Historical Society of Pennsylvania, Philadelphia.

[4]Ames to George Richards Minot, Mar. 25, 1789, Seth Ames, ed., *Works of Fisher Ames*, 2 vols. (Boston, 1854), 1:31.

[5]William Maclay to Benjamin Rush, Mar. 26, 1789, Rush Papers, Library of Congress, Washington, D.C.

[6]Huntington to William Samuel Johnson and Oliver Ellsworth, Mar. 30, 1789, W. S. Johnson Papers, Connecticut Historical Society, Hartford.

prodded to start his journey to New York immediately. His arrival would create a quorum in the Senate, almost three weeks overdue. Charles Thomson, longtime secretary of the Continental and Confederation Congresses, applied the heaviest pressure:

> Those who feel for the honor and are solicitous for the happiness of this country are pained to the heart at the dilatory attendance of the members appointed to form the two houses while those who are averse to the new constitution and those who are unfriendly to the liberty & consequently to the happiness and prosperity of this country, exult at our languor & inattention to public concerns & flatter themselves that we shall continue as we have been for some time past the scoff of our enemies. . . . What must the world think of us? . . . the eyes of the continent will be turned on you, & all the great & important business of the Union be at a stand because you are not here.[7]

It should be noted that although the absence of a quorum prevented members in New York from taking any formal action, their letters reveal that they were not idly biding their time. Members met at the hall and paid visits to each other, discussing the form of the new government, the organization of the judiciary, and the establishment of a revenue system. The eventual location of the seat of government was perhaps the primary topic of these conversations.

The House of Representatives was finally able to proceed to business on April 1, a date some members thought inauspicious, being All Fools' Day. They immediately began work on internal House business, such as the appointment of a Speaker — the experienced parliamentarian Rep. Frederick Augustus Muhlenberg of Pennsylvania — the choice of staff, and the establishment of rules of operation.

With the attendance of the twelfth senator at the April 6 meeting, the Senate could elect a president pro tempore and establish the procedures for counting the electoral votes. John Langdon of New Hampshire was chosen for this position and tellers from each House were appointed to tally the votes in the presence of all the senators and representatives. Congress counted the votes for president and vice president, and Charles Thomson and Sylvanus Bourne were dispatched as

---

[7]Charles Thomson to Read, Mar. 21, 1789, Judge Richard S. Rodney Collection of Read Papers, Book B, Historical Society of Delaware, Wilmington.

messengers with letters from Langdon and certificates of election for George Washington and John Adams.

The First Federal Congress did not experience similar problems with attaining a quorum at its second and third sessions, and understanding representatives refused to censure the tardiness of their colleagues by forcing the withdrawal of a motion to list in the journal the names of absent members at the opening of the second session.[8] Fortunately, the inauspicious delay in its formation was not an omen of future impotence, and any negative image created by this delay was counteracted by the impressive and substantial legislative output of this Congress.

At every opportunity Congress took additional steps to signal its commitment to fulfilling its ambitious agenda. Among the preliminary House rules proposed on April 9 was the stipulation that no member absent himself without official leave, except in cases of illness. Rep. Fisher Ames did not wait the two days until the rule was formally adopted before rising to request leave on behalf of his absent colleague George Leonard. A firsthand witness to the disgraceful lethargy of the Confederation Congress's last months, Rep. George Thatcher led a spirited fight for strict accountability, arguing that leave ought to be granted only in cases of personal or family illness. Rep. James Madison offered the more moderate proposal that members respect each others' private reasons for requesting leaves, but that they be of limited duration with the possibility of extensions. This seems to have been the procedure actually followed.[9]

At least one constituent thought his congressman worked too many hours. When Samuel Nasson of Maine expressed frustration that the sessions should drag on so long — at the exorbitant cost to the public of six dollars a day per member — Thatcher reminded him that when the Constitution was ratified it was generally expected that the First Congress would be in permanent session. In fact, congressmen — including Thatcher — surprised themselves at the length of the first and second sessions. Adjournment dates agreed to in joint committee were

---

[8]*DHFFC*, vol. 12 (Helen E. Veit, Bickford, Kenneth R. Bowling, and William C. diGiacomantonio, eds.), p. 4.

[9]Ibid., vol. 10 (Bickford, Bowling, and Veit, eds.), pp. 7–8.

repeatedly rescinded and postponed. Part of their reports listed the business that was considered necessary to be finished before the end of the respective session, "and such as may be conveniently postponed to the next sessions."[10]

Despite the implications of this wording, a week after the second session convened, the House entertained the question of whether unfinished business was to be considered as uninterrupted by the adjournment or as terminated by it, to be taken up de novo. Rep. Thomas Hartley opposed the latter and sought to confirm his interpretation by moving to resume consideration of the first session's Copyright (and Patents) Bill (HR-10). The motion was tabled, and on January 25 both houses agreed to a joint resolution that unfinished business "ought to be regarded as if it had not been passed upon by either."[11]

Rules and Procedures[12]

The new Congress faced the challenge of fleshing out the body of the new federal government under the Constitution and providing a new order, while further defining federalism and the new republican form of government. But the first tasks that the House and Senate took up related to their organizational structure. The rules and procedures agreed upon would send a message to the people of the United States about their new government's direction, even before any substantive matters had been decided.

The House immediately began work on organizational matters by appointing a grand committee of a member from each state represented to draft its rules. The committee was also directed to report the duties of a sergeant at arms or other officer proper for enforcing the rules of the House. On April 7 the committee reported numerous rules divided into four sections covering the duties of the Speaker, debate and decorum, bills, and procedures in the Committee of the

---

[10]Thatcher to Samuel Nasson, July 18, 1790, George Thatcher Papers, Massachusetts Historical Society, Boston; *DHFFC*, vol. 8 (Bowling, Bickford, and diGiacomantonio, eds.), p. 467.

[11]*DHFFC*, 12:21–22, vol. 3 (DePauw, Bickford, and Hauptman, eds.), p. 273.

[12]For the texts of rules agreed to in the First Federal Congress, see ibid., 8:748–87.

Whole House. Because the House debates had not yet been opened to the public, there is no documentary evidence, but it is likely that these rules were passed without much discussion. On the other hand, the committee's second report on April 9 did evoke some reaction. As is the case with most debates on House rules and procedures, the only extant account comes from the shorthand notes taken on the floor by Thomas Lloyd. Lloyd, who had previously recorded debates in two state ratifying conventions, had come to New York City with the announced intention of covering the debates of the House of Representatives and publishing a complete account of them in a new publication called *The Congressional Register*.[13] Unfortunately, these notes are quite sketchy and unclear, but the subject of excused absences did come under discussion.

The provisions relating to the duties of the sergeant at arms and the use of the mace, a symbolic representation of the authority of the House, caused a more extensive discussion and provoked Rep. George Thatcher to question the need for such protocol. The outlined procedure called for the placement of the mace either on top of or under a table in the House chamber as an indicator of whether the House was sitting as the House or as a committee of the whole, as was done in the House of Commons. Again, Lloyd's notes are sketchy, but Thatcher was certainly arguing against the need for such symbolism, noting that it would be obvious when the House was in the Committee of the Whole because someone other than the Speaker would be in the chair. When discussion continued on April 13, Thatcher challenged the whole concept of the mace, saying that it was a "pointed stick" that "would only be the object of ridicule by boys."[14] Thatcher and others seemed to be arguing against the adoption of a British precedent if it was not suitable for the American form of government and absolutely necessary to the operation of Congress. In the end the proposed rules relating to the sergeant at arms and the mace were recommitted, and the committee resolved the problem by substituting vague language for what had been more specific. The rule relating to the mace ul-

---

[13]For more information on Thomas Lloyd, see ibid., 10:xxix–xxxiii and Marion Tinling, "Thomas Lloyd's Reports of the First Federal Congress," *William and Mary Quarterly*, 3d. ser. 18 (1961):521–45.

[14]*DHFFC*, 10:68.

timately read: "A proper symbol of office shall be provided for the serjeant at arms, of such form and device as the Speaker shall direct, which shall be borne by the serjeant when in the execution of his office."[15]

Another aspect of the second report on House rules that caused discussion was the question of how far the powers of a standing committee of elections extended, since the responsibility for elections rested with the states, while the Congress had only the power to decide whom to seat. The committee on elections was precedent setting as the first standing committee in the House. It heard two cases during the first session.[16]

The first case was referred to the committee only two days after it was established: a petition from David Ramsay disputing the eligibility for office of Rep. William Smith of South Carolina. The committee expressly refused to render a judgment, limiting itself to collecting the facts. The House rejected the committee's recommendation that Smith be denied his seat pending a resolution of the case, which ended in a favorable ruling based primarily on Smith's implied eligibility under South Carolina law. The second dispute, over New Jersey's contested election returns, also addressed the question of the primacy of states' election laws, as well as committees' proper mode of obtaining evidence.

Mourning a member carried far fewer constitutional implications than unseating one. The reactions of the House and Senate to the passing of one of their own varied significantly. When Antifederalist William Grayson died in March 1790 — the first member of the federal Congress to die in office — his colleagues in the Senate took no official notice, probably because Grayson was not in New York City when he died. The House responded very differently when Rep. Theodorick Bland died in June of the same year, a victim of the influenza epidemic that had ravaged New York City during the late spring. Upon being notified of his death, the House immediately appointed a formal committee composed of the representatives from Virginia that were present to superintend his funeral the next day. Shortly before adjourning to

---

[15]Ibid., 3:21.

[16]For the documentary record on these two disputed elections, see ibid., 8:541–68.

attend the ceremony as a body, it resolved unanimously to don black crepe around the left arm for one month, the traditional sign of mourning. The Speaker notified Governor Randolph of Virginia of Bland's death and enclosed extracts of the House proceedings relating to the funeral and mourning for Bland.[17]

The House found it necessary to modify or rescind rules four times during the First Congress. Changes or additions to the rules seem to have resulted from a commonsense approach to accomplishing the business of the House. For example, they apparently found the requirement that members go to different sides of the House chamber when a division was called for to be too cumbersome and unworkable and so modified the rule to allow members to stand at their seats for either the ayes or nays.

Perhaps the most important feature of the House rules governed the Committee of the Whole House. The House often made use of this parliamentary device by which some member other than the Speaker assumed the chair and the members engaged in debate under less formal rules than in the House. This method of consideration provided an easier opportunity for members to be heard and gave them two chances to amend bills. Rep. Fisher Ames criticized the Committee of the Whole House as slowing progress: "Our great committee is too unwieldy for this operation. A great, clumsy machine is applied to the slightest and most delicate operations — the hoof of an elephant to the strokes of mezzotinto."[18]

One simple action did more than any of its rules to define the public's perceptions of its representative legislative body, the House of Representatives. On April 9, 1789, the *New-York Daily Gazette* prefaced its first account of the debates of the U.S. House of Representatives with a deceptively simple statement: "Yesterday the doors of the House of Representatives, were thrown open for the admission of the Citizens." Behind this statement and the historic event it heralded lay more than a century and a half of constitutional struggle in Great Britain, the colonies, and the states over the public's access to legislative debate and the freedom of the press to print it. The opening of the House

---

[17]Ibid., 8:474–75.
[18]Ames to George R. Minot, July 8, 1789, Ames, *Works of Fisher Ames,* 1:61.

debates to the public represented a radical change in practice and happened without any official action being recorded by the House.[19]

The delegates to the First Federal Congress's antecedent bodies, the Continental and Confederation Congresses, had met in secret, simply publishing a journal of their proceedings. The Federal Convention also practiced secrecy, and the Constitution it proposed required only that "Each House shall keep a Journal of its Proceedings, and from time to time publish the same, excepting such Parts as may in their Judgement require Secrecy" (Art. I, sec. 5). By the First Federal Congress the debates in some state legislatures were open. Of the states that proposed amendments to the Constitution when ratifying it, only New York suggested an amendment to require open sessions of both houses.

The institutions that had resulted from the drawing together of the colonies or states, the Continental Congresses, the Confederation Congress, and the Federal Convention, were all representative of and accountable to the state governments. The Senate was designed for this same purpose, but the House of Representatives was conceived as an innovation, a national body representative of the people. Individual members of that body held a personal responsibility to the people of their district. Perhaps more than any other factor, this personal accountability made opening the House doors during debate inevitable. Also, in light of the history of the issue in England and the States, it must have seemed natural for the body that represented the people — the democratic component of the new government — to open its doors. During a debate in July 1789 on the procedure for considering Madison's proposed amendments to the Constitution, Rep. Elbridge Gerry of Massachusetts gave voice to this concept of accountability: "Are gentlemen afraid to meet the public ear on this topic? Do they wish to shut the gallery doors? Perhaps nothing would be attended with more dangerous consequences — No, sir, let us not be afraid of full and public investigations; let our means, like our conclusions, be justified; let our constituents see, hear, and judge for themselves."[20]

The House went far beyond the minimal nature of the constitu-

---

[19]For a complete discussion of the coverage of House debates, see *DHFFC*, 10:xi–xl.
[20]Ibid., vol. 11 (Bickford, Bowling, and Veit, eds.), p. 1163.

tional requirement when it exposed its deliberations to public scrutiny. The only extant evidence that the House discussed opening its doors comes from Rep. Elias Boudinot's journal for April 17, which notes a motion to open the doors and that he opposed making it a rule but did not object to allowing access to debates. Letters written by members during March, while they awaited their absent colleagues, include no indication that the issue was discussed privately. The House rules passed in early April do not mention it. Comments made by members in late September 1789 in a debate on a motion to banish reporters from the floor of the House show that this omission was probably deliberate. Members expressed reluctance to put any motion relating to the publication of the debates on the record for fear of giving the reporters a quasi-official sanction.

Despite the sparse documentation for this decision, its importance cannot be overemphasized. By allowing citizens and reporters to observe from the galleries, with the declared intention of publishing accounts of the debates, the House substantially increased public access to information about legislative business and process. Sitting in the House gallery that first day was the future constitutional commentator James Kent. Years later he described the event:

> All ranks & degrees of men seemed to be actuated by one common impulse, to fill the galleries, as soon as the doors of the House of Representatives were opened for the first time, & to gaze on one of the most interesting fruits of their struggle, a popular assembly summoned from all parts of the United States. Col. [Alexander] Hamilton remarked to me that . . . such impatient crowds were evidence of the powerful principle of curiosity. . . . I considered it to be a proud & glorious day, the consummation of our wishes; & that I was looking upon an organ of popular will, just beginning to breathe the Breath of Life, & which might in some future age, much more truly than the Roman Senate, be regarded as "the refuge of nations."[21]

Not all procedures, even in the House, lent themselves to the type of candor and disclosure of which Chancellor Kent boasted. Committee meetings, for example, were apparently off limits to the merely curi-

---

[21] Boudinot Papers, Historical Society of Pennsylvania; Kent to Elizabeth Hamilton, Dec. 2, 1832, Hamilton-McLane Papers, Library of Congress, Washington, D.C.

ous, unless they were specially invited to provide testimony or for some other purpose. In the case of the Senate committee to whom the Bailey Bill (HR-44) had been referred, Philadelphia lawyer Miers Fisher seems not only to have drafted the original House bill under the committee's consideration, but also to have served as its ad hoc clerk transcribing written testimony (possibly his own) that became part of the committee's report.[22] Fisher's hand can also be seen in the draft revision of the lighthouses bill presented to a Senate committee on behalf of Philadelphia merchants. Representatives of the Pennsylvania Quakers who petitioned for regulation of the slave trade attended House committee sessions and provided the committee with testimony, recommendations, and information.[23]

After the Senate achieved a quorum on April 6, its members also began to create a structure of rules of operation. The amended report of a five-member committee agreed to on April 16 included nineteen rules, and a twentieth rule was adopted on April 18.[24] Though most of the Senate's rules had parallels in the House rules, the House rules were much more extensive than those of the Senate. Given the fact that by its nature the Senate was a less democratic body, it is interesting that, at least in the case of its rules, it settled for less protocol. One example of this is that the Senate did not immediately establish a sergeant at arms position. Instead, it chose to appoint a doorkeeper, James Mathers. Neither this position nor the responsibilities of its occupant were mentioned in the Senate rules, but Mathers was generally at the service of the Senate, barring the doors to maintain the secrecy of the sessions, stoking the fires, and maintaining the Senate chamber. It was not until 1797 that the doorkeeper's functions were extended to include the authority to compel attendance by members at sessions, and this was in response to the fact that Sen. William Blount had escaped to Tennessee rather than face his impeachment trial in the Senate.[25]

Because of the invaluable diary kept by Sen. William Maclay, we

---

[22]*DHFFC*, 8:77–84.

[23]Ibid., 8:317.

[24]Ibid., 1:18–20.

[25]Robert C. Byrd, *The Senate, 1789–1989: Addresses on the History of the United States Senate,* 3 vols. to date (Washington, D.C., 1988–), 2:282.

know more about the application of the rules in the Senate. For example, on May 21, 1789, Oliver Ellsworth introduced another rule that required that all bills on the second reading would be considered as though the Senate were in a committee of the whole house. But in his May 25 entry Maclay noted that "according to Elsworth's resolution, we were to act as if in Committee of the Whole. But the President kept the Chair," implying that the proposed rule was passed, but that it did not work as intended with a senator substituting for the presiding officer.[26] Other entries in Maclay's diary reveal the turmoil that John Adams went through while attempting to define the role of the vice president, and this was one case in which he clearly would not relinquish any power. Since he was not a senator, he would have had no role at all if he had abandoned his chair, and this clearly would have been unsatisfactory to him. Thus, the Senate apparently settled for a hybrid committee of the whole, with the vice president presiding on second readings.

A total of twenty-two rules eventually governed the Senate during the First Congress, but the most revolutionary of the rules proposed during this period did not pass. During both the second and third sessions a proposed rule that would have thrown open the doors of the Senate to those who wished to attend its debates garnered only lukewarm support. The first attempt came from Virginia's Richard Henry Lee and John Walker, but only Maclay joined them in voting for it. When Lee and his new colleague James Monroe raised the issue again in the third session they were backed by instructions from the Virginia General Assembly that urged them to "use your utmost endeavors" to secure access to Senate debates.[27] These instructions served to divert the debate to the issue of whether or not state legislatures could instruct senators. Opening the doors of the Senate failed with nine voting for and seventeen against.

The Senate's status as a branch of the legislature sharing certain executive functions with the president necessitated special rules pertaining primarily to the manner of communications between the two.

---

[26] *DHFFC*, vol. 9 (Bowling and Veit, eds.), pp. 51–52.

[27] Gov. Beverley Randolph conveyed these instructions to Lee and Monroe in a letter of Jan. 3, 1790 (Executive Letterbook, Library of Virginia, Richmond).

But the Senate did not appoint a committee on how executive business would be transacted until August 6, 1789, one day after it notified the president that his nomination of Benjamin Fishbourn as the naval officer for the port of Savannah, Georgia, had not been consented to by the Senate. It is probable that Washington's reaction to this rejection precipitated the appointment of the committee. Although there is no contemporary account of this incident in existence, the story told years later was that Washington appeared in the Senate that day to express his displeasure with its decision and to find out the cause for the rejection of Fishbourn. This account of the incident was found in the papers of the president's secretary, Tobias Lear, and was apparently drafted as a correction to a different version of the story printed in the *Daily National Intelligencer* on March 11, 1818. The letter, in the hand of Lear's son, Benjamin Lincoln Lear, states that:

> after the president learned of the rejection he immediately repaired to the Senate Chambers & entered, to the astonishment of every one. The Vice President left his chair & offered it to the President, who accepted it & then told the Senate that he had come to ask their reasons for rejecting his nomination of Collector & c. After many minutes of embarrassing silence, Genl. [James] Gunn [Georgia], rose and said, that as he had been the person who had first objected to the nomination, & had probably been the cause of its rejection, it was perhaps his office to speak on this occasion. That his personal respect for the personal character of Genl. Washington was such that he would inform him of his grounds for recommending this rejection (and he did so,) but that he would have it distinctly understood to be the sense of the Senate that no explanation of their motives or proceedings was ever due or would ever be given to any President of the United States. Upon which the President withdrew.[28]

Benjamin Lincoln Lear implies that the story was recounted by his father, who also said that Washington immediately regretted his impulsive trip to the Senate.[29]

Since the entry in the Senate Executive Journal for this date records only the appointment of this committee and no other business, it

---

[28]Dorothy Twohig, ed., *The Papers of George Washington: Presidential Series* (Charlottesville, 1993), 4:82 n.

[29]Ibid., 4:81–83 n relates this entire story.

seems likely that there was some impetus for establishment of the committee not recorded in the journal. Unfortunately, the usual source for this kind of information, Senator Maclay, was on a three-week leave of absence during this period, but he did note in his diary on August 16 that "the President, shewed want of temper, (as Mr. Z [Ralph Izard of South Carolina] said) when One of his Nominations was rejected."[30]

If this incident actually occurred, it only expands the importance of the Fishbourn case, clearly the first application of what we know as the principle of senatorial privilege (the right of an individual senator to prevent the nomination of someone from his state or for his state). Gunn's statement of an understanding that the Senate would never owe or give a president any explanation of why it acted the way it did is a strong assertion of both the Senate's role and its independence. Washington, whose August 7 letter to the Senate outlined Fishbourn's background, originally seems to have believed the Senate to be a rubber stamp on nominees that he thought were well qualified.[31]

Clearly something happened to cause the Senate to decide that procedures needed to be established. The committee was charged with the task of conferring with the president on the "mode of communication proper to be pursued between him and the Senate, in the formation of Treaties, and making appointments to Offices."[32] Senator Izard wrote to the president requesting that he meet with the committee at his pleasure. Washington's own notes are the only record that we have of the negotiations that went on in two meetings between the committee (Izard, Rufus King of Massachusetts, and Charles Carroll of Maryland) and the president. These notes reveal that he preferred oral consideration in matters of foreign affairs but was concerned about procedural matters such as whether or not the vice president would leave the chair in favor of the president. At the August 8 meeting, after the Fishbourn incident, he was wary about appearing personally to "hear the propriety of his nominations questioned." He contended that "as the President has a right to nominate without assigning reasons, so has the Senate a right to dissent without giving theirs," thus

---

[30]*DHFFC,* 9:120–21.
[31]Ibid., vol. 2 (DePauw, Bickford, and Hauptman, eds.), pp. 24–25.
[32]Ibid., 2:24.

accepting the position that Gunn had espoused. After the August 10 Senate postponement of a motion to commit the president's message on the Fishbourn rejection until the committee's report was received, Izard requested another meeting with the president that was held that evening. Washington's notes argue that the Senate in the executive capacity was a "Council only to the President" and that he should decide the time, place, and manner of consultation. He suggested that when the government had its own buildings that a chamber would be set aside for this purpose. He saw the procedures as needing to be flexible according to circumstances, such as the president's indisposition, stating that not just the time and place but also the mode and manner of consultation could vary.[33]

The committee's report agreed with most of Washington's points and recommended that the Senate "accommodate their Rules to the uncertainty of the particular mode, and place that may be adopted." They recommended a resolution to establish procedures for the president's personal appearances in the Senate chamber and for when the president called the Senate to a meeting elsewhere. This resolution, agreed to by the Senate on August 21, also contained the provision: "That all questions shall be put by the President of the Senate, either in the presence, or absence of the President of the United States; and the Senators shall signify their assent, or dissent, by answering viva voce ay, or no."[34] Washington's first official appearance in the Senate chamber to consult on a treaty came one day later and this part of the resolution was put to the test.

Accompanied by Secretary of War Henry Knox, the president came before the Senate to report on the status of hostilities and treaties with the southeastern Indian tribes and to obtain the Senate's answers to questions relating to the positions the federal government should take in future negotiations. Treaties existed with the Cherokee, Choctaw, and Chickasaw nations, but the Creeks had refused to negotiate.

Senators clearly found themselves in an uncomfortable spot. According to the procedures just established, the president obviously expected an immediate consent. Vice President Adams began to put

---

[33] Ibid., 8:756–58.
[34] Ibid., 8:759.

the questions in the president's message to a vote as soon as the report had been read. Senator Maclay immediately rose to voice his objections: "The business is new to the Senate, it is of importance, it is our duty to inform ourselves as well as possible on the Subject. I therefore call for the reading of the Treaties and other documents alluded to." Eventually Sen. Robert Morris moved to commit the president's message and questions in order to give the Senate time for consideration and discussion. The president "started up in a Violent fret. This defeats every purpose of my coming here."[35]

In the end compromise was reached when it was agreed to postpone the issue to the following Monday, the motion to commit having been overruled and withdrawn.[36] While the president did return on that day to complete the business, he never sought to consult the Senate in person again, setting a precedent that continues to this day.

The delicacy with which the chief executive and the Senate strove to respect the other's independence and prerogatives while at the same time asserting its own is perhaps most revealingly evidenced in the little-known episode surrounding the official acknowledgment of a French eulogy for Benjamin Franklin in December 1790. Two packets, addressed to "The President and Members of the American Congress" by the city of Paris, circulated for a day while Washington and John Adams, as president of the Senate, refused to open them out of deference to the other.[37]

Conscious of the need to establish a procedure for receiving communications from the president, the House and Senate established a joint committee on this subject in late May 1789. It was determined that until the executive offices were established, the president could

---

[35] Ibid., 9:130.

[36] Secretary of the Senate Samuel A. Otis's account of this incident is printed in ibid., 8:760. Otis's notes are from the journal that he kept, where he recorded precedents, and they indicate that Washington thought committing the message in an executive capacity was improper. In addition he answered questions addressed to the secretary of war. A question about adjournment arose: "The President leaving it dissolves the [privy] council — But the question of adjournment of Senate not put by Vice President until President retires." In the end Washington withdrew before the Senate adjourned.

[37] Washington passed the responsibility for deciding what to do with the packets to Secretary of State Jefferson, see ibid., 8:574–75.

send messages to either house, directed to either the president of the Senate or the Speaker of the House.

Another early order of business was the establishment of joint rules for the "inrollment, attestation, publication and preservation of the Acts of Congress and also the mode of presenting addresses, bills, votes or resolutions to the President of the United States." These joint rules provided the formal structure that established the authenticity of legislation, and a joint committee on enrollment established under them became the first standing joint committee. During the second session additional joint rules were agreed to establishing procedures in cases of disagreement between the two houses. In addition the two houses agreed to rules for conferencing on disagreements between them and for appointing chaplains — the chambers to appoint one chaplain each who then alternated their responsibilities between the two houses. Less formal joint resolutions established procedures for such matters of mutual convenience as the allocation of contracts for the printing of reports, resolutions, bills, and enrolled acts, as agreed upon by the House clerk and Senate secretary. Conscious that a system for receiving messages and bills from the president also should be established, the Congress appointed a joint committee to recommend such a procedure in late May 1789.

One procedural dispute that illustrates the struggle that occurred and the resultant leveling out of the prestige and image of the two houses was the conflict over how messages between the two houses should be delivered. The original joint committee report on these communications proposed a system by which bills sent from the Senate to the House would be carried by the secretary of the Senate, while bills sent from the House to the Senate would be carried by two House members, and all other messages from the House were to be carried by one House member.[38] The distinction implicit in the requirement equating the Senate secretary to two representatives was anathema to the House. Maclay, in his journal for April 24, recorded: "Mr. Izard had Yesterday, been very anxious to get a report adopted, respectg. the communications between the Houses. [I]t was so, but now we hear the

---

[38]Ibid., 1:23–24.

House below laugh at it."[39] After a considerable amount of consideration and reconsideration, the Senate was forced to agree to a system whereby all messages were delivered to it by the clerk of the House.

Record Keeping and Staff

One of the real bonuses for those working in the history of the early Congresses is the completeness of the Senate documentary record. The Senate chose a man with an archivist's nature as its first secretary. Samuel A. Otis, brother of Massachusetts Revolutionary leader James Otis, Jr., and historian Mercy Otis Warren, not only saved everything that documented the process, including little slips of paper with proposed amendments written on them by senators, but also organized the records in a highly intelligible manner. His docketing procedures do much to help one understand the order of things. In addition to such treasures as the first draft of the Judiciary Act of 1789, complete with numerous changes attached and a stack of amendments on separate pieces of paper, the Senate records contain a document of special interest for students of congressional procedures. This is a volume that was discovered in a safe in the office of the secretary of the Senate in the 1980s. In this volume, the journal of the secretary of the Senate, Otis recorded precedent-setting decisions and actions as they occurred. For example, an undated entry from the First Congress time period describes the following tiebreaker on appropriations: "In case of equal votes on a money bill the Vice President or Speaker is to decide, He is always in favor of the highest sum."[40] It is also from this journal that we know what books were in the Senate's collection in the early 1790s.

Unfortunately, the records of the House of Representatives did not have the benefit of such meticulous care. The House elected John Beckley of Virginia as its first clerk. Despite his extensive and varied experience as a clerk, Beckley's desire for neatness apparently outweighed his sense of history. Beckley would certainly have found the

---

[39]Ibid., 9:4.

[40]Journal of the Secretary of the Senate, Records of the United States Senate, Record Group 46, National Archives and Records Administration, Washington, D.C.

document shredders of today useful, since both internal and external evidence suggest that he routinely destroyed all original documents that he believed were superseded by revised or perfected copies. For instance, no House bills were preserved in House records in the form in which they were originally introduced, and no original engrossed House bills remain in the House records when such bills were subsequently passed by the Senate and became law. In such cases Beckley apparently believed that the enrolled act was all the record necessary to save. On the other hand, if the Senate and the House could not reach agreement on a bill, Beckley preserved the earlier engrossed form — all but four of the bills in this category survive. Another gap in the House files that may be explained by Beckley's records management is the absence of original House committee reports and most executive department reports. For almost all of these, transcribed copies prepared in Beckley's office still exist, suggesting that he disposed of the originals after they had been copied into bound volumes. Except for petitions and miscellaneous papers, Beckley put his assistants to work transcribing all the important materials entrusted to his keeping, and these bound volumes are, with very few exceptions, the only House records that have survived. His own assistants reported that he saw loose papers as "lumbering up the office" and routinely eliminated office clutter by destroying records he saw as no longer useful.[41] Consequently, most of the official records that would have detailed the step-by-step House legislative process were destroyed by its own clerk. In 1814, when the British burned the U.S. Capitol in retaliation for a similar American action in Canada, the bulk of the records of the early House of Representatives were not endangered because they had long since disappeared.

The issue of staffing presents one of the most striking contrasts between the standard today and the situation in the First Federal Congress. The grand total of congressional employees was around a dozen. Samuel Otis and John Beckley each had two or three assistant clerks. Both bodies had doorkeepers and the House doorkeeper had an assistant. The Senate hired a messenger while the House employed the

---

[41] U.S. Congress, Senate, *Register of Debates in Congress*, 24th Cong., 1st sess., 1836, vol. 12, pt. 2:1594; Samuel Burch to Walter S. Franklin, Apr. 6, 1836.

sergeant at arms discussed previously. Imagine a Congress with no personal or professional staffs! For example, when members of the committee to draft the revenue laws needed state-by-state statistics on imports and exports, they were the ones who wrote each governor requesting such information. And, the long and detailed Judiciary Act as introduced in the Senate clearly demonstrates that a three-member subcommittee divided up the drafting responsibilities into the topics of jurisdiction, structure, and procedures, personally authoring and writing out large portions of the bill — the kind of work done by committee staffs and others today. The impact of individual members is very easy to trace in the extant documentary record. Conversely, the lack of active participation in the Congress's business makes it easy to determine what members did not speak in debate, serve on committees, or show leadership in other ways.

In the absence of any support staff, First Congress members relied on their own expertise brought to bear in the smaller committee setting. Responsibility for the composition of most House committees initially lay with the Speaker, with committees consisting of more than three members to be elected by ballot. This process was streamlined in the second session, when the rule was amended to allow the Speaker to appoint all committees unless otherwise directed by the House. Rules permitted a member to excuse himself only if he was already serving on two other committees.[42]

Besides the expertise gained in their respective fields of occupation or previous public service, congressmen kept themselves (and their constituents) informed by taking advantage of a decade-long policy of providing, at public expense, each member with newspapers printed at the seat of government. The policy apparently continued uninterrupted, largely through the perseverance of local newspaper editors, although it was only officially renewed by identical House and Senate orders passed early in the third session. Congressmen also had at their disposal the three-thousand-volume collection of the New York Society Library, the state statute books kept at the office of the secretary of state, and the Library Company of Philadelphia. The House rejected two initiatives to form an official "Library of Congress" during the

----

[42]*DHFFC*, 3:12, 19, 261.

First Congress; evidence indicates that the Senate rejected a similar measure in the second session but that Secretary Otis nevertheless began a process of buying books for a Senate library that was well established by the Second Congress, as indicated by the records he kept of his acquisitions.[43]

In addition to framing legislation, the First Congress began to develop procedures for implementing its oversight functions. The House appointed committees to examine and verify the treasury accounts submitted periodically to it under the terms of the Treasury Act (HR-9). Congressional committees' investigative powers were called into question when Sen. Robert Morris petitioned the House and Senate in February 1790 for an official investigation and exoneration of his role as superintendent of finance during the Revolutionary War. In the House the question sparked a minor debate over the separation of powers and whether Congress could investigate the conduct of prior executive officers, or whether specially appointed commissioners were more competent to the task, as proposed by the Senate. Expenses may have been a more important factor than constitutional form in the decision to appoint a committee to investigate. Less sensitivity but more secrecy was required in the case of the House committee appointed in the second session to investigate allegations that Assistant Secretary of the Treasury William Duer used inside information and his control over access to public accounts to speculate in the public debt. Committee members shared the evidence with Secretary of the Treasury Alexander Hamilton, who forced Duer's resignation a few days later. The existence of the committee was not even acknowledged in the legislative journal, although it may have been recorded in the "secret" journal of the House, which is not extant.[44]

The Titles Issue

On April 24 George Washington arrived in New York City. The only official action taken by Congress to mark his arrival was the appointment of a joint committee to escort the president-elect from New

[43]Ibid., 8:676–80, 653–54.
[44]Ibid., 8:790–91, 664–65.

Jersey to New York, but New Yorkers put on a grand celebration with large crowds heralding his entrance into the city. The Hudson River was filled with decorated boats and crowds lined its shore; entertainers sang, danced, and played music on both boats and shore; red carpets were spread and strains of "Hail thou Auspicious Day," sung to the tune of "God Save the King," could be heard.

Three days earlier John Adams had presided over the Senate for the first time, and by April 23 the Senate had begun the consideration of a largely symbolic matter that would occupy it intermittently for the next three weeks—the question of titles of address for the president and vice president. Richard H. Lee, seconded by William Paterson, moved for a committee "to consider and report, what Style or Titles it will be proper to annex to the Offices of President and of Vice President of the United States—if any other than those given in the Constitution."[45] Maclay states that "this base business, had been went into Yesterday solely on the Motion of our President," referring to John Adams. Maclay, believing the subject to be absurd, was unsuccessful in stopping the appointment of the committee.[46] The report of the joint committee was simply that no titles should be used and that "President of the United States" and "Vice President of the United States" would suffice.[47] But although the House quickly agreed to this report, the Senate, after a lengthy debate in which Lee and Maclay were the chief protagonists, rejected it. The two sides of the debate can be summarized using statements reported by Maclay. The first was made by Lee: "All the World civilized and Savage called for titles, that there must be something in human Nature that occasioned this general Consent." The second is Maclay's response: "Answered . . . with . . . arguments from the Constitution . . . I mentioned that within a Space of 20 Years back, more light had been thrown on the Subject of Government, and on human affairs in General than for several Generations before. That this light of knowledge had diminished the veneration for Titles, and that Mankind now considered themselves as little bound to imitate the follies of civilized Nations, as the Brutality of

---

[45]Ibid., 1:24, 9:51–52.
[46]Ibid., 9:4.
[47]Ibid., 3:45.

Savages, that the Abuse of Power, and fear of bloody Masters, had extorted Titles, as well as adoration in some instances from the Trembling crowd."[48]

While Maclay's views were those of the minority in the Senate, House members almost unanimously opposed titles. Fisher Ames wrote to George Richards Minot on May 14, relating the House happenings when the subject of titles came up: "The House was soon in a ferment. The antispeakers edified all aristocratic hearts by their zeal against titles. They were not warranted by the Constitution; repugnant to republican principles; dangerous, vain, ridiculous, arrogant, and damnable. Not a soul said a word *for* titles."[49]

Even before this subject came under debate, some senators and House members were concerned about indications that the people were attracted to monarchical forms and wanted to stem any tide in that direction. The tremendous popular adulation of George Washington as evidenced by the ceremonial processions that marked his progress at nearly every village and town on his triumphal trip to New York City from Mount Vernon, plus the images of red carpets and the strains of "God Save the King" from Washington's arrival, gave credence to the theory of a monarchical leaning in the populace. "With concern I perceive that it has infused into the Minds of People here the most intolerable Rage for Monarchy that can be imagined. Verily I believe that a very great Proportion are ripe for a King & would salute the President as such with all the Folly of Enthusiasm," wrote Representative Tucker.[50] While the joint committee had planned and executed a modest ceremony for Washington's inaugural and Washington had struck just the right note with both his demeanor and his brown suit tailored from American-made cloth, Washington's personal popularity intensified the fear that the people might want to transform him into an elected monarch.

For several days the Senate's time was consumed by extensive and repetitive debate on this issue, with the protitle faction in the majority. A second Senate committee on titles was appointed to reconsider the

---

[48]Ibid., 9:27–28.
[49]Ames to George Richards Minot, May 14, 1789, Ames, *Works of Fisher Ames*, 1:36.
[50]Thomas Tudor Tucker to St. George Tucker, May 13, 1789, Tucker-Coleman Papers, Swem Library, College of William and Mary.

issue and confer with a House committee on the disagreement existing
between the two houses. On May 14 they reported that no agreement
with the House had been reached and the committee's opinion was
that the president should be addressed as "His Highness the President
of the United States of America, and Protector of their Liberties."
Eventually, in a strongly worded resolution stating its continued belief
in the need for a respectable title for the office of president, the Senate, in the interest of preserving harmony with the House, capitulated
and agreed "that the present address be — 'To the President of the
United States' " — without addition of title. The Senate opponents of
titles tried to defeat the part of the resolution that stressed the Senate's
reasons for supporting titles, but the language was kept in and the
divide between the two houses was exposed in the Senate journal.[51]

A related complication of the Senate's stubbornness on the issue of
titles was its inability to present a reply to the president's inaugural
address. Unconcerned about how to formally address the president,
the House replied on May 5, while the Senate kept postponing its reply
pending a settlement of the titles issue. The Senate reply was finally delivered on May 18, two and a half weeks after the inaugural ceremony.

Although the debate on titles was over in both houses, John Adams
continued to express his opinion that titles were necessary to give
prestige to these offices. Unfortunately for Adams, one of the first
converts to the cause of American independence, this advocacy of
titles and other monarchical embellishments caused some members to
lose respect for him and to ridicule his position, as evidenced by the
fact that he was referred to by the mocking title, "His Rotundity" and
the following riddle passed around the House floor:

> *Quis? by T. T. T. M. D.*
>
> In gravity clad,
> He has nought in his Head,
>   But Visions of Nobles & Kings,
> With Commons below,
>   Who respectfully bow,
> And worship the dignified *Things*

---

[51] *DHFFC,* 1:45.

The Answer Impromptu' by P

I'll tell in a Trice —
 'Tis Old Daddy *Vice*
Who carries of Pride an Ass-load;
 Who turns up his Nose,
Wherever he goes
With Vanity swell'd like a Toad[52]

Pay of Members

The decision on titles was another real and also symbolic step on the road toward breaking with monarchical traditions — a process begun in 1776. And it kept the title provided by the Constitution, unembellished by congressional changes. The conclusion of the titles debate was also a victory for the House in a period when the relative position of the two houses was taking shape.

Later in the session, Congress made another decision that contradicted the theory of Senate superiority. The Senate majority tried to ensure that there would be a discrimination in the daily pay of representatives and senators, with senators being paid more. Although James Madison supported this concept in the House, he lacked the votes to gain approval. The bill passed by the House provided for a daily pay of six dollars for both senators and representatives. The Senate responded by resolving that there ought to be a discrimination between the salaries and amended the bill to provide for an increase to seven dollars daily for senators in 1795. The House's refusal to agree and the Senate's insistence forced a conference on the issue. The conference committee's report demonstrates how firmly each house held its stance: "That they had come to no precise agreement — that the Senate could not be induced to recede from their amendment — but by way of compromise, the committee on the part of the Senate proposed, that the compensation provided for by the present bill should be limited to seven years — the last of which the compensation

---

[52] "Quis?" by Thomas Tudor Tucker and "The Answer" by John Page enclosed in a letter of Page to St. George Tucker, Feb. 25, 1790, Tucker-Coleman Papers, Swem Library, College of William and Mary.

of the Senate to be at 7 dollars — Or, they proposed that the House should pass a law providing for their own compensation, without including the Senate."[53]

The first compromise suggested in the report was accepted. Thus, the Senate may have won a skirmish in the battle to exert a degree of superiority, but the House won the war. For the year 1795 senators were paid more, but in 1796 the daily compensations were again made equal. This precedent was not broken until fiscal year 1983. For that one year House members actually received higher salaries than senators, while senators were allowed unlimited outside income.

Freedom of Debate

In early April 1790 the members of the First Federal Congress found themselves faced with the possibility of a duel between Rep. Aedanus Burke and Secretary of the Treasury Alexander Hamilton. The episode arose from a challenge issued by Burke on the House floor on March 31, 1790. Burke took offense at a eulogy that Hamilton had delivered for Gen. Nathanael Greene in front of members of the Society of the Cincinnati and others gathered at St. Paul's Church on July 4, 1789, and voiced his displeasure on the floor of the House. He believed that Hamilton's remarks were an insult to the honor of the southern militia that served during the Revolutionary War. A secret committee of four House members (Lambert Cadwalader, Elbridge Gerry, James Jackson, and George Mathews) and two senators (John Henry and Rufus King) was chosen to mediate a resolution of the affair. The British House of Common's unanimous resolution that the Speaker should intervene in a potential duel between two of its members in 1717 might have served as a precedent for Congress's intervention. The settlement of the Burke-Hamilton "affair of honor" by this group of mediators averted a duel and set yet another precedent, this one relating to the freedom of debate in the Congress.[54]

When the members of the First Federal Congress set about to organize the ship of state, they took actions serving notice on their constitu-

---

[53] *DHFFC*, vol. 6 (Bickford and Veit, eds.), pp. 1844–45.
[54] Ibid., 8:476–80.

ency of the seriousness of their intentions, their refusal to adopt any royal forms, and their rejection of the theory that either house of Congress was above or superior to the other. In this way they established a republican tone for the government that would endure and be elaborated over the following two centuries.

Charlene Bangs Bickford

Throwing Open the Doors

The First Federal Congress and the Eighteenth-Century Media

ON APRIL 8, 1789, the first House of Representatives opened its doors to public attendance and exposed its debates to media coverage and public scrutiny. The *New-York Daily Gazette* prefaced its first account of the debates with the following: "Yesterday the doors of the House of Representatives, were thrown open for the admission of the Citizens."[1] This deceptively simple statement announced a radical departure from past practices that served to symbolize the nature of the House of Representatives as representative of the people under the new Constitution.

By allowing citizens and reporters with the declared intention of publishing accounts of the debates to observe from Federal Hall's galleries, the House began a practice that substantially increased both the access to information about legislative business and process and the individual member's accountability to his constituents. This quiet revolution resulted inevitably from the constitutional framework of the House of Representatives. The shift from delegates answerable to state legislatures to representatives elected by the voters in their dis-

---

[1] *Documentary History of the First Federal Congress, 1789–1791*, 14 vols. to date (Baltimore, 1972–), vol. 10 (Charlene Bangs Bickford, Kenneth R. Bowling, William C. diGiacomantonio, and Helen E. Veit, eds.), p. 3. Hereafter cited as *DHFFC*.

tricts radically changed the dynamics and created a political imperative for informing the people.

The opening of House debates was also the end result of an evolutionary process that began in Great Britain. Even though the states had
fought a long war to free themselves from English rule, citizens of the
United States and their leaders still looked to the more liberal of British traditions for guidance. America's leaders were familiar with the
struggle in England over the ancient parliamentary privilege of deliberating out of the public eye and the progress of the British press and
people in winning access to legislative debates. Therefore it is useful to
review the history of the issue of access to and publication of the
debates of Parliament.

By the seventeenth century, Parliament believed the ancient privilege that its debates were neither seen nor heard by the public to be
an essential tool in its struggle for power against the stronger Crown.
At the same time, it recognized that publication of its proceedings
could enhance the parliamentary cause with the public, and in 1650
Parliament gave official sanction to the daily publication of its proceedings and votes. But with an eye to its political advantage, it desired
control over which debates were published and which were not. The
rise of printing as both a profession and a business and the birth of
magazines and newspapers led to a confrontation with this desire for
control, because a printer's success depended on a constant supply of
information.

A variety of rules and orders governed the conduct of members.
They were forbidden to discuss any statement made in the Lords or
Commons with anyone except a member of the same House; to provide anyone with notes on, or copies of, anything spoken on the floor;
and even to read their speeches, because the written words could fall
into the hands of outsiders. Nevertheless, some members kept private
records of debate. Between 1667 and 1694, Anchitell Grey, a member
of Parliament, clandestinely took notes at his seat, but they did not appear in print until the mid-eighteenth century. When information did
leak out, the responsible parties were punished. For example, in 1641
a member was censured for publishing a speech he had delivered, and
the printed speech was ordered burned by the common hangman.

Parliament took several actions during the seventeenth century to discourage the unauthorized disclosure of its proceedings by printers. Closing the doors of Parliament to nonmembers became essential to this increasing concern for secrecy. After a series of incidents, the Commons resolved in 1650 that the sergeant at arms forbid strangers' entrance to the House. By 1700 a single member could have the gallery cleared simply by saying, "Mr. Speaker, I spy strangers."

With the Revolution of 1688 and the establishment of a limited monarchy, the custom and tradition of keeping its deliberations secret had become an affirmation of the special status of Parliament. Since secrecy was no longer necessary to protect it from the Crown, Parliament's only reason for insisting on the practice was to protect itself from the people. Indeed, as soon as it had won the contest with the Crown, a new struggle over the issue arose between Parliament and the public and its ally, the popular press. Public curiosity and willingness to pay for knowledge spurred editors to seek out information and played an important role in the history of the publication of the debates of English-speaking legislative bodies.

The eighteenth century witnessed an ebb and flow in Parliament's willingness to enforce its rules. Gradually the people won access to the views of members of Parliament through the publication of its debates. The first man to challenge the Commons on this issue was John Dyer. In 1694 he was summoned before the House for presuming to "take notice of the proceedings" of the House in his newsletter. He acknowledged his offense, begged the pardon of the House, and, on his knees, received the reprimand of the Speaker. After paying the various fees associated with his arrest, he was discharged. Other writers faced the wrath of the Commons, but it was Dyer who persisted: again and again he was brought to the Bar of the House, confessed his fault, asked forgiveness, paid his fees, and was discharged.

In 1711 Abel Boyer began publication of *The Political State of Great Britain.* It regularly included proceedings and occasionally debates with the speakers' names sometimes slightly veiled but easily recognizable. Boyer was extremely circumspect and nonpartisan. He reported the speeches of men he knew would not object; indeed, some members provided him with copies of their remarks. Although Parliament ignored Boyer's activities, both the institution and the editor remained aware of the potential for parliamentary censure or even fines and imprisonment.

In 1732 two monthly magazines began publishing the debates of Parliament: Edward Cave's *Gentleman's Magazine* and Thomas Astley's *London Magazine.* Their rivalry furthered the cause of the people's right to know the details of legislative proceedings. Edward Cave left an account of how his magazine prepared the debates for publication. He and some friends sitting in the gallery of the House of Commons would take notes of speeches or their substance and then repair to a tavern, where they compared and adjusted their notes with the help of memory. The crude text that resulted was then turned over to a stylist who put it in proper form. The most famous of these stylists, the essayist Samuel Johnson, was employed by Cave. The resulting text naturally varied considerably from what had actually been said.

The House of Commons took action against the magazines in 1738. Robert Walpole complained of reading reports of his speeches in which he was made to speak the reverse of what he had said, and accounts of debates where all the weighty arguments were on one side and the other side was made to look ridiculous. The House then reaffirmed that it was a breach of privilege to report any unofficial account of the proceedings and promised in the future to proceed harshly against anyone so doing. Both magazines found ways to circumvent the order. The *Gentleman's Magazine,* in an introduction by Samuel Johnson, explained that as the reporting of parliamentary debates had been forbidden, it had space to publish a sequel to Gulliver's travels. The "sequel" proved to be an account of debates in Lilliput's legislature that happened to be on matters then under debate in the British Parliament. Even before a key to speakers was published, few readers would have had difficulty recognizing that Lilliput's Sir Rubs Waleup was England's Sir Robert Walpole. In 1747 both Astley and Cave were arrested for reporting an account of a trial before the House of Lords. Prime Minister Henry Pelham refused to follow suit in Commons, allegedly saying, "Let them alone, they make better speeches for us than we can ourselves."

Matters came to a head during the so-called "unreported parliament" of 1768 to 1774. That controversial body, which contended with the American colonies and expelled the popular political radical and former periodical editor John Wilkes from his seat, strictly enforced the order for the expulsion of nonmembers. Fortunately, Sir Henry Cavendish, a member of Commons, filled forty-eight quarto volumes with shorthand notes of the speeches. The constitutional and political importance of the issues faced by this Parliament created a public demand for information on its debates. As a result a popular uprising against Parliament, backed by the press and the Lord Mayor of powerful London, occurred in 1771. Although the House of Commons arrested the Lord Mayor and placed him in the Tower of London, thereby establishing the priority of its privileges, it yielded on the question of the public's right to know, and in 1772 did not renew its contest with the London press. Secrecy was still enjoined but not enforced, except that the device of clearing the galleries was resorted to more frequently.

Even the House of Lords yielded. In 1775 the Lords ordered a London printer arrested, but he was not at home when the sergeant at arms called. At the instigation of the new Lord Mayor of London — none other than John Wilkes — the printer notified the sergeant of the time that he would be home and invited a visit. If the Lords had sent the sergeant, Wilkes would have arrested him, forcing the Lords in turn to arrest the popular Lord Mayor.

The freedom of the press to publish the debates was further abetted by the political process itself, for the opposition party generally wished to have the comments and actions of the ministry placed before the public. Thus in the mid-1770s opposition leader Charles James Fox advocated publication as strongly as he had formerly opposed it, declaring in 1778 that the only way to prevent the misrepresentation of parliamentary debates was to make them as public as possible.

The decision by Parliament not to enforce its rules against publication of its proceedings came simultaneously with a major change in the manner of reporting the debates. Newspapers, not magazines, became the primary vehicle for publication and the accuracy of the reports increased dramatically. They were written for the newspapers by reporters who had actually heard the speeches rather than by stylists who prepared them as literary compositions from notes supplied by others. The most famous of these new reporters was William Woodfall, the first editor to publish the debates the day after they occurred. Relying entirely on his memory, Woodfall would listen intently to the debate and then, going back to his office, write out column after column of what had been said. In 1783 James Perry introduced the system of a corps of reporters who took turns in the galleries taking notes, transcribing them at the printing office and then returning to take more. Even though reporters had access to the debates with only minor harassment after 1775, it was not until 1909 that full and official publication of the debates began.[2]

American colonial and early state legislatures also proved hostile to the publication of their proceedings and often sparred with printers. Nevertheless, by the mid-1780s some American newspapers were beginning to report debates without legislative harassment. Perhaps the earliest was the *Charleston Evening Gazette,* which in 1785 began to cover debates in the South Carolina House of Representatives. In 1786 Mathew Carey published a pamphlet containing excerpts from the debate over the rechartering of the Bank of North America in the Pennsylvania Assembly. Legislative debates proved so popular among readers that Carey's *Pennsylvania Evening Herald* became a triweekly, rather than a biweekly, publication during sittings of the legislature. Excerpts from the legislative debates of Massachusetts, Rhode Island, and New York were also published. The practice exploded with the intense public interest in the debates over the proposed Constitution in 1787–88, and the debates of most state ratification conventions were published in newspapers or in pamphlets, although not without controversy over their content.

The delegates to the antecedent bodies to the First Federal Congress, the Continental and Confederation Congresses, had met in secret, simply publishing a journal of their proceedings. During this time, the most famous breach of privilege case occurred in 1779, when Congress called Philadelphia printer John Dunlap to its bar for revealing that France was secretly supplying the United States with military aid while it denied the fact to Great Britain. Dunlap named congressional employee Thomas Paine as his source, an assertion that surprised no one.[3]

---

[2] For more on the history of Parliament and the press, see Lawrence W. Hanson, *Government and the Press, 1695–1793* (London, 1936).

[3] For more on the Continental Congress and the press, see Dwight L. Teeter, "A Legacy of Expression: Philadelphia Newspapers and Congress during the War of Independence, 1775–1783," Ph.D. diss., University of Wisconsin, 1966.

The Federal Convention also practiced secrecy and the Constitution it proposed required only that, "Each House shall keep a Journal of its Proceedings, and from time to time publish the same, excepting such Parts as may in their Judgement require Secrecy." Of the states that proposed amendments to the Constitution when ratifying it, only New York suggested an amendment to require open sessions of both houses. The Senate chose to keep its doors closed to the public. But, given the history of this issue, it was inevitable that the House, representing the people and the most democratic component of the new government, would open its doors.

The institutions that had resulted from the drawing together of the colonies or states, the Continental Congresses, the Confederation Congress, and the Federal Convention, were all representative of the individual states. The Senate was designed for this same purpose, but the House of Representatives was conceived as an innovation, a national body representative of the people. Individual members of that body held a personal responsibility to the people of their district. Perhaps more than any other factor, this personal accountability made opening the House doors during debate inevitable. Also, in light of the history of the issue in England and the states, it must have seemed natural for the body that represented the people — the democratic component of the new government — to open its doors. During a debate in July 1789 on the procedure for considering Madison's proposed amendments to the Constitution, Rep. Elbridge Gerry of Massachusetts gave voice to this concept of accountability: "Are gentlemen afraid to meet the public ear on this topic? Do they wish to shut the gallery doors? Perhaps nothing would be attended with more dangerous consequences — No, sir, let us not be afraid of full and public investigations; let our means, like our conclusions, be justified; let our constituents see, hear, and judge for themselves."[4]

The House went far beyond the minimal nature of the constitutional requirement when it exposed its deliberations to public scrutiny. The only extant evidence that the House discussed opening its doors comes from Rep. Elias Boudinot's journal for April 17, which notes a motion to open the doors and that he opposed making it a rule

---

[4]*DHFFC,* vol. 11 (Charlene Bangs Bickford, Kenneth R. Bowling, and Helen E. Veit, eds.), p. 1163.

but did not object to allowing access to debates. Letters written by members during March, while they awaited their absent colleagues, include no indication that the issue was discussed privately. The House rules passed in early April do not mention it. Comments made by members in late September 1789 in a debate on a motion to banish reporters from the floor of the House show that this omission was probably deliberate. Members expressed reluctance to put any motion relating to the publication of the debates on the record for fear of giving the reporters a quasi-official sanction.

Despite the sparse evidentiary "paper trail" for this decision, its importance cannot be overemphasized. By allowing citizens and reporters with the declared intention of publishing accounts of the debates to observe from the galleries, the House substantially increased public access to information about legislative business and process.

The citizenry of New York City, then the federal seat of government, reacted enthusiastically to the opening of the House doors, as the following description demonstrates:

> All ranks & degrees of men seemed to be actuated by one common impulse, to fill the galleries, as soon as the doors of the House of Representatives were opened for the first time, & to gaze on one of the most interesting fruits of their struggle, a popular assembly summoned from all parts of the United States. Col. Hamilton remarked to me that . . . such impatient crowds were evidence of the powerful principle of curiosity. . . . I considered it to be a proud & glorious day, the consummation of our wishes; & that I was looking upon an organ of popular will, just beginning to breathe the Breath of Life, & which might in some future age, more truly than the Roman Senate, be regarded as "the refuge of nations."[5]

Undoubtedly newspaper publishers in New York City recognized that the debates would add substance to their papers and thus increase sales, but the lure of covering the new government even drew entrepreneurs to the temporary capital. Two such individuals, Thomas Lloyd and John Fenno, arrived with the intention of making a living publishing the debates.

Pennsylvanian Thomas Lloyd (August 14, 1756–January 19, 1827),

---

[5]Boudinot Papers, Historical Society of Pennsylvania; James Kent to Elizabeth Hamilton, Dec. 2, 1832, Hamilton-McLane Papers, Library of Congress Manuscript Division.

who was born in England and educated at a Catholic boy's school in St. Omer's, Flanders, had apparently learned a form of shorthand in school that he adapted for his own use.[6] After emigrating to the colony of Maryland, he quickly became a supporter of the Revolutionary cause and was both wounded and taken prisoner at the Battle of Brandywine. After the war, Lloyd established himself as a shorthand writer and teacher in Philadelphia and did some work for the Confederation Congress. He also began to cover and publish the debates of the Pennsylvania General Assembly by 1787.

After failing in his effort to become the clerk of the Pennsylvania ratifying convention, Lloyd chose to publish privately the deliberations of that body. Although he promised two volumes, the second one was never printed. This seems to have been related more to politics than to Lloyd's ability to get the job done. Volume one contained only the speeches of proponents of the Constitution. Accusations by the Antifederalist "Centinel" (Samuel Bryan) that Lloyd had been persuaded through Federalist threats or bribes not to continue his venture remain unsubstantiated. The fact remains that although he continued to advertise the second volume, Lloyd never published any of the opposition arguments made during the Pennsylvania convention.

Lloyd maintained his interest in producing a record of the ratifying debates and traveled to Annapolis to cover the Maryland convention. To his dismay, the Federalists, in order to push the Constitution through the convention quickly, avoided responding to the Antifederalist arguments. Lloyd found himself faced with a dilemma: should he publish only the arguments against the Constitution with no rebuttals? A Maryland newspaper carried the following "Anecdote" alleging that Lloyd received payments not to publish: "Mr. Lloyd, a warm and decided friend to the *new* constitution, *frequently* expressed his *concern* at the silence of the majority; and declared that it would never do to publish the objections and arguments against the constitution, without any answer. After the convention was dissolved, the *majority* made a collection for Mr. Lloyd, *to defray his expences;* and he declared his intention not to publish what he had taken down."[7]

---

[6]For more on Lloyd, see Marion Tinling, "Thomas Lloyd's Reports on the First Federal Congress," *William and Mary Quarterly,* 3rd ser. 18 (1961):519–45.

[7]*Maryland Journal* (Annapolis), May 20, 1788.

These incidents cast some doubt on Lloyd's ability and willingness to produce an unbiased account of the debates of the House of Representatives. Although his failure to publish any antifederal arguments in each case could be attributed to his pro-constitution fervor, purely economic considerations must also have influenced his decisions. Lloyd launched these publications to make a living through selling subscriptions, and if not enough subscriptions were sold to make the publication profitable, he would certainly have been forced to abandon the effort. His motivations for not completing what he started remain a mystery.

On March 11, 1789, John Fenno wrote to a friend in Boston: "We have a Man arrived here from Philadelphia, with a design to publish the Debates of Congress &c in weekly numbers a Mr. Lloyd."[8] Like Fenno, Lloyd took the risk of moving to New York in the belief that the Congress, or at least the House, would open its debates to the public. He was obviously sanguine about the possibility that enough subscriptions could be sold to make the project financially viable and set up his offices at 56 Water Street. Because the bulk of the papers of the House of Representatives were destroyed, it cannot be ascertained whether or not Lloyd sought some form of official House sanction or support for his publication, but it seems likely that he would have solicited such assistance either formally or informally. The Congress provided no financial support for Lloyd's venture other than through subscriptions purchased by individual members.

On April 11, Lloyd placed the following advertisement in the *Daily Gazette:*

PROPOSALS
For Publishing by Subscription.
The Congressional Register

Or History of the Proceedings and Debates of the House of Representatives of the United States of America. Containing an impartial account of the most interesting Speeches and Motions; and accurate Copies of remarkable Papers laid before and offered to the House
Taken in shorthand by THOMAS LLOYD.

---

[8]Fenno to Joseph Ward, Mar. 11, 1789, Joseph Ward Papers, Chicago Historical Society.

The list of subscribers for the new publication soon included most of the representatives and senators, President Washington, and many other individuals of influence. The first fifty-six page issue appeared on May 6 and included the proceedings for April 1–7 and debates for April 8–14.

Lloyd faced innumerable challenges as he launched his new publication. No records have survived that would suggest that he was blessed with financial backers to assist him in establishing himself at New York City. His publication, which would contain only the proceedings and debates of the House, could not be supported by advertisements and thus he depended completely on subscriptions to pay his costs and make a living. Unlike the newspaper editors, who could skip days of the debate or shorten their accounts drastically, Lloyd had committed himself to providing as complete a record as possible. He seems to have been working alone during the first session, and thus he faced several hours of work transcribing his notes into publishable form after spending five to six hours painstakingly taking down the debates in shorthand. From his early notes it is clear that he did not know many of the members on sight and that he had to do research to attribute the speeches correctly in the *Register.* Imagine sitting in the gallery or on the floor of a legislative chamber and attempting to record everything said, equipped with only a quill pen and ink bottle, a primitive shorthand method, and small rag paper notebooks, and without even a pictorial directory to assist in identifying the speakers! Little wonder that early in the notes several speakers are identified with descriptions such as "gentleman in blue, tall man" or "bald-headed gentleman on right of chair," or with question marks after their names.[9]

Two volumes of Lloyd's shorthand notes have survived and are part of the manuscript collections of the Library of Congress. The library purchased these volumes containing the notes for April 8 through May 15, 1789, and January 19 through June 3, 1790, in 1940. Since they are completely filled, it is logical to assume that additional volumes containing the remainder of the notes for the first session and probably notes covering the rest of the second and perhaps the third session

---

[9]*DHFFC,* 10:45, 49.

existed at one time. These notebooks may be extant, but either un-identified for what they are or in private hands.

The extant notes were transcribed for the National Historical Pub-lications Commission in the late 1950s by Marion Tinling, a shorthand expert who made an extensive study of Lloyd and his methodology. The transcript contains much information that is not part of the *Con-gressional Register,* and the *Register* expands substantially upon what is in the notes. We know that Lloyd drew only what he called the "most interesting speeches" from the notes and presented them with a great deal of embellishment. How much was from memory and how much was invention we cannot know. But on many days, particularly toward the end of first session and in the second session, Lloyd did not print from his notes at all but "borrowed" from the most complete contem-porary newspaper version.

Lloyd printed his first issue only three weeks after the date of the latest debates that it contained. Then a large gap occurred between the publication of that issue (May 6) and the next on June 23. On May 20, Rep. Henry Wynkoop of Pennsylvania wrote to Reading Beattie that he had "spoke to Loyd respecting his Register being so far behind, he lay's it to Difficulties in getting them Printed, the second Number not out yet."[10]

By the end of July the lag was six weeks long, and a real disaster occurred when the House debated the constitutional issue of who had the power to remove executive officers. This June 16–19 debate took up three entire issues of the *Register* and threw Lloyd's publication schedule totally to the winds. As the first session drew to a close, Lloyd was struggling to keep up with his ambitious project. He was not able to catch up during the three-month intersession; and when the second session began, the publication of the first session debates remained incomplete and Lloyd resorted to wholesale "borrowing" of accounts of the September 1789 debates printed in the New York newspapers. The last extant issue of the *Congressional Register* ends an account of the debate of March 8, 1790, in midsentence.[11]

Despite flaws in his product and his failure to publish as advertised,

---

[10]Wynkoop Papers, Bucks County Historical Society, Doylestown, Pa.
[11]For a publication history of the *Congressional Register,* see *DHFFC,* 10:xxxi–ii.

Lloyd deserves credit for pioneering the reporting of House debates. Those who have been quick to fault Lloyd's work, citing his doodles in the notes, his inability to publish on time, and his "technical skills dulled by excessive drinking,"[12] applied twentieth-century standards to an art still in its infant stages in 1789. Some documentary evidence suggests that Lloyd drank too freely, but he could have been reduced to this condition by overwork and discouragement.

On January 1, 1789, Bostonian John Fenno announced his intention of founding a "publication to be entirely devoted to the support of the Constitution, & the Administration formed upon its national principles — to be entitled — The Federal Oracle & the Register of Freedom."[13] Fenno promised that the newspaper, to be published at the seat of the federal legislature, would print essays in support of the Constitution, domestic intelligence from every part of the union, foreign news, and "every species of intelligence which may affect the commercial, agricultural, manufacturing, or political interests of the several States." In addition, he stated his intention to provide: "Early & authentick accounts of the proceedings of the Federal Legislature, its laws, acts & resolutions. . . . A succinct & impartial sketch of the Debates of Congress, by which the Characters, abilities & views of the members will be developed." Fenno made an open plea for private patrons to assist in funding this new periodical but assured his prospective donors that, given his personal acquaintance with many of the members, it was not "improbable that he may receive the patronage of congress."[14]

Fenno (August 12, 1751–September 14, 1798) was educated at the Old South Writing School in Boston and assumed a position there as assistant teacher after his schooling. Joseph Ward, who was to become Fenno's firm friend and patron despite the fourteen-year difference in their ages, was a master at the school. Fenno's printing experience began when he worked in some capacity for Benjamin Russell, the editor of the *Massachusetts Centinel*. Near the end of the Revolutionary War, his wife's uncle had set him up in the importing business, but

---

[12]James H. Hutson, "The Creation of the Constitution: The Integrity of the Documentary Record," *Texas Law Review* 65 (1986).

[13]John Fenno: An Address, Jan. 1, 1789, Ward Papers, Chicago Historical Society.

[14]Ibid.

the business failed, probably from Fenno's importing too much at too little profit.[15]

Fenno had settled with his creditors from his unsuccessful business venture when he decided to move to New York and launch his new publication. Jeremy Belknap described him as "having a poetical Talent — is industrious — has a retentive memory — & is a person respected & beloved by his friends." Belknap advised his friend Ebenezer Hazard to encourage and assist Fenno because it was "probable that the fertility of his Genius may produce redundancies wh. may need the pruning knife."[16] Private loans, totaling at least £225, were obtained from several of Boston's leading citizens, including former Massachusetts Gov. James Bowdoin and future U.S. Sen. Christopher Gore.[17] In addition, prominent individuals supplied him with letters of introduction to influential men at New York.

By the end of January he had arrived in New York, presented his plan and letters to several individuals, and expressed confidence that "the project has met with universal approbation."[18] Although individuals such as Rufus King and Alexander Hamilton were encouraging, Fenno acknowledged that "the enterprise must depend for success upon my own exertions ultimately."[19] In late February he reported to Ward that only one New Yorker was willing to finance the venture and for only thirty pounds. He admitted "that it is rather a Speculation with the Sum I have, as it will require *the whole* to push off with, & keep the boat afloat for a few months at farthest."[20]

Although Fenno deplored the delay, the inability of Congress to muster a quorum during March worked to his advantage. During February and early March he was frustrated in his efforts to locate an office for his paper; and finding that he could not obtain the necessary type in New York at an affordable cost, he was forced to make a trip

---

[15]American Antiquarian Society *Proceedings* 89, no. 2 (1979):299–302.

[16]Jeremy Belknap to [Ebenezer Hazard], May 8, 1789, Belknap Papers, Massachusetts Historical Society, Boston, Mass.

[17]List of Subscribers to the Plan of a New Publication, Jan. 1, 1789, Ward Papers, Chicago Historical Society.

[18]John Fenno to Joseph Ward, Jan. 28, 1789, Ward Papers, Chicago Historical Society.

[19]Ibid.

[20]Fenno to Ward, Feb. 23, 1789, Ward Papers, Chicago Historical Society.

to Philadelphia. While there he visited the famous printer Benjamin Franklin.[21] By late February Fenno was in a position to send for Benjamin Russell, who probably had been assigned the task of bringing a printing press from Boston to New York. When Russell arrived in New York in mid-March, Fenno was still searching for suitable housing for both his paper and family. By April 15, when the first of the twice-weekly issues of the *Gazette of the United States* appeared, he had located his offices at 86 William Street and sent for his family.

Despite the verbal enthusiasm expressed by New York Federalists and members of Congress for his project, Fenno continued to be dogged by financial woes. Clearly, Fenno, who has often been portrayed as Alexander Hamilton's tool, began his venture as an independent businessman, taking all the risks that status brings with it. Neither Fenno's letters nor Hamilton's correspondence provide evidence that the future secretary of the Treasury backed the paper in any significant way during the first session.

On May 16, the day after Congress appointed a joint committee on printing services, Fenno sought to alleviate his financial problems by petitioning the House for what he referred to as "a slice of the Printing Loaf."[22] Possibly because of the new and unproven nature of his operation, Fenno received no printing jobs during the first session from the Clerk of the House or the Secretary of the Senate, to whom Congress had delegated the task of choosing printers. Instead they hired Francis Childs and John Swaine, publishers of *The Daily Advertiser* (New York), to print the laws and Thomas Greenleaf, the Antifederalist publisher of *The New-York Journal and Weekly Register,* to print bills and other documents as they were ordered printed. Clerk of the House John Beckley contracted with Childs and Swaine for publication of the House journals, while Secretary of the Senate Samuel Otis chose Greenleaf as the printer of the Senate journals.[23] It seems likely that Greenleaf's excess

---

[21]John to Mary Fenno, Mar. 8, 1789, Fenno-Hoffman Collection, Clements Library, University of Michigan, Ann Arbor.

[22]*DHFFC,* vol. 3 (Linda Grant DePauw, Charlene Bangs Bickford, and LaVonne Siegel Hauptman, eds.), p. 63; Fenno to Ward, Apr. 5, 1789, Ward Papers, Chicago Historical Society.

[23]See *DHFFC,* vol. 1 (DePauw, Bickford, and Siegel, eds.), p. 57 n. 3. The bibliography of documents printed for the First Federal Congress in *DHFFC,* vol. 4 (Bickford and Veit, eds.), pp. xxvii–lv, provides a complete record of the printing that was done for the Congress.

press capacity, caused by the changeover of his paper from a daily to a weekly, combined with his previous experience in printing for both the Confederation Congress and the State of New York, won him the contract even though he was a much-disliked and vociferous opponent of the new Constitution. During the second session, Fenno replaced Greenleaf as the printer of bills and documents ordered printed and the Senate journals.

By late July, Fenno, who had earlier admitted to his wife and Ward his fears that he might have to abandon his project, told Ward that: "the Gazette is jogging on—I have generally from 6 to 12 new Subscribers per Week. The whole Number is now 600—which will just about pay the expences of printing only—so that my time Labour & subsistence have hitherto gone for nothing." Fenno did report that he had obtained a small executive printing job, possibly an "entering wedge" to a more steady flow of such additional work to help sustain him and his family. He thanked Ward for his praise of the *Gazette* and admitted: "Was my Situation less embarrassed, there would be greater variety & correctness—Your approbation goes beyond that of all other persons (I hope it is not merely the effect of your partiality) for altho' the original plan was supposed to be important, & no complaints have been made of a falling off, or a deviation, yet it is not propped by many advocates in this City—Gentlemen from the Southward have paid it the greatest Compliments."[24]

In October 1789 Fenno printed a "Plan Of the Gazette of the United States (A National Paper)." This plan, which did not vary greatly from the one that he had unveiled in Boston on New Year's Day, included additional specifics, such as the facts that the paper was published every Wednesday and Saturday and that the price of an annual subscription was three dollars. The announcement that subscriptions would be taken at each capital town on the continent and also at 9 Maiden Lane indicates both that the offices of the newspaper had moved and that Fenno took seriously his claim that the *Gazette of the United States* was a national paper.

When he began, Fenno had intended to print the paper without advertisements, but in November he found himself so strapped for funds that "with great regret" he notified the public that the *Gazette* would

---

[24]Fenno to Ward, July 26, 1789, Ward Papers, Chicago Historical Society.

begin to accept advertisements. Fenno told Ward: "You say, I must touch up H.K. [Henry Knox] &c they are friendly — and do employ me — but at the present moment I want some effectual assistance — by an Advance of 5 or 600 Dollars — this they cannot do. As to H [Hamilton] he is cautious, sage *prudent & economical* as a public man to the greatest degree."[25]

During most of 1789, Fenno published primarily debate summaries, including the names of the speakers and a brief synopsis of their arguments. He seldom printed speeches with the detail presented by *The Daily Advertiser* or Thomas Lloyd's *Congressional Register,* but the *Gazette of the United States* was more consistent than the other newspapers in presenting at least a brief account for most days the House met. While the paper's pages served as a forum for Federalist viewpoints, Fenno strongly believed that the reporting of the debates should be done without bias of any kind. When the Boston *Herald of Freedom* published separately a speech by Elbridge Gerry taken from the extensive constitutional debate on the issue of power of removal from office, Fenno had this reaction: "The printer that can be made the tool of a party in so flagrant a manner merits universal contempt — I should equally reprobate similar conduct on the other side — the strictest impartiality has been discovered in the publication of the debates — and Mr. G. — has equal justice done him, with the other speakers."[26]

Despite the numerous hardships encountered, by the end of the first session Fenno was publishing a four-page semiweekly paper that was expanding its coverage of the debates and building a creditable reputation as a major source of congressional information. Even before the demise of the *Congressional Register* in February 1790, the *Gazette of the United States*'s accounts of the debates were the most timely and complete available.

Fenno moved his paper to Philadelphia with the Congress in the fall of 1790. The last issue of the *Gazette* published in New York was dated October 13, 1790; the first at Philadelphia, November 3, 1790. A partnership that he had hoped to form with Benjamin Franklin Bache did not materialize, but Fenno did obtain the job of printing most of the

---

[25] Fenno to Ward, Nov. 28, 1789, Ward Papers, Chicago Historical Society.
[26] Fenno to Ward, June 30, 1789, Ward Papers, Chicago Historical Society.

bills for the House and Senate during the third session. In Philadelphia he ran a bookstore as well as a print shop.

Fenno seems to have gotten off to a slow start during the third session, covering only half as many days of debate in December as the other two major papers. But in January the *Gazette of the United States* covered more days than the other two combined. In February and March Fenno's paper is the source for proceedings not in the *House Journal,* but like the others, it is virtually devoid of debate after the conclusion of its coverage of the Bank Act (S-15) debate on February 8. Fenno was often weeks late in publishing debates. For example, the February 8 debate appeared in the April 16 and 20 issues.

Independent debate accounts also appeared in two other New York papers (*The Daily Advertiser* and the *New-York Daily Gazette*) and in three Philadelphia papers (*The General Advertiser, The Federal Gazette,* and *The Pennsylvania Packet,* which became *Dunlap's American Daily Advertiser* in January 1791). For many days their accounts are the most complete, but Lloyd's and Fenno's ventures stand out because of their concentration on covering the new government and their American entrepreneurial attitude that publishing debates could be a viable business venture. To those familiar with today's substantial governmental investment in the creation of a permanent official record in different formats, this concept must seem a pipe dream.

Despite their unofficial status, reporters recording the debates were soon allowed to move from the galleries to the floor, perhaps in an effort to improve the quality of the published record. Virginia's James Madison had complained that "reasonings on both sides are mutilated, often misapprehended, and not infrequently reversed,"[27] but nevertheless members referred constituents to these accounts to learn what happened in Congress. On September 26, 1789, the accuracy issue came to a head when Aedanus Burke of South Carolina called for debate on a resolution that he had previously introduced condemning the reporters for misrepresenting

> these debates in the most glaring deviations from the truth — often distorting the arguments of the members from the true meaning . . .

---

[27]Madison to Edmund Randolph, June 24, 1789, Madison Papers, Library of Congress Manuscript Division.

and, in a great many instances, mutilating, and not infrequently, suppressing whole arguments, upon subjects of the greatest moment; thus, throwing over the whole proceedings a thick veil of misrepresentation and error; which being done within the house, at the very foot of the speaker's chair, gives a sanction and authenticity to those publications, that reflects upon the house a ridicule and absurdity highly injurious to its privileges and dignity.[28]

Burke was trying to force the reporters off the floor.

John Page of Virginia warned that such a measure was "the first step toward driving them . . . out of the House."[29] Burke responded by withdrawing his motion after saying that "the misrepresentation, he complained of, was principally occasioned by the partiality of the printer, who sat at the foot of the chair [presumably Thomas Lloyd]. . . . He did not see him there now; but if he saw him there again, and he continued to print falsely, . . . he would renew the motion."[30] During the debate, Burke's motion was called an attack on the freedom of the press and another member suggested that the House authorize publication of its debates in an "able and impartial manner."[31]

Gerry echoed Burke's complaints about one-sided accounts. Perhaps the defense of the *Congressional Register*'s accounts by Michael Jenifer Stone of Maryland, noting that "gentlemen delivered their sentiments on the floor without system, or grammatical precision," is the most revealing for those using First Congress debates today.[32] Think about how disjointed and disorganized individuals sometimes sound when forced to put their thoughts into words on the spur of the moment. Today, speeches are "revised and extended" before being printed in the *Congressional Record,* but in 1789 printers had to rely primarily on their notes and recollections.

The opening of the second session found the reporters in the galleries rather than on the floor. On January 15 Page stated that he supposed "they had modestly withdrawn on the supposition that the debates which took place just before the adjournment, shewed that

---

[28]*DHFFC,* vol. 11 (Bickford, Bowling, and Veit, eds.), p. 1503.
[29]Ibid., p. 1505.
[30]Ibid.
[31]Ibid.
[32]Ibid., p. 1504.

the sense of the members was against their sitting in the house" and argued against this conclusion.[33] Members expressed both a willingness to have the reporters on the floor and a reluctance to formally establish a policy, fearing it might be looked upon as official House sanction for the reports. No action was taken, but the reporters returned to the floor.

More than one hundred different newspapers were in publication in the United States during all or part of the two-year tenure of the First Federal Congress. Most published one issue a week, several appeared semiweekly, and less than ten appeared daily (except Sunday). The fact that virtually all of these newspapers made some attempt to keep their readers informed about what was occurring in Congress is indicative of the high public interest in legislative happenings. But it is clear that citizens distant from New York or Philadelphia had access to much less information than those at the seat of government. The majority of newspapers were forced by space restrictions to print only short summaries of House debates or excerpts from them at best. More frequently they relayed only the bare-bones proceedings of the Congress. Occasionally newspapers printed a letter by a member of Congress or some other well-informed person at the seat of government. Far more often, editors reprinted portions of the proceedings or debates of the House either directly from newspapers based at the seat of government or from newspapers that had themselves reprinted from these sources. The lucky few had access to issues of the New York and Philadelphia newspapers sent to them (or to an acquaintance) by a member of Congress or someone else at the seat of government. Often letters from members mention the enclosure, or mailing under separate cover, of newspapers. It was undoubtedly the coverage given to the legislature in newspapers that caused John Adams to comment, "The Continent is a kind of a Whispering Gallery and Acts and Speeches are reverberated round from N. York in all Directions. The Report is very loud at a distance, when the Whisper is very gentle at the center."[34]

Publication of its debates and public attendance at its sessions ex-

---

[33]Ibid., vol. 12 (Veit, Bickford, Bowling, and diGiacomantonio, eds.), p. 24.

[34]John Adams to Benjamin Rush, Apr. 18, 1790, Rush Papers, Library of Congress Manuscript Division.

posed the House's actions and opened it to both praise and ridicule in the popular press, while senators were criticized for meeting in secret, their fondness for titles, and seeking a higher rate of pay than that of the representatives. Much of this public comment appeared over pseudonyms or with a heading such as "a correspondent writes." Senators and representatives had set their own salaries at six dollars for each day they were in session and endured considerable criticism for what was seen by some as generous spending on themselves. The following anonymous satirical epigram entitled "On the Detention of an Honorable Member from his seat in Congress, on account of the sickness of his Lady" rings familiar today, even given its eighteenth-century flavor:

> Maria, dear Lady, how blest is thy lot,
>   O'er so noble a Consort to bear *such a sway*
> For sure *very dear* must that Woman be thought
>   Who is valued at more than *"Six Dollars a day."*[35]

Similarly, a motion by Gerry for a committee to draw up a list of books to form a library for Congress evoked this comment in the *Boston Gazette:* "As [Massachusetts] is furnished with a number of Academies, it is proposed by a correspondent, that the Members of Congress should spend a few months in them for the improvement of their Education, rather than put their Constituents to the expence of tutoring them at New York, with the additional charge of a Library, Preceptor, etc."[36]

The legislative issues that caused the most intense debates were also those most often commented upon in the newspapers. For example, the debate of April 12, 1790, the day the House voted against assumption of the states' Revolutionary War debts was parodied in a mock eulogy:

> Last Monday Mr. [Massachusetts Rep. Theodore] Sedgwick delivered a funeral oration on the death of Miss Assumption. . . . Her death was much lamented by her parents who were from New-England. . . . This orator being manly and grave, and the language being alternately threatning and soothing, caused unusual sensations — a pause ensued — her southern relations bore the loss with fortitude (except her

[35] *Western Star* (Stockbridge, Mass.), Jan. 19, 1790.
[36] *Boston Gazette,* May 10, 1790.

aunt South Carolina) reflecting, that her disorder might have been contagious, and general consumption in the family the consequence.

Sixty-one of the political fathers of the nation were present, and a crouded audience of weepers and rejoicers. Mrs. Speculator was the chief mourner, and acted her part to admiration: She being the mother of Miss Assumption, who was the hope of her family. . . . Twenty-nine of the political fathers cried out aloud. Thirty one bore the loss with manly fortitude, being in full hope of a glorious resurrection, when she might appear again in angelic shape and virgin innocence, unattended by any monstrous appendage.[37]

When Congress finally decided to build the federal capital on the Potomac and to make Philadelphia its temporary home until 1800, New Yorkers were incensed. Poems, letters, cartoons, and other commentary in the media accused Congress of wasting the public's money, abandoning New Yorkers with the debt they had incurred for refurbishing Federal Hall, causing a decline in the public's respect for George Washington, and other things. But their strongest criticisms were aimed at the Pennsylvania delegation, particularly Sen. Robert Morris and Rep. Thomas Fitzsimons. Even popular and quiet Speaker Frederick Augustus Muhlenberg was subject to parody, as is shown in the following excerpt from a "Valedictory" to the Pennsylvania members:

> Yet had not Fitzsimons supported the scheme
> The whole would have ended in smoke like a dream;
> For Fitz has more influence whenever he wills;
> Than staggering Bob [Morris] with his noted long bills:
> Mark this Philadelphia; Fitz alone was the man
> Who led in the residence plan
> Tis to Fitz you should pay the debt of thanks due,
> For Fitz was the man that sent Congress to you.
>
> · · ·
>
> Fred Augustus, God bless his red nose and fat head
> Has little more influence than a speaker of lead;
> And now sister Phila, we return you your clowns
> Transformed into shapes like men bred in towns.

---

[37] *Gazette of the United States,* June 2, 1790.

When some of them first made their 'pearance in York,
They scarcely knew how to hold a knife or fork.
But by living some time 'mongst people wellbred,
They've learned to walk and to hold up a head.

Our taylors and Sailors have learn'd them some taste
Yet these wandering Members have departed in haste,
Farewell silly Congress — repent all your lives,
For following the devil wherever he Drives.[38]

Reaction in the press to the Compromise of 1790 also produced the first attempt by a member of Congress to call the press to account for personal attacks on members. During the summer of 1790, after the bargain relating to the location of the capital city and the assumption of the states' Revolutionary War debts had been struck, printed sketches about the congressional behavior of various members appeared in three newspapers, the *New-York Daily Gazette, The New York Journal,* and the New York *Morning Packet.* These pieces closed with "D. G.," or "D. G. and P. N." or "M. N. P.," and the members were identified only by first initials and dashes or asterisks to indicate the number of letters in their names. Sometimes even the first initials were left out. The judgments expressed and overall pictures painted of some members of Congress were quite complimentary. For example, Rep. James Jackson of Georgia was called a man "without artifice, just without pride, sanguine without prejudice, elegant without deceit, faithful without ostentation, and uniformly brave in the contempt he shews for the sycophants of the cabinet."[39] Others vividly criticized members in potentially libelous terms. Sen. Pierce Butler of South Carolina was roundly castigated for his behavior on the residence issue and declared by the author to be: "stigmatized by infidelity to the Citizens of New York, Treachery to his private friends, and cruelty to those whose unfortunate situations deprived them of the means of calling him to an account. I say, that thus covered over, with the blackest robes of ingratitude, treachery, dissimulation and unmanly unprovoked revenge. His

---

[38] "The Valedictory," *New-York Morning Post,* Aug. 21, 1790.
[39] *New York Journal,* July 20, 1790, signed "D. G." The term "cabinet" was applied to the ministers of state in England in the seventeenth century. Its use to describe the heads of executive departments during the First Federal Congress was rare.

character will ever be detested, either on the banks of the Potowmac, or amongst the discerning inhabitants of Pennsylvania."[40]

Eventually these "biographies" drew a reaction and a piece entitled "The Biographer Biographized" that called the author a " *'Bull Dog'* of Faction," " *'Pimp'* of discord," and " *'Puppy'* among whelps" appeared in the *New-York Morning Post.* The article concluded: "He snarls at his friends, and grins at his foes, / And leaves marks of his folly wherever he goes."[41] The same day a letter signed "D. G. & P. N." appeared in the *Morning Post* stating that they had received a letter from the publisher informing them that a member of Congress had "this day sent several commanding messages, to desire your attendance at Foederal Hall, respecting a publication in your paper, and threatening you by one of the Messengers of the House." Since the printer had sought their instructions on how to act, the anonymous authors assured the publisher that he was under no obligation to reveal who the authors were and that "the Constitution of the United States does not empower any member of Congress to send threatening message by an Attendant on the House." They promised to support and indemnify the publisher in the event of his being arrested or sued.[42] No records exist of any official House or Senate action on this issue or any real confrontation between the free press and the Congress. Two days later an unsigned item appeared that identified and satirized Rep. John Vining of Delaware as the author of a "Biographer Biographized" and after that the anonymous series ended.[43]

Members of the First Federal Congress, particularly the representatives, found themselves in the spotlight as no previous federal legislators had been. While the coverage of their debates and actions lacked the completeness and immediacy of today's gavel to gavel C-SPAN broadcasts and their actions were not continuously analyzed and dissected, those familiar with today's coverage would recognize its beginnings in the first valiant attempts to publish the House debates. And they would find both the criticism of and cynicism about Congress and its members all too familiar. But the First Federal Congress

---

[40] *New-York Morning Post,* July 19, 1790, signed "M. N. P."
[41] Ibid., July 24, 1790.
[42] Ibid.
[43] Ibid., July 26, 1790.

received much praise through the press and it is fitting to conclude with an example:

> The third inst. closed the political career of the first Congress of the United States, under the new Constitution: As a skilful pilot, after he has conducted the vessel, committed to his charge, through straits, abounding with rocks, quicksands, and shoals, and has given her a fair offing to the port of destination, experiences indescribable sensations of pleasure, so our political fathers may congratulate themselves on the success of the endeavors in conducting our political affairs through paths before untried. From this auspicious period, may they behold the labours of their hands maturing to a happy state of perfection.[44]

[44] *Pennsylvania Journal* (Philadelphia), Mar. 9, 1791.

Marie Sauer Lambremont

Rep. James Jackson of Georgia and the Establishment of the Southern States' Rights Tradition in Congress

Historians have written about the First Federal Congress as though two men dominated the politics of the House of Representatives: Fisher Ames of Massachusetts, who spoke for northern commercial interests, and James Madison of Virginia, who represented southern agrarian interests. This interpretation is too simplistic. Madison voiced the interests shared by many late-eighteenth-century Virginians in a diversified commercial and agrarian economy that characterized the Middle Atlantic states of Pennsylvania and New Jersey more than the plantation economy of the Carolinas and Georgia. The real spokesman for the interests of these southern states in the First Federal Congress was James Jackson, the passionate and outspoken representative from Georgia's low-country First Congressional District.[1]

Jackson was born in Devonshire, England, in 1757 and immigrated to Georgia in 1772. Five years later he sat in the state's first constitutional convention, an amazing accomplishment for someone only twenty years old. Jackson became the most renowned officer in the Georgia militia, serving six years during the Revolutionary War and earning for his efforts an honorary membership in the Society of the Cincinnati. After the war, he practiced law and acquired rice and

---

[1] Interview with Kenneth R. Bowling of the First Federal Congress Project.

cotton plantations while sitting for several terms in the Georgia legislature. He helped found the University of Georgia and was an aggressive expansionist in the state's postwar drive against the Creek Nation. In 1785 he married Mary Charlotte Young, with whom he had five sons, four of whom later became prominent in the state's public affairs.

Post-Revolutionary Georgia was a rapidly expanding state dominated by planters. It was bordered by Spanish Florida to the south, and until 1802 it claimed all the territory west to the Mississippi River, lands inhabited by various indigenous tribes, most prominently the Creek Nation, with whom Georgia had a long and hostile relationship. In 1788 Jackson was elected governor of Georgia at the age of thirty-one, an honor he declined on the grounds of youth and inexperience. These excuses, however, were not sufficient to discourage him from accepting the seat in the First Federal Congress that he won in the most contested race in the state. Jackson defeated two more experienced candidates in an election in which personality and political rivalries played more significant roles than issues.[2] Catherine Greene, widow of Continental Army Gen. Nathanael Greene, described the young Georgian at the time as a lawyer of tolerable reputation and an honest, but hotheaded, man.[3]

As a member of the First Federal Congress, Jackson consistently argued for southern interests, especially those of his home state. He was an impassioned, colorful orator who filled his speeches with biblical and historical allusions. As the editors of the *Documentary History of the First Federal Congress* point out in their introduction to the debates in the House of Representatives, "The consistently fiery speeches of James Jackson of Georgia can be recognized even with no name attached to them."[4] Jackson used his oratorical gift in attempts to persuade his colleagues. Unfortunately, he was not often successful; his argumentative speeches were generally long and repetitive, leading to

---

[2]"James Jackson," *Dictionary of American Biography; Documentary History of the First Federal Congress, 1789–1791,* 14 vols. to date (Baltimore, 1972–), vol. 14 (William C. diGiacomantonio, Kenneth R. Bowling, Charlene Bangs Bickford, and Helen E. Veit, eds.), pp. 555–61 (hereafter *DHFFC*).

[3]Catherine Greene to Jeremiah Wadsworth, Apr. 18, 1789, Wadsworth Papers, Connecticut Historical Society, Hartford.

[4]*DHFFC,* vol. 10 (Charlene Bangs Bickford, Kenneth R. Bowling, and Helen E. Veit, eds.), p. xxi.

a less than favorable reputation with his colleagues. Jackson was consistent in most of his positions: his first concern always was Georgia, after which he supported southern interests in general, and invariably the Constitution as he understood it, referring to it again and again as an untested ship ready to leave port. He took pride in supporting the Constitution: "My heart, sir, is federal," he declared on the House floor.[5] Nevertheless, from the beginning his positions demonstrated a strong states' rights stance.

Jackson was sensitive to the delicate relationship between the state and federal governments. One of the first matters on which he spoke concerned the act requiring officers of state governments to take the oath of allegiance to the federal Constitution. Jackson thought this provision would only excite jealousy between the state and federal governments. The Georgian argued that since the Constitution was the supreme law of the land and applied to everyone, a special act was unnecessary and impolitic. It would be better for the state governments to regulate this, Jackson believed, for an involuntary oath is seldom held sacred. He compared the act to the British attempt to force those residing in territory it conquered during the Revolutionary War to swear allegiance to the Crown. Jackson admitted that the federal government had the power to enact the Oath Act, but he preferred to give the state governments the opportunity to enforce taking the oaths.[6]

Jackson again expressed his opposition to expanding the Constitution through legislative interpretation in the August 1789 debate on the federal judiciary bill. His initial concern simply was to ensure that there would be an uneven number of Supreme Court justices so that decisions could not be equally split. After "mature consideration," he later voiced opposition to the creation of a system of federal district courts. In a long-winded speech, Jackson argued that because laws and rules were formed for the convenience of society, "the conveniency of the people is, or ought to be the first privilege of every government; and people have a right to expect it."[7] The establishment of inferior

---

[5]Ibid., vol. 11 (Charlene Bangs Bickford, Kenneth R. Bowling, and Helen E. Veit, eds.), p. 1387.

[6]Ibid., 10:309, 484.

[7]Ibid., 11:1487.

federal courts, however, was "unnecessary, vexatious, and expensive, and calculated to destroy the harmony of the people."

The Constitution, Jackson argued, permitted but did not require Congress to establish district courts. When members expressed fear that state courts would not rule according to federal law but state law, Jackson countered that the Constitution was the supreme law of the land and the states would have no basis to dispute federal law. The Supreme Court could reverse any state court decision, therefore the liberties guaranteed by the Constitution would remain intact. Jackson's arguments on the judiciary bill evidenced the same principles as his arguments against the Oath Act; in both he favored permitting the state governments to implement the Constitution before federal government intervention.[8]

In the second session of the First Congress, the House debated for several weeks the assumption of state war debts in conjunction with the Funding Act. Ames described one of Jackson's speeches on the subject as so loud that the Senate was forced to close its windows.[9] The Georgian was appointed to the committee to consider assumption and made several motions on the subject, one attempting to postpone the discussion until the next session. The issue, he claimed, had "more or less convulsed the whole people of the United States," and the bill "has in short, been the centre pin of visionary projectors and interested men, whilst its future effects have been viewed with horror by disinterested men."[10] He felt it was unjust for the federal government to ask the citizens of states that had already paid their war debts to assist in paying the debts of delinquent states. It might have been acceptable at the end of the war, but certainly not in 1790, after several states had burdened their inhabitants with heavy taxes to pay their war debt. If it were proper for the federal government to assume state debts, Jackson claimed, then the Constitution would have provided for it. In particular, he worried about where the money would come from. The Senate, in its attempt to fund the state debts, he argued, had undertaken to

---

[8]Ibid., 11:1328, 1353 (quoted), 1360, 1387–89.

[9]Fisher Ames to Thomas Dwight, July 25, 1790, Fisher Ames Papers, Dedham Historical Society, Dedham, Mass.

[10]*DHFFC,* vol. 12 (Helen E. Veit, Charlene Bangs Bickford, Kenneth R. Bowling, and William C. diGiacomantonio, eds.), p. 1694.

load the citizens of the United States with enormous taxes that encroached on their constitutional rights. When it was proposed that the debt be funded from tariff duties on imported goods, Jackson objected because he believed such duties fell more on the agricultural South than the commercial North.[11] At one point he even implied that some members of the House had been bribed into favoring assumption, an accusation that helps explain Jackson's unpopularity with some of his colleagues.[12] Nevertheless, once it became obvious that assumption would pass, Jackson quickly jumped on the bandwagon, preparing a bill to assume an additional three hundred thousand dollars of Georgia's state debt.[13] The bill's failure by one vote must have galled him.

One of Jackson's most enduring and consistent views was his absolute and complete faith in the Constitution as he interpreted it. He repeatedly referred to the document to support his positions and to challenge anything he did not support. Several times he implied, with thinly veiled threats, that if a motion he considered unconstitutional was passed, Georgia might have to look elsewhere than the union for protection. Jackson advocated caution when considering constitutional matters; his views were generally conservative, based on his belief that the government should be given a chance to operate under the Constitution before changes were made.[14]

Jackson did not oppose amendments per se; he even stated that he would support those that would help other states, provided that experience, not theory, proved them necessary.[15] In his most famous and frequently cited metaphor, Jackson compared the Constitution to "a ship that has never yet put to sea — she is now laying in the dock — we have had no tryal as yet; we can not determine with any precision, whether she sails upon an even keel or not — Upon experiment she may prove faultless, or her defects may be very obvious — but the present is not the time for alterations."[16] Jackson said that when amendments were necessary, he trusted the country to be virtuous enough to

---

[11] Ibid., 12:1694–97.
[12] Ibid., 12:1696.
[13] Ibid., vol. 5 (Charlene Bangs Bickford and Helen E. Veit, eds.), p. 938.
[14] Ibid., vol. 4 (Charlene Bangs Bickford and Helen E. Veit, eds.), p. 3.
[15] Ibid., 11:812.
[16] Ibid., 11:805.

make them, but reminded the House that England had not amended Magna Charta.[17] However, as a letter to the editor of a New York newspaper pointed out, Jackson's knowledge of the British Constitution was faulty; Magna Charta had indeed been altered.[18] In one of his many biblical allusions, he worried that a constitution with amendments would be like Joseph's coat of many colors.[19] The amendments proposed by Madison were, in the Georgian's opinion, a mere *ignis fatuus*, or "fool's fire," amusing by appearances but often leading to dangerous conclusions.[20] Jackson, who admired the simplicity of the Constitution, feared that amendments would render the document "complex and obscure," and if any inconsistencies between the original document and the amendments arose, they would lead to "a government of opposite principles." Therefore, he also emphasized that any amendments should be entirely supplementary to the original document.[21]

When specific amendments were debated, Jackson objected to their content. During the discussion of what became the Second Amendment, he argued that the exclusion of conscientious objectors from the militia was unfair unless those excused paid a fine. He raised the same objection when debate on the militia bill came up during the third session. At that time, he supported an exemption for members of Congress on the grounds that they should always be available to consider the nation's business.[22] His comments in the first session on the amendment to allow constituents "to instruct their representatives" were particularly interesting. Jackson fervently objected. Constituents should offer their opinions, but the elected representative ultimately should judge for himself and be able to reject their advice. He worried about a conflict between a legislator's conscience and the instruction of his constituents if they differed; the representative would breach his solemn oath to support the Constitution if he did not follow his conscience.[23]

Jackson's commitment to the Constitution motivated his opposition

---

[17] Ibid., 11:1209.
[18] "A Spectator," *Daily Advertiser* (New York), Aug. 17, 1789.
[19] *DHFFC,* 11:1228.
[20] Ibid., 11:809.
[21] Ibid., 11:1209.
[22] Ibid., 11:1286.
[23] Ibid., 11:1258.

to an amendment to drastically limit the taxation power of the federal government. He insisted that the amendment would return the union to the situation that existed under the Articles of Confederation, when the central government had an extremely difficult time raising money. The federal government needed a secure source of revenue, Jackson argued, to defray expenses and to protect the nation against foreign foes. He was particularly passionate about the issue because of Georgia's vulnerability on its southern and western frontiers. In his typical exaggeration and fervor, Jackson tried to convince his colleagues that if the federal government could not tax directly, it would be destroyed either by internal commotion or external assault, and the Revolution would have been for naught.[24]

One constitutional question that particularly concerned Jackson was the relationship between the executive and legislative branches. At issue in the debate over the foreign affairs bill was the power of the president to remove executive officials. Madison did not want to blend executive and legislative powers, while Jackson argued that that was what the Constitution established, given the requirement for Senate approval of nominees. Jackson also argued that no government had ever succeeded in completely dividing executive and legislative powers, not even Great Britain, where the "deadly influence of the crown" constrained government.[25]

Jackson worried that giving the president so much power would make him a despot, which could happen if he were given the power of the purse as well as the power of the sword. The president, if given the power to remove executive officials, would have complete control over the executive departments, including the treasury. Jackson wanted an efficient government, but not at the expense of personal liberty. He believed the people agreed with him, because they too feared a powerful president.[26]

Those who advocated giving so much authority to the chief executive, Jackson believed, put too much faith in their current leader without considering what might happen under future presidents.

---

[24] Ibid., 11:1316, 1320.
[25] Ibid., 11:889.
[26] Ibid., 11:889, 911–15, 948–49, 993.

"Suppose the President should be taken with a fit of lunacy?" he asked. What then would happen to a government that was completely under his control? Any minor deviations from the exact words of the Constitution would be a step toward arbitrary government.[27]

Jackson's commitment to southern, and especially Georgian, interests was clearly evident in his position on the debate over the location of the national capital. Keeping his home state in mind, Jackson wanted a geographically central seat of government. In his usual dramatic way, he tried to turn the debate into something larger than it was, claiming that the continuation of the union depended on the capital's location. He aptly said the capital "might be compared to the heart in the human body; it was a center from which the principles of life were carried to the extremities."[28] Georgia was certainly such an extremity. Jackson objected to the sites proposed on the Delaware and Susquehanna Rivers as too far from Georgia. Showing his pride and arrogance concerning his home state, he reminded the other members that Georgia's population would grow rapidly, for "one of the finest countries in the world could not but rapidly extend her population" and only Indian attacks stunted its growth.[29] In the end, Jackson supported the Potomac site.[30] However, he may not have been happy that Congress would reside in Philadelphia for a decade before moving to the permanent capital, because he saw the city as a bastion of antislavery Quakers and consequently inhospitable to southerners.

The debate on salaries of members of Congress showed an amusing yet consistent side of Jackson. When higher salaries were proposed for senators, an outraged Jackson asked: "Can a senator eat more — or does he drink better than a Representative? I presume not." In one of his more sarcastic remarks, he attacked the argument that "the wisdom of the Senate" should be rewarded with higher pay, saying he did not see any special wisdom in the other house, but if a distinction was to be made on this account, a difference in pay should be made

---

[27]Ibid., 11:729, 889, 890, quote on p. 890.
[28]Ibid., 11:1338.
[29]Ibid., 11:1406.
[30]Ibid., 11:1483.

among various members of the House as well.[31] Once again, one can easily see why Jackson was not the most-liked member of the House of Representatives.

The debate on various Quaker groups' antislavery petitions to the First Federal Congress in February and March 1790 provided Jackson an ideal rostrum for elaborating several favorite themes: the "meddling" of Quakers whose pacifism during the Revolutionary War had placed them beyond the pale of citizenship; the moral imperative to Christianize Africans; the Judeo-Christian tradition's countenance of slavery; the economic imperative of cultivating fertile land inhospitable to "northern constitutions"; and the political imperative for the states to tolerate each other's "ill habits." As the most outspoken southern apologist in Congress, Jackson's display of racial paranoia was perhaps predictable. What was unusual was the amount of erudition and scholarship he mustered to justify it. In one anti-Quaker, proslavery speech alone, he cited both Old and New Testaments, Jefferson's Notes on the State of Virginia, a Virginia newspaper editorial, and the work of a famous contemporary Scottish law professor.[32]

Jackson's second session defense of slavery echoed an earlier attack against a brief and unsuccessful effort to regulate the slave trade. When Josiah Parker of Virginia proposed that the tariff bill include a duty of ten dollars per slave imported into the United States, Jackson said he understood how someone from Virginia might propose such a duty, since that state no longer had to import slaves but merely breed the ones it had. He asked the members from the North to sympathize with the South, on which such a duty would be a great burden. He argued that the tariff bill already proposed to tax southerners for every comfort and enjoyment in life; the duty on slaves sought to take away the South's means for raising the money to procure those comforts. This would surely destroy the South at once, Jackson claimed. He hoped the motion would be withdrawn, and that if it ever came up again, it would include "white slaves" as well, those people who were "imported from all the gaols of Europe; wretches, convicted of the

---

[31] Ibid., 11:1136, 1139.
[32] Ibid., 12:719–34 passim.

most flagrant crimes, who were brought in and sold without any duty whatever." According to the Constitution, Jackson claimed, white slaves could be taxed equally with African slaves. He admitted it was the "fashion of the day, to favor the liberty of slaves," but he hoped the northern members of Congress would sympathize with the South and reject the motion.

Jackson attempted to convince his colleagues that African Americans were better off in slavery than in freedom. What would they do if they were free, he asked. The experience of freed slaves in Maryland, he argued, proved that they would turn to crime to support themselves. Slaves lived better in the United States, he contended, than they had lived as free men in Africa, where, in times of peace, parents sold their children, and, in times of war, tribes enslaved one another. At least in the United States, he argued, slaves had masters who were bound by interest and law to provide for their comfort and support in old age and infirmity.[33]

Economic issues elicited Jackson's strongest statements of support for states' rights and particularly the interests of his beloved Georgia. When tariff duties were debated in the first session, Jackson consistently argued for southern interests. He wanted the duty on imported rum lowered because a high tariff damaged the South's economy, especially Georgia's.[34] He claimed that if imported rum had a high duty, it would be too expensive for most people to purchase. They would be forced to drink domestically manufactured rum instead, which, he maintained, was "five hundred times as bad in its effects as any from the West-Indies." To Jackson, the issue was one of morality and health; the duty on foreign rum should remain low so that the government could discourage the use of bad spirits.[35]

Although Jackson framed his argument against high tariffs in terms of moral posturing, he could just as easily rail against government policies designed to regulate morality. He was adamantly opposed to excise duties on domestically distilled spirits, proposed in the third session as a means to raise additional revenue to pay the interest on the

[33]Ibid., 10:644–46.
[34]Ibid., 10:282.
[35]Ibid., 10:335.

assumed state debts. Jackson thought these duties would unfairly burden the South. When a petition from the Philadelphia College of Physicians supported high excises as a means of discouraging the consumption of alcohol, Jackson fumed in opposition, asserting that if the federal government responded to such arguments it would soon find itself in the absurd position of regulating the quality of ketchup on the grounds that one of its ingredients might be poisonous.[36] Though he might not have been consistent in his arguments, Jackson preferred direct taxes to tariffs and excises that he believed fell disproportionately on the southern states.

As the First Federal Congress progressed, Jackson grew increasingly upset that northern concerns, especially commerce, received more attention than the agricultural concerns of the South. Does the prosperity and safety of the nation depend on a navy and the protection of commerce, he asked. No, the nation must rely upon agriculture for its future. If more attention were not paid to the southern agricultural states, he threatened, they would become dissatisfied with the federal government. Jackson called on the House not to make any regulations that would promote the interests of one part of the union at the expense of another.[37] In a letter to a constituent, Jackson admitted that his state delegation was "decidedly of opinion that the time is not far distant when the interests of Georgia will be to support the navigation of the [New England states, but] these, however, are sentiments we did not chuse to express to the House."[38] Considering the passionate battle he waged against New England's commercial interests, this intriguing comment perhaps indicates that Jackson was not as parochial as he presented himself.

Georgia's support for the ratification of the Constitution had hinged on the expectation of federal military aid in securing Georgia against its indigenous tribes and the neighboring Spanish. In the 1780s Georgia witnessed a population explosion of immigrants from Virginia and the Carolinas. Expansion westward and northward along the Savannah River met armed opposition from the Creek Nation. One of Jackson's

---

[36] Ibid., 14:210.

[37] Ibid., 10:664.

[38] James Jackson to Anthony Wayne, May 10, 1789, Anthony Wayne Papers, William L. Clements Library, University of Michigan, Ann Arbor.

biggest concerns in Congress was to secure federal military protection for Georgia. He believed that the only way to overcome the Indian threat was by force. To this end, he used the Indian Treaties Act to push for military protection from the Creeks. Almost immediately after arriving in New York in 1789, he wrote his mentor, George Walton, then governor of Georgia, to request official papers. Jackson had found that gentlemen from other states had come "furnished with information on every possible topic," and if the Indian business came up, he would need "the most exact and Minute facts." Jackson noted that he found many of his colleagues in the House "not favorable to our politics" and asked Walton for his "sentiments of what will benefit the State."[39] From the prominence given to the Creek issue in this letter, its magnitude to the interests of Georgia is unmistakable.

When Jackson spoke on the issue in the House, he provided another glimpse of his racial sentiments. He made several derogatory remarks about Alexander McGillivray, the powerful and well-educated leader of the Creek Nation, calling him a "half-bred chief" who had dared to treat the United States with "indignity."[40] Jackson reminded his colleagues of the reason Georgia ratified the Constitution, threatening to seek protection elsewhere if they could not find it from the federal government.[41] Thomas Sumter of South Carolina observed that the Georgian was "too much affected by the situation of his [state] to apply his arguments to the reason of his hearers."[42]

The terms of the Treaty of New York that the federal government negotiated with McGillivray in the summer of 1790 outraged Jackson. When the third session of the First Congress convened in December, Jackson demanded, without success, that the treaty's secret articles be published. He particularly opposed the manner in which the executive branch had treated McGillivray, whom he referred to as "a savage of the Creek Nation." One of the treaty's secret articles had awarded the Indian leader the rank of brigadier general in the U.S. Army and a

---

[39]James Jackson to George Walton, Apr. 29, 1789, James Jackson Papers, Georgia Department of Archives and History, Atlanta.

[40]*DHFFC*, 11:1197.

[41]Ibid., 11:1204.

[42]Ibid., 11:1203–4.

salary of twelve hundred dollars as an agent of the United States, a salary slightly higher than Jackson himself received.[43]

Jackson's comments on the second session naturalization bill were also extreme. He characterized it as essential to the respectability and character of the American name that the title of citizen of the United States should be as highly venerated as that of a citizen of ancient Rome. The nation should "trust to the natural increase of our population for inhabitants," he argued, rather than let the common class of European immigrants become citizens. "I think," he said, "before a man is admitted to enjoy the high and inestimable privileges of a citizen of America, that something more than a mere residence among us is necessary." His idea of the proper way to merit citizenship was a long period of probation, after which the candidate must bring testimonials of a proper and decent character before a grand jury, which could then determine admissibility."[44] This elitist attitude is quite interesting when one considers that Jackson himself was an immigrant who had quickly become a political leader. His xenophobia was again apparent when later in 1790 the trade and navigation bill was debated. He said he would consent to prohibiting all foreign ships from American ports.[45]

Jackson expressed his strong support for his home state in the Second Appropriations Act. On March 8, 1790, he moved to appropriate funds for removing obstructions left in the Savannah River from the Revolutionary War. He tried in vain to convince his colleagues that the government lost revenue from the commerce interrupted by these obstructions. When his motion was passed over for a discussion of the salary of the doorman of the House, an irate Jackson cried, "If we can pay this attention to a private person we ought to pay attention to what will be advantageous to the state." Later he supported a motion for a lighthouse in Charleston's harbor and stated "he hoped the

---

[43]Ibid., vol. 2 (Linda Grant DePauw, Charlene Bangs Bickford, and LaVonne Marlene Siegel, eds.), p. 249; 14:35.

[44]Ibid., vol. 12 (Helen E. Veit, Charlene Bangs Bickford, Kenneth R. Bowling, and William Charles diGiacomantonio, eds.), pp. 151–52.

[45]Ibid., vol. 13 (Helen E. Veit, Charlene Bangs Bickford, Kenneth R. Bowling, and William Charles diGiacomantonio, eds.), pp. 1599–1611.

gentlemen from South Carolina would give their vote for certain improvements in the navigation of the Savannah River, which he mentioned and which he designed to move for." Not above political games, Jackson was quite capable of bargaining and maneuvering for what he wanted.[46]

More than any other member of the First Federal Congress, except perhaps Madison, Jackson sparked attention in the press. His speeches on the Quakers and slavery led to an anonymous attack by Benjamin Franklin, the last publication authored by that venerable statesman.[47] Similarly, his comments on the petition of the College of Physicians prompted "A Friend to the College" to comment on Jackson's "vehement harangue."[48]

Throughout his service in the First Federal Congress, Jackson was lively and vocal; however, he often was too brash to be truly effective. In fact, an observer from North Carolina claimed that no congressman had attempted to divide the House by setting up a southern interest in opposition to the eastern interest "except Mr. Jackson, from Georgia, the violence of whose passions sometimes hurries him into expressions which have, or appear to have, such a tendency."[49] Nonetheless, his opposition to aristocracy in government, high tariffs, the excise, the establishment of inferior federal courts, a northern capital, and the assumption of state debts show that while he believed strongly in the virtue of the Constitution, he refused to sacrifice the rights and interests of Georgia to those of the union. By the second session he had distanced himself from other Federalists, becoming an early leader of what would develop into the Jeffersonian Republican party.[50]

Jackson was not reelected to the Second Congress. In a bitter campaign, he lost to Anthony Wayne, a Revolutionary War hero from Pennsylvania who had settled in Georgia.[51] Massachusetts Rep. Theodore Sedgwick, upon hearing of Jackson's defeat, rejoiced: "May every de-

---

[46]Ibid., 12:709–15.

[47]Historicus, *Federal Gazette* (Philadelphia), Mar. 5, 1790.

[48]*General Advertiser* (Philadelphia), Jan. 18, 1791.

[49]Thomas Lowther to James Iredell, May 9, 1789, Griffith J. McRee, *Life and Correspondence of James Iredell*, 2 vols. (New York, 1857–58), 1:258.

[50]William Foster, *James Jackson: Duellist and Militant Statesman* (Athens, Ga., 1960), p. 102.

[51]Ibid., p. 98.

claiming demagogue who attempts to lay a foundation for popularity, by inflaming the passions of the people meet their deserved fate."[52] Jackson returned to Georgia in 1791 and reentered state politics. He contested by every means at hand, including several duels, the election that he had lost, but he was unable to win back the seat. However, he did succeed in having Wayne unseated on the grounds of corrupt election practices. In 1793 Jackson was elected to the Senate, where he attacked the excise and supported a motion to open the proceedings to the public. In 1795, when Georgia was stirred by controversy over the sale of its western lands, Jackson resigned from the Senate and returned home. He devoted the next six years to state politics, including serving as governor from 1798 to 1801.[53]

In 1800 Jackson was elected to the Senate for a second time, declining the position of president pro tempore. He strongly supported the Jefferson administration, which looked to him as its chief spokesman in Georgia. The mature legislator was instrumental in the purchase of the Louisiana Territory, supporting several bills that facilitated the acquisition and arguing persuasively to win his colleagues' support. When discussion arose about moving the capital from the Potomac, Jackson expressed his hope that his grandchildren would not see the time when the capital might move to the newly acquired territory west of the Mississippi River. The Potomac site was sacred, he maintained, because it was the choice of George Washington, "perhaps the most illustrious man who ever lived." During the debate, he referred to the First Congress and the compromise under whose terms the capital was located on the Potomac and the federal government assumed the states' war debts. If the capital were ever moved, he said, the assumed debt would have to be returned to the states.[54]

As a senator, Jackson still argued vehemently for the removal of the Creek Indians from the Southeast. He differed with the administration on the question; Jefferson sought to accomplish with persuasion what Jackson would do by force. The Georgian did, however, show considerable patience in dealing with the president on this matter,

---

[52]Theodore Sedgwick to Williams, Jan. 27, 1791, Theodore Sedgwick Papers, Massachusetts Historical Society, Boston.

[53]Foster, *James Jackson*, pp. 104, 144–67.

[54]*Annals of Congress*, 13:282–87, quote on p. 285.

demonstrating a maturity from his rash days in the First Federal Congress. He spoke in support of a bill to repeal the excise, a cause he had always championed. Jackson was now ready to support amendments to the Constitution, particularly one limiting the president to two terms. Yet, Jackson was still foremost a Georgian. Sen. Jonathan Dayton of New Jersey wrote: "If there was a single member who had more warmly, ably, perseveringly, and successfully contended for the rights and interests of his particular state than all the others — Jackson was that person."[55] Jackson's political career was cut short toward the end of his term by serious illness, and on March 19, 1806, he died at the age of forty-nine. No one had done more to establish the tradition of a southern states' rights viewpoint in Congress.

He did, however, leave us with an autobiography. In it he penned his own obituary:

> In public life he was patriotic and zealous for the preservation of those liberties America had so perseveringly obtained — Strenuous against the least invasion of the people's rights and totally opposed to any other measure of either Titles or otherwise which might endanger true Republicanism — In private life he was affectionate to his Family and kind to his servants; his slaves lived & were clothed much better than those of most of his Neighbors — The mechanics loved him for his punctuality in payment and the poor were never dismissed from his door empty handed — He had however (& where is the Mortal without them) his Foibles — He had a sensibility to extreme and frequently took amiss from even his Friends what was never intended as such — which rendered him frequently unhappy in his disposition and he gave too much way to violent passions which for the moment led him too far — Reason however soon resumed her sway & his natural good temper returned with all but himself; with himself he would be angry for having been so with others. On the whole we may safely conclude that his good qualities far exceeded those of a contrary tendency and that he is a real loss to the community who sincerely lament him.[56]

This passage provides a unique insight into James Jackson; it tells much about how he wanted to be viewed by others and how he viewed

---

[55] Foster, *James Jackson*, p. 177.

[56] "Character of James Jackson Drawn by Himself," *Georgia Historical Quarterly* 37 (1953):160.

himself. Jackson claimed to be a patriot, and there is no doubt that he was. It is also clear that he did in fact believe in the rights of the people. Not enough evidence exists to evaluate the analysis of his private life; there is no way of knowing if, in fact, his slaves "lived & were clothed much better than those of most of his Neighbors." His passionate oratory certainly demonstrated his "sensibility to extreme," and his frequent duels also indicated "violent passions which for the moment led him too far." The validity of Jackson's final assertion, that "his good qualities far exceeded those of a contrary tendency," is up to the reader to decide. In any event, James Jackson played a unique and important role in the formative period of American history and should not be overlooked or underestimated.

William C. diGiacomantonio

To Form the Character
of the American People

*Public Support for the Arts, Sciences, and Morality
in the First Federal Congress*

I N M A Y 1780 John Adams took time out from his new assignment as
peace commissioner in Paris to remind Abigail back in Braintree: "I
must study Politicks and War that my sons may have liberty to study
Mathematicks and Philosophy. My sons ought to study Mathematicks
and Philosophy, Geography, natural History, Naval Architecture, navigation, Commerce and Agriculture, in order to give their children a
right to study Painting, Poetry, Musick, Architecture, Statuary, Tapes-
try and Porcelaine."[1]

The author of this beautiful Whitmanesque passage has often been
depicted as the stereotypically colorless Yankee, a Boston lawyer passionate about two things only: abstract political theorizing and his own
reputation in history. But in utterances like these the author proves
himself a true and passionate visionary. The striking thing about the
passage is not that Adams wrote it, nor even that he was inspired to
write it during one of the darkest periods of the Revolutionary War.
The most striking things about the passage are the nature of its content and the direction of its perspective.

Two assumptions seem to underlie Adams's insistence that he "*must*

---

[1]John Adams to Abigail Adams, ca. May 12, 1780, Lyman H. Butterfield, ed., *The
Book of Abigail and John: Selected Letters of the Adams Family, 1762–1784* (Cambridge,
Mass., 1975), p. 260.

study Politicks and War" so that his sons might study mathematics and philosophy, and that their sons in turn might study poetry, music, and architecture. The first assumption is that the progress of human achievement would be measured by increasingly refined endeavors. The second assumption is that, in practicing the art of painting and porcelain, succeeding generations would actually be completing the work of the American Revolution.

Adams isn't necessarily arguing that poetry is more important than national defense. But the forceful parallel structure of his prose strongly suggests that, for Adams at least, the one is fully as important as the other. His political and martial pursuits would only experience their full realization — indeed, would only make sense — in light of the scientific, literary, and artistic pursuits of his children and grandchildren. This is because the Revolutionary generation had merely created an "America," whereas subsequent generations would have to people it with "Americans."

The task was formidable. "The American continent," notes one historian of the early republic, "had acquired no shared history outside the British context. . . . The logic of national identity pointed back to Britain, to counterrevolution, to a repudiation of the bizarre events of 1776."[2] As late as the 1830s, Tocqueville observed how America's rampant commercialism, the business of taming its vast continent, and the nearness of Europe and its commodities similarly discouraged attempts to elevate the American mind to a conception of itself and its cultural achievement: "His desires, needs, education, and circumstances all seem united to draw the American's mind earthward. Only religion from time to time makes him turn a transient and distracted glance toward heaven."[3]

What role would the arts and sciences play in developing a novel and unique American character? The arts express ideas around which private will and public virtues coalesce. If they do not guarantee a

---

[2]John M. Murrin, "A Roof without Walls: The Dilemma of American National Identity," in *Beyond Confederation: Origins of the Constitution and American National Identity,* ed. Richard Beeman, Stephen Botein, and Edward C. Carter II (Chapel Hill, 1987), p. 342.

[3]Alexis de Tocqueville, *Democracy in America,* ed. J. P. Mayer, 2 vols. (Garden City, N.Y., 1969), 2:chap. 9; quote on pp. 455–56.

unified worldview, they at least indulge a united desire to debate the same issues. In the process, those issues become national issues, and citizens become practiced in the habit of exchanging native ideas in a native idiom. The sciences encourage an inventive self-reliance among citizens, while those among them who become tinkers and scientists create the conditions necessary for economic independence and growth. Add to these a public morality capable of propounding and enforcing a common national identity through shared values, and one begins to uncover the origins of a national character.

The work of creating a national character did not wait for the public career of Adams's sons and grandsons. The first steps under the Constitution to place the encouragement of the arts, sciences, and morality on the national agenda occurred, like so much else, during the First Federal Congress.

Subsidies, Patents, and Copyrights

Government encouragement of the arts and sciences was extremely limited under the Articles of Confederation. Congress's minimal powers meant it could do little more than recommend favorable measures to the individual states. Even when there was a willingness to subsidize specific projects, like Ebenezer Hazard's publication of historic manuscripts, lack of money prevented Congress from acting on its resolve.[4] In 1783, as peace neared, a congressional committee deemed it "indispensably necessary" that a "just and impartial Account of our Contest for public freedom and happiness should be handed down to posterity" by an official "historiographer to the United States . . . governed by the most disinterested principles of public good, totally uninfluenced by party of every kind." Thomas Paine was proposed for the job, but it never materialized. It took another two years for Congress to award Paine a three-thousand-dollar "gratification" for his "unsolicited and

---

[4]Worthington C. Ford et al., eds., *Journal of the Continental Congress, 1774–1789*, 34 vols. (Washington, D.C., 1904–37), 11:705 (hereafter *JCC*). See also Congress's favorable response to the petition of Pierre Eugene du Simitiere for government funds to publish his *Memoirs and observations on the origin and present state of North America* in *JCC*, 15:1316–18.

continuous labors" as a propagandist during the war. These measures were actively promoted by many future members of the First Congress, including Antifederalists Elbridge Gerry of Massachusetts and William Grayson of Virginia, and Federalists Charles Carroll of Maryland and Benjamin Hawkins and Hugh Williamson of North Carolina. Their support demonstrates an early understanding about the government's role in encouraging the arts and sciences, an understanding, more-over, that transcended ideological and sectional interests.[5]

The Constitutional Convention reached beyond the Confederation Congress's meager achievements when it considered Madison's pro-posals to empower Congress to grant patents and copyrights, establish a university, and reward "useful discoveries." Charles Pinckney of South Carolina proposed federal support for "seminaries for the pro-motion of literature and the arts & sciences" as well.[6] Ultimately, the Convention agreed only to the pared-down provision we read today in Article I, section 8, paragraph 8: "That Congress shall have Power . . . To promote the Progress of Science and the useful Arts, by securing for limited Times to Authors and Inventors the exclusive Right to their respective Writings and Discoveries." The clause raised little discussion during ratification. An Antifederalist warned that federal copyrights threatened freedom of the press, but more commentators greeted the clause as a victory over the "principles of barbarism."[7]

Some Americans believed that the federal government's "exclusive jurisdiction" over the national capital and federal territories would encourage Congress to venture beyond the limited scope of patents and copyrights, and establish there such institutions as a national ar-chives, museums, botanical gardens, and a national university. One scientist, anticipating the name ultimately bestowed on the capital, proposed a "Washington Society of Sciences" as early as May 1789. Meeting periodically at the seat of government, the society was in-tended to settle disputes over who qualified for potential protection as an original inventor. One "Lover of the Arts" was even more assertive,

---

[5]*JCC*, 24:512–13, 29:662, 774 n. 2, 775, 796.

[6]Max Farrand, ed., *Records of the Federal Convention of 1787*, 4 vols. (1911; reprint, New Haven, 1966), 2:325.

[7]John P. Kaminski et al., eds., *The Documentary History of the Ratification of the Constitu-tion*, 17 vols. to date (Madison, Wis., 1976–), 16:386, 229.

proposing a "permanent fund" and the appropriation of land in the Northwest Territory for a colony of poets and painters, "a kind of elisium."[8]

The nationalizing purposes of a publicly funded university were to be seen in Paris's College of the Four Nations, where since 1661 the best and brightest from France's four ethnic borderlands had been sent to become Frenchmen. When a "Foreign Spectator" defended the idea of a national university during the ratification debate in 1787, his purpose was less to ensure the indoctrination of a new republican ideology than to break down sectional barriers and instill an orthodox allegiance. "From a *concourse of her best sons at the temple of wisdom,*" he hoped, America's "Federal University" would send forth students like "so many powerful centripetal forces" to give "eternal stability" to the union. "Infinitely above the local prejudices of vulgar bosoms, they will think and feel as genuine sons of America."[9]

Washington himself gave voice to expectations of this magnitude in his second annual message to the First Congress on January 8, 1790. "In resuming your consultations for the general good," Washington recommended a number of concerns worthy of attention, including the establishment of a militia, a post office, and a diplomatic corps, relations with Native Americans, and naturalization for (white) immigrants. Significantly, the president omitted reference to such outstanding business as locating the seat of the federal government while devoting almost the entire second half of his annual message to the encouragement of the arts and sciences.

The bulk of this section is a lengthy reflection on the role of education in the young republic: "There is nothing which can better deserve your patronage than the promotion of science & literature. Knowledge is, in every country, the surest basis of public happiness. In one, in which the measures of government receive their impression so immediately from the sense of the community, as in our's, it is propor-

---

[8]Kenneth R. Bowling, *The Creation of Washington, D.C.: The Idea and Location of the American Capital* (Fairfax, Va., 1991), pp. 5–6; John Churchman to George Washington, May 7, 1789, George Washington Papers, series 7, 6:15, Library of Congress, Washington, D.C.; *Daily Advertiser* (New York), Mar. 15, 1790.

[9]John O'Connor, *Political Opinions Particularly Respecting the Seat of Government* (Georgetown, Md., 1789); "Foreign Spectator" [Nicholas Collins], *Independent Gazetteer* (Philadelphia), Sept. 13, 1787.

tionably essential." Washington concluded his address with the suggestion that Congress consider subsidizing existing "seminaries of public learning" and establishing a "national university."[10]

Several months later, the House considered a motion to refer to a select committee "that part of the President's speech which respects the encouragement of science and literature." At the time the motion was made, legislation providing for patent and copyright protection had either already been passed or was under consideration; the subject of the motion could only have been a national university. Only amateur scientist John Page of Virginia is known to have challenged the objection that such an expenditure was unconstitutional. The House adjourned for the day without arriving at a decision.[11]

The first legislation in which Congress registered its support for the arts and sciences was the Impost Act (HR-2), the provisions of which were introduced one week after the House officially assembled. Early in the debate, George Thatcher of Maine proposed listing grammar books, Bibles, novels, and plays among the enumerated imports to be taxed at a higher rate. Roger Sherman of Connecticut reproached his colleague for lumping Bibles with "plays, farces, tragedies, and novels" for taxation purposes. Whether Sherman's object was to keep imported Bibles more affordable or to repudiate the profane implication of Thatcher's suggestion, it shows the strong Puritan values for which the Connecticut congressman earned his nickname, "Father Sherman."[12]

The Impost Act's ultimate failure to tax books above the common rate of 5 percent suggests that a majority of congressmen felt the impost was an improper means of encouraging or protecting America's cultural resources. But one other belated gesture suggests the opposite. On January 27, 1790, Sherman presented the House with a petition from President Ezra Stiles and the fellows of Yale College requesting a refund on the duties paid for importing "philosophical apparatus." The collection of instruments included an air pump, an

---

[10] *The Documentary History of the First Federal Congress, 1789–1791*, 14 vols. to date (Baltimore, 1972–), vol. 3 (Linda Grant DePauw, Charlene Bangs Bickford, and LaVonne Siegel Hauptman, eds.), p. 253 (hereafter *DHFFC*).

[11] *DHFFC*, vol. 13 (Helen E. Veit, Charlene Bangs Bickford, Kenneth R. Bowling, and William Charles diGiacomantonio, eds.), p. 1221.

[12] Ibid., vol. 10 (Charlene Bangs Bickford, Kenneth R. Bowling, and Helen E. Veit, eds.), p. 177.

astronomical clock, a solar microscope, a three-foot reflecting tele-
scope, and a device intriguingly listed simply as "a machine for demonstrating mechanical powers."[13] The petition also sought a general exemption for such goods in the future. "It is humbly presumed," wrote
Stiles, "that the small diminishments of Revenue from even an universal Exemption of such Importations for public literary use would be
compensated by the speedy Promotion of the useful arts & by the
accelerated Advance of Science & Literature in America."[14]

The Ways and Means Act (HR-83) of August 1790 exempted from
future taxation "philosophical apparatus specially imported for any
seminary of learning," while Secretary of the Treasury Alexander
Hamilton's report on Yale's petition recommended restitution for the
impost duties the school had already paid. At almost the same time
that Stiles petitioned Congress, Harvard's president presented a similar if less formal request to Massachusetts Rep. Benjamin Goodhue
proposing an exemption for books imported for the use of public
libraries.[15]

Even before Congress was scheduled to convene in 1789, individual
citizens were eagerly contemplating the possibility of more direct government aid in the form of subsidies for books and inventions. In mid-
February 1789, the Reverend Jedidiah Morse of Charlestown, Massachusetts, drafted a petition seeking temporary franking privileges.
Some know of Morse's controversial career as a Congregational minister; others know he was the father of the noted inventor Samuel F. B.
Morse. But every member of the first Congress knew him as the author
of *The American Geography,* for which succeeding generations bestowed
on him the reputation of "father of American Geography." Echoing
the public education theme of Washington's second annual message
to Congress, an advertisement declared the usefulness of Morse's book
derived from the fact that "no national government holds out to its
subjects so many alluring motives to obtain an accurate knowledge of

---

[13]Edmund S. Morgan, *The Gentle Puritan: A Life of Ezra Stiles* (New Haven, 1962), pp.
379–81.

[14]Petition (draft), Dec. 29, 1789, Ezra Stiles Papers, Yale University, New Haven,
Conn.

[15]*DHFFC,* vol. 5 (Charlene Bangs Bickford and Helen E. Veit, eds.), p. 942, vol. 6
(Bickford and Veit, eds.), p. 2035; Joseph Willard to Benjamin Goodhue, Jan. 16, 1790,
Goodhue Papers, New York Society Library, New York.

their own country."[16] Compiling information for his magnificent one-volume edition of *The American Geography* was a costly endeavor; free postage was viewed as an appropriate way for government to subsidize the cost. Morse's petition never reached the floor of Congress. Perhaps no congressman was willing to present it, but more likely Morse never sent it.[17]

The First Congress did receive six petitions seeking federal government subsidies for literary or scientific purposes. The first was presented to the House only two weeks after a quorum had assembled. The noted Pennsylvania surveyor and cartographer John Churchman personally delivered his petition to New York City, armed with a letter of introduction to James Madison from the vice president of Madison's alma mater, Princeton. Churchman's petition, the first of two on the subject, contained a request for funds to undertake an Arctic expedition that would verify the cause of magnetic variation.

The petition radically challenged Congress to assert its constitutional role in encouraging scientific discoveries. A select committee acknowledged the potential benefit of the expedition but failed to recommend the expenditure, citing "the present deranged state of our finances." Floor debate also focused initially on the question of expediency and benefits. For his part, Madison thought that a project that might "throw any valuable light on the discovery of longitude . . . certainly comports with the honor and dignity of government to give it their countenance and support." He reminded the House that "some of the most important discoveries, both in arts and sciences, have come forward under very unpromising and suspicious appearances." Madison's Virginia colleague, Alexander White, pointed out that Churchman's request related only to establishing the cause of magnetic variation, not the consequences: "If the principle is true, it could be applied to practice without knowing the cause which produced it."[18]

Only South Carolina's Thomas Tudor Tucker and Maryland's Joshua Seney—both strict constructionists—are known to have raised the question of Congress's constitutional power to subsidize the sci-

---

[16] *New-York Daily Gazette,* Mar. 20, 1790.

[17] Petition to Congress, Feb. 19, 1789, Morse Family Collection, Yale University, New Haven, Conn.

[18] *DHFFC,* 3:28–29, 10:218–19.

ences in this way. "In the case of a doubt," cautioned Tucker, it was "best to err on the safe side."[19] In tabling that part of the committee report relating to Churchman's subsidy, the House apparently was swayed more by Tucker's arguments than by White's, since a rejection based only on financial considerations would have implicitly conceded the constitutionality of the measure. During the third session, Churchman petitioned the House again on the subject. A select committee this time acknowledged that his request involved a deeper inquiry into Congress's constitutional powers, and it declined making a recommendation. The House concurred with no recorded debate.

Christopher Colles remains, like Churchman, best known as a surveyor and cartographer. But it was as a hydraulic engineer that the First Congress petitioner advertised his services upon his emigration from England shortly before the Revolutionary War. In 1789 he began to raise subscriptions for his *Survey of the Roads of the United States of America*. He appealed to the New York legislature for additional aid, but that body recommended instead that he apply to the federal government since the surveys were "considered and intended to be of national utility."[20] Colles's petition to the House was referred without recorded debate to the postmaster general, the federal official with the most to gain from accurate road maps. He supported the proposal, but the Senate ultimately struck the relevant provision from the House's post office bill (HR-74). Colles went on to publish his road maps serially until 1792, when he abandoned the project, having covered the major coastal route from Albany to Yorktown, Virginia.

Yet another petition for a "reward or gratuity" came from Jacob Isaacs, a member of the once-vibrant Jewish mercantile community in Newport, Rhode Island. Isaacs's experiments in distilling fresh water out of sea water began to attract the attention of the local scientific community early in 1790, although Isaacs did not deliver his petition to Philadelphia until barely two weeks before the First Congress adjourned. The same day, the House referred it to Secretary of State Jefferson, who, with characteristic thoroughness, assembled and consulted an ad hoc board of Philadelphia's leading scientific authorities.

---

[19]Ibid., 10:220.

[20]Walter W. Ristow, ed., *A Survey of the Roads of the United States of America by Christopher Colles* (Cambridge, Mass., 1961), p. 50.

The resulting report outlined the history of distilling sea water and concluded that Isaacs's method, while sound, was not original. Ironically, Isaacs's "discovery" did ultimately yield an indirect benefit to the public; the Second Congress authorized customs officers to issue clearance forms with Jefferson's highly informative report printed on the reverse.[21]

The last petitioner for a government subsidy, John Macpherson, was without a doubt one of the oddest petitioners to appear in the records of the First Congress. A Scottish-born American sympathizer, he claimed to have immigrated to Philadelphia during the Revolutionary War and to have donated a considerable fortune to the war effort. In a Second Congress petition for compensation for wartime services, Macpherson boasted of having spied for Washington and of having single-handedly "changed the face of the War, as he was the cause of the taking the Hessians at Trenton." Previous petitions to the Confederation Congress sought protection for his design of a fort which, he claimed, "all the Cannon and Mortars in the World cannot Injure."[22]

For unknown reasons, the petition Macpherson addressed to the Senate only weeks after the First Congress convened was not presented until just before Congress adjourned, almost two years later. Equally strange, while the Senate Journal entry describes Macpherson's request for patent protection, it omits any mention of his rambling petition's principal object—money to consult with scientists in France about his own theories of determining longitude by magnetic variation. The Journal's silence probably was a tacit acknowledgment of the upper body's constitutional prohibition against introducing money bills. Macpherson's claim clearly challenged that of Churchman, whom Macpherson accused of plagiarism and fraud. In a follow-up petition to the Second Congress, he derided Churchman's proposed Arctic expedition by assuring the Senate, "I do not wish to obtain Sea Otters and Seal Skins by deceiving my Country."[23]

Another First Congress petition sought a government reward for

---

[21] See Julian P. Boyd et al., eds., *The Papers of Thomas Jefferson*, 25 vols. to date (Princeton, 1950–), 19:608–24, 22:318–22.

[22] W. W. Abbot et al., eds., *The Papers of George Washington*, Presidential Series, 4 vols. to date (Charlottesville, 1987–), 4:148 n. 1.

[23] Petition to the Senate, Mar. 19, 1792, Record Group 46, National Archives and Records Administration, Washington, D.C.

curing diphtheria. Ultimately, none of these prayers were granted, but not primarily because of lingering constitutional doubts. Four of the six were referred either to a committee or an executive department head; only one of their reports acknowledged that the request involved a deeper inquiry into constitutional powers. Implicit behind Congress's response was a distinction between a public concern and a public role, for which the measure of legitimate government intervention was its pragmatic effect.

The First Congress's most assertive and comprehensive initiatives for promoting the arts and sciences were the Patents and Copyright Acts (HR-41 and 43) of April and May 1790. The federal government's power to grant patents and copyrights figures eighth among the powers of Congress enumerated in the Constitution, providing a reliable index of its importance to the Founding Fathers. Apart from its intrinsic contribution to the progress of cultural nationalism, patent and copyright protection was a matter of considerable political and historiographic significance as well. Property was among the foremost "blessings of liberty" the Constitution had been ordained to secure. And, like today, no form of property was more resistant to regulation or more needy of protection than intellectual property. The widespread diffusion of ideas and blueprints directly tested the new government's control over interstate commerce in a way that the trade in casks of rum or hogsheads of tobacco did not.

Colonial and state legislatures passed a few bills for patents and even fewer for copyrights before the adoption of the Constitution. Connecticut led the country by passing the first general copyright law "for the Encouragement of Literature and Genius" in early 1783. By 1786 every state except Delaware had enacted copyright legislation, assigning penalties for violations and guaranteeing periods of protection from fourteen to twenty-one years.[24]

Congress was prompted to consider its own copyright legislation only two weeks after the House formally assembled, when it received the first two of seven petitions for copyright protection. David Ramsay's petition of April 15, 1789, enjoys the distinction of being the first petition presented to the First Federal Congress. The second petition,

---

[24]James Gilreath, ed., *Federal Copyright Records, 1790–1800* (Washington, D.C., 1987), pp. xv–xxv.

one of Churchman's two, was submitted immediately afterward. South Carolinian Ramsay sought a copyright for his two-volume *History of the Revolution of South Carolina* (1785) and for his *History of the American Revolution*, due out later that year. Churchman sought protection for all globes, maps, and charts based on his principles of magnetism. Another Churchman petition, submitted during the brief third session of the First Congress, asked for an increase of the penalties listed under the Copyright Act (HR-39). The resulting copyright bill (HR-123) provided for such an increase but died with the end of the session.

The third copyright petition received by the First Federal Congress came from Rev. Jedidiah Morse. In addition to his own petition for a copyright for his book, Morse drafted and delivered another copyright petition on behalf of a friend, Newburyport schoolteacher Nicholas Pike, for his *New and Complete System of Arithmetick* (1788). Although the House Journal notes that the next petitioner, Hannah Adams, sought "an exclusive privilege" for her *Alphabetical Compendium of Various Sects*, she later claimed that she petitioned for a general copyright law.[25]

Copyright legislation passed without significant recorded debate on May 17, 1790. Under the terms of the Copyright Act (HR-43), copyrights were issued by federal district courts and deposited, along with a copy of the work, with the secretary of state.[26] The First Congress heard from only one new copyright petitioner after passage of the law. Like Morse, Rev. Enos Hitchcock was a Congregational minister. But unlike Morse, he was often absent from his flock while serving as a chaplain in the Continental Army. (For his participation in the Saratoga campaign, he was honored with a cameo appearance in John Trumbull's painting *Surrender of Burgoyne* [1822], now in the Capitol rotunda.) Also unlike Morse, Hitchcock never journeyed to the federal capital for the purpose of copyrighting his book *Memoirs of the Bloomsgrove Family . . . Containing Sentiments on the Mode of Domestic Education* (1790). But he did have an aggressive promoter on the spot in the person of New York City merchant and bookseller Royal Flint.

---

[25] Hannah F. S. Lee, ed., *A Memoir of Miss Hannah Adams* (Boston, 1832), pp. 16–20.

[26] For the language of the Copyright Act (HR-43), see the complete legislative history of the act in *DHFFC*, vol. 4 (Charlene Bangs Bickford and Helen E. Veit, eds.), pp. 522–28. Brief debates on the Copyright (and Patents) Bill (HR-10) and the Copyright Bill (HR-39) that preceded HR-43 and anticipated all the arguments posed on the subject can be found in *DHFFC*, 10:215–16, vol. 12 (Helen E. Veit, Charlene Bangs Bickford, Kenneth R. Bowling, and William Charles diGiacomantonio, eds.), pp. 122–23.

It was Flint who urged Hitchcock to send complimentary copies of his book to potential patrons, such as Mrs. John Jay, Mrs. Henry Knox, and Mrs. William Smith, wife of the South Carolina representative and daughter of Sen. Ralph Izard. Hitchcock apparently needed all the inside influence he could find; as a citizen of Providence, Rhode Island, he had the unique disadvantage among these petitioners of not being a citizen of the United States at the time he petitioned on May 26, 1790. Rhode Island's ratification of the Constitution three days later extended the provisions of the Copyright Act to him, and the *Memoirs* became the first book registered for federal copyright protection in Rhode Island.

While all of these authors, except Pike and possibly Ramsay, availed themselves of the First Congress's copyright legislation, inventors had still more to gain by passage of a general patent law, since the national government's aid to inventors was weaker even than its aid to authors had been before 1790. The only encouragement given by the Continental Congress was a resolution drafted by John Adams in early 1776, calling on each colony to establish a society for the promotion of "Agriculture, Arts, Manufactures and Commerce." Congress rejected another resolution for a congressional committee "to receive all Plans and Proposals for encouraging and improving the Agriculture, Arts, Manufactures and Commerce both foreign and domestic."[27]

The first Patents Act (HR-41) was approved on April 10, 1790. Under its provisions, patents were issued by at least two members of a board consisting of the secretaries of state and war and the attorney general. Upon favorable consideration, the commission issued letters patent valid for fourteen years, which were then forwarded to the attorney general for examination, certified by the president, and registered with the Department of State. House debate on the bill seems to have been limited to striking a clause that permitted trial by jury in cases of appeal. Sen. William Maclay's diary describes Senate debate on the bill only as "considerable."[28]

---

[27]Paul H. Smith et al., eds., *Letters of Delegates to Congress, 1774–1789,* 21 vols. to date (Washington, D.C., 1976–), 3:420–21 (hereafter *LDC*); *JCC,* 24:211, 326.

[28]*DHFFC,* vol. 9 (Kenneth R. Bowling and Helen E. Veit, eds.), p. 236. For the legislative history of the Patent Act (HR-41), see ibid., 6:620–42. For House debate, see ibid., 12:639.

The House received its first petition for a patent on May 4, 1789, one month after a quorum had assembled and two weeks after forming a committee on the general subject of patents and copyrights. Following this in rapid succession, no fewer than twenty patent petitions were submitted to the House prior to passage of the Patents Act (HR-41). Two of these petitioners applied directly to the Senate as well, while one petition was submitted exclusively to that body.

The first two patent petitions were unusual in specifying the duration of the patents they sought, in each case, twenty-one years. The third patent petition, the oldest still in existence, was submitted by the most dynamic and prolific patent petitioner in the history of the First Federal Congress. John Fitch's claims to the invention of the steamboat embroiled him in a highly publicized controversy with fellow petitioner James Rumsey. A "Rumseian Society" was formed in 1788 to provide financial support in the looming legal battle with Fitch over title to the invention of the steam engine, but Rumsey himself was in Europe throughout the First Congress period. Fitch's network was less extensive, owing perhaps to his forthright personality. Only days before Congress convened he publicly identified representatives George Clymer and Thomas Fitzsimons of Philadelphia as two of his "professed enemies on this subject," who "will leave no stone unturned to hurt my interest with that honorable body."[29] But Fitch had persistence and submitted a total of four petitions before the First Congress adjourned.

Neither party felt its exclusive interests served by the provisions of the Patents Act. Fitch protested the failure to guarantee trial by jury in cases of appeal, while both he and Rumsey felt the bill's language invited opportunities to plagiarize their ideas. Fitch's initial response was to withdraw from the competition and seek other patrons; he mentioned the Spanish in Mississippi. Then he sought a private bill. The regular steamboat service he inaugurated along the Delaware River between Wilmington and Trenton apparently encouraged his prospects as the sole inventor, because his fourth and last petition actually opposed changes in the law proposed by an amendatory patents bill (HR-121). Fitch canvassed members of both houses prior

---

[29] *Independent Gazetteer*, Mar. 31, 1789.

to submitting this petition; his tally is a rare and fascinating record of early congressional lobbying activity. After temporarily suspending consideration of all applications related to steam engines in January 1791, the patents commission issued patents to both Fitch and Rumsey, leaving open ended the question of origin. Fitch's muted victory did little to stem the flight of investors. After a fruitless five-year search for patronage, he migrated to Kentucky, where he committed suicide. Rumsey died in London trying to perfect his steamboat.

John Stevens, Nathan Read, and Angelhart Cruse joined the swelling tide of patent applications relating to modifications or improvements on the steam engine. The first two became prominent state officeholders and industrialists. Cruse remains a nearly anonymous figure, a fate largely shared by several of these patent petitioners. For a handful of others, biographical information is sketchy, or unreliable, or both. Among this group, John Macpherson represents an especially intriguing case, as we have already seen. The mystery extends even to his purported inventions, which seem to have been adaptations of the lightning rod involving, among other things, an umbrella.

Two petitioners who failed to receive patents for their inventions, but nevertheless attained notable recognition in related fields of endeavor, were Christopher Colles and Leonard Harbaugh. Colles — the same person who later petitioned for a subsidy for surveying America's roads — sought protection for his "perambulator," a type of odometer. Harbaugh was a Baltimore mechanic and self-taught architect who followed his failure as an inventor of a reaper and dock-cleaning devices with a relatively successful career designing and constructing public buildings in the new federal city.

The only First Congress patent petition to result in a private bill was that of Francis Bailey, a Philadelphia newspaper publisher who laid claim to an innovative technique for preventing counterfeiting. In the House the only recorded objection to bringing in a bill came from Samuel Livermore. The shrewd New Hampshire farmer logically pointed out that Bailey was "one of the last persons that needed a special interference in his favor, as it is impossible, by his own words, for any person to find out his invention."[30] Bailey managed to recruit

---

[30] *DHFFC,* 12:580.

the support of several notable Pennsylvanians in and out of Congress. They included the noted Philadelphia lawyer Miers Fisher, who not only provided testimony to a Senate committee on Bailey's behalf but even seems to have served as the committee's unofficial clerk.[31] The Senate eventually referred the Bailey bill (HR-44) to the committee considering the Patents Act, where its individually tailored provisions were lost. The patent commission later issued one of its first patents to Bailey on January 29, 1791.

What do the petitions for general subsidies, copyrights, and patents tell us about public support for the arts and sciences during the First Congress? On the most basic level, of course, they merely tell us what fewer than three dozen individuals — scientists, writers, and in some cases, cranks — considered to be the legitimate concerns of government. The European origins of three out of the five petitioners for general subsidies may explain the inflated expectations implicit in requests of that type. Such entitlements were easier to get in Europe, where the tradition of government patronage for the arts and sciences was more deeply rooted and more freely exercised. By contrast, all of those who petitioned for copyrights were native Americans, while only two out of the twenty patent petitioners are known to have been born abroad.

The patent petitions paint a very vibrant and human picture of America's infant Industrial Revolution. The variety of inventions submitted for congressional approval, before the establishment of a more standardized patent-approval system, run from the sublime to the absurd. Like Churchman and Macpherson, Arthur Greer presented a machine which, he claimed, "reduced to a certainty the discovery of the true longitude or departure from any given meridian north of the equator." To an economy heavily dependent on transatlantic commerce, that three petitioners addressed the improvement of navigation hardly seems inappropriate. Similarly, the five petitioners who joined Fitch and Rumsey in promoting or protecting some version of the steam engine speak eloquently to the adaptive uses of steam

---

[31]Changes made by Fisher's hand to the text of the Bailey Bill (HR-44) in the Senate committee may be his own recommendations or the committee's proposed amendments.

power and to the importance of inland navigation in an increasingly westward-looking nation. At the other end of the spectrum we find Abraham Westervelt's exclusive process for manufacturing something called "shell buttons." In between are more predictable inventions — at least six relate to the improvement of mills. Strangely, given what we know of consumer habits in the early republic, only one petitioner offered a new method of distilling alcohol.

The identities of so many of these inventors may be instructive for what they do not reveal. The relative anonymity of so many of them, especially compared to the copyright petitioners, may be a tribute to the government's perceived accessibility to the "common man." It goes without saying that one reason the copyright petitions are so well documented is precisely because they were undertaken by writers. More than almost any other group of petitioners to the First Congress, their thoughts and deeds have been passed down in the only durable form of remembrance available at the time.

Neither were the copyright petitioners timid about exhausting the avenues of influence open to them. Unlike the overwhelming majority of patent petitioners, most of those seeking copyrights were socially and politically well connected. Hitchcock was a member of the Society of the Cincinnati, a fraternal organization of former Continental Army officers that included twenty-five members of the First Congress; Hannah Adams was a distant relation of the vice president; and Pike was a local officeholder and a fellow of the American Academy of Arts and Sciences. The close correspondence Pike maintained with Massachusetts Sen. Tristram Dalton and Rep. Benjamin Goodhue enabled him to closely monitor relevant legislation and even to offer revisions.

Popular support for copyright and patent legislation can be inferred from the justifiable expressions of pride and support expressed in the newspapers. In 1790 such cultural and scientific advances as a reliable road map or the distilling of sea water were sufficient to guarantee momentary celebrity for a hometown hero. In the months preceding William Stoy's unsuccessful First Congress petition for a reward for his cure of diphtheria, New York City papers carried reports of his having saved more than three hundred lives through "extraordinary cures performed . . . on persons bit by mad dogs." The recovery of one anonymous merchant was said to have been witnessed "by thousands."[32] At a time when very few First Congress petitions were reprinted in the public press, Christopher Colles's petition enjoyed the distinction of appearing in the *New-York Daily Gazette* the day after it was presented. This reflects either a high level of interest in Colles's project or an unknown connection between Colles and the editor. Shortly after Churchman's second unsuccessful bid for a federally subsidized Arctic expedition, Philadelphia and New York newspapers carried a satirical poem that dismissed the constitutional question and sympathized with the petitioner for failing to excite Congress's feeble curiosity:

> The men, whom you petition for some dollars,
> Tho' willing to be thought prodigious scholars,
> Yet care no more for variation charts
> Than ace of spades, or king of hearts.[33]

Indirect Support for the Arts and Sciences

In addition to providing patent and copyright protection, the First Congress acknowledged or debated the federal government's role in encouraging the arts and sciences through six other initiatives. The first was the House's decision to grant newspaper reporters a privileged view of its proceedings. At a time when the Senate's doors were not even open to the general public, providing a reserved space for reporters at the foot of the Speaker's chair was a courtesy of which the press, as well as congressmen, understandably made much.

In the last days of the first session, Aedanus Burke of South Carolina introduced a resolution that condemned the printed debates for their "most glaring deviations from the truth" and threatened to deny reporters the future "sanction and countenance of the House."[34] Content that he had made his point, Burke consented to withdraw his

---

[32] "Extract of a letter . . . dated May 24," *Gazette of the United States* (New York), June 17, 1789.

[33] *Daily Advertiser,* Feb. 2, 1791.

[34] *DHFFC,* 10:1502–3. For more on newspapers' access to and reporting on debates, see 10:xvi–xxii, 11:xi–xii.

resolution after brief debate, at which point his colleague, Thomas Sumter, suggested that the House authorize an official publication of its debates. A handful of members, including Madison, opposed making congressmen accountable for what was said about them, and the measure was not brought up again.

Midway through the second session, the House took up the related issue of whether to continue to supply its members with newspapers at public expense. The practice was defended, not as a means of keeping representatives informed at the seat of government, but as their means of sharing information with constituents back home. Upstate New York's Egbert Benson, who opposed the practice, insisted that the Confederation Congress had distributed newspapers only as a way of amusing the often bored delegates "to keep them in their places." Massachusetts Rep. Elbridge Gerry disputed that "curious anecdote." And, in any case, the tradition had come to be valued by the citizens, especially at the farther reaches of the republic. Moreover, congressional patronage of newspapers constituted a considerable source of income to their often fledgling editors; any budget-saving measure that limited the circulation of the largest possible number of newspapers, or threatened to limit it to one or two powerful organs, he regarded as a "contemptible economy." For this reason, and to avoid partiality, the House voted to continue to supply each member with every newspaper published at the seat of government.[35]

By underwriting newspapers in these ways, Congress intended to do more than encourage an important medium of literature, although the press's contribution to the early republic's cultural nationalism cannot be overstated. The House's actions aimed at making the press an active agent of political nationalism as well. Just as science would make Americans independent of European imports, and literature would make them independent of European values, a free and objective press was valued as the nursery of republicanism, which would make Americans free of factionalism and dishonest government.

Although receiving newspapers at public expense was viewed primarily as a way of educating constituents, the First Congress did not neglect to look to its own house as well. The concept of a library of

---

[35]Ibid., 13:1016–17.

Congress was first advanced in 1783 by a committee of the Confederation Congress, which reported a list of books to be purchased. Future First Congress representatives Theodorick Bland and James Madison of Virginia and Hugh Williamson of North Carolina were among its original proponents. The debate at the time weighed financial constraints against the need for books in anticipation of defending future territorial claims against Spain and other European powers, and for books on international law to render Congress's proceedings "conformable to propriety." Madison also advocated the measure as a way of collecting "American Antiquities" for the intended authorized history of the Revolution. Financial considerations prevailed and the committee's report was rejected.

While meeting in New York City's Federal Hall, Congress had access to the New-York Society Library housed on the third floor. Soon after its move to Philadelphia in December 1790, it received a similar invitation to use the Library Company of Philadelphia. There is internal evidence from the recorded debates that some books were kept on hand in the House chamber as well.[36] But Congress's first official motion to establish its own library occurred on April 30, 1790, the same day it approved the Copyright Act. On that date the House agreed to a motion by Elbridge Gerry for a committee to recommend a catalogue of "books necessary for the use of the executive and legislature . . . such as are not readily to be found in public libraries or in book stores."[37]

Gerry's motion kindled a colorful debate, both privately and in the public press. Penny-pinching colleagues like Benjamin Goodhue considered a library of Congress merely "one of Gerry's follies." Newspaper editorials lamented the prospect of having to educate congressmen at public expense, especially at a time when establishing the public credit required Congress's strict attention and austerity. Other supporters of public credit noted that speakers would stand to benefit by having books on political economy readily available to them. The

---

[36] *JCC*, 24:92; *The Papers of James Madison*, 17 vols. to date (Chicago and Charlottesville, 1962–), vol. 6 (William T. Hutchinson and William M. E. Rachal, eds.), p. 116. An extensively annotated printing of the committee's recommended list of books to be purchased in 1783 can be found in *JCC*, 6:62–115; *DHFFC*, 9:3 n. 1, 14:218; Resolution of the Directors of the Library, Jan. 19, 1791, Senate Records, RG 46, NARA.

[37] *New-York Daily Gazette*, June 24, 1790.

committee, chaired by Gerry, submitted its report on June 23, 1790; but its recommendation for an initial investment of one thousand dollars and an annual appropriation of five hundred dollars thereafter for books on political economy, parliamentary law and debates, history, and legal codes was tabled without debate and not taken up again during the First Congress.[38]

Thomas Jefferson's disappointment over the lack of an adequate government library was no more evident than when he tackled the problem of reporting on a single, uniform, and integrated system of currency, weights, and measures. It was a task the House assigned to him on January 15, 1790. Prior to submitting his report in July 1790, the secretary of state—with characteristic thoroughness—consulted several men of science in New York and Philadelphia, constituting, in effect, the first federal commission on science.

Congress's interest in weights and measures, and Jefferson's resulting report, allowed America to claim its status as a near equal to the most scientifically advanced European countries. In this way it served the cause of cultural nationalism. Paradoxically, by tying his proposed system to the French Revolution's aspirations for a universal scientific system, Jefferson consciously signed America on as a full partner in the crusade for a cultural internationalism promised, but ultimately betrayed, by the Enlightenment. Jefferson sent copies of his report to university professors throughout the nation; the House only tabled it. It was not substantially taken up again until Secretary of State John Quincy Adams consulted it in compiling his own famous report on weights and measures in 1821.[39]

Closely related to the concept of a congressional library was Madison's motion to expand the first census schedule to include categories "specifying the number of persons employed in the various arts and

---

[38]For opposition to the measure, see Benjamin Goodhue to Stephen Goodhue, May 25, 1790, Benjamin Goodhue Papers, Essex Institute, Salem, Mass.; *Boston Gazette,* May 10, 1790; *Independent Chronicle* (Boston), May 13, 1790; *Connecticut Journal* (New Haven), June 9, 1790; *New York Journal,* June 29, 1790; *American Mercury* (Hartford, Conn.), July 12, 1790. In defense of the library, see *Massachusetts Centinel* (Boston), May 12, 1790; Solomon Drowne to Theodore Foster, July 25, 1790, Brown Deposit, Special Collections, Brown University, Providence, R.I.

[39]See Boyd, *Jefferson Papers,* 16:602–17.

professions carried on in the United States." Madison believed that reliable statistics on the thirty specified classes of people, from ship-builders to sugar refiners, would allow Congress "to know in what proportion to distribute the benefits resulting from an efficient general government."[40]

Some challenged the measure's expediency. Samuel Livermore, for example, thought that his New Hampshire constituents "would suspect that government was so particular, in order to learn their ability to bear the burden of direct or other taxes." But Virginia's John Page laid his finger on the profounder implications behind Madison's motion when he warned his colleague that "their purposes cannot be supposed the same as the historian's or philosopher's — they are statesmen, and all their measures are suspected of policy." The Senate struck Madison's ambitious schedule from the final version of the Enumeration Act (HR-34) on February 12, 1790, but the attempt stands as an early indirect encouragement of the nascent science of sociology.[41]

A sixth and final initiative in support of the arts and sciences was the work of the five lawyers in the Senate who drafted the Punishment of Crimes Act (S-6) of April 1790. Buried among the thirty-one sections that make up the country's first federal criminal code is a clause permitting the corpses of capital punishment offenders to be handed over to surgeons for dissection. There is no other language in the bill describing the intended purpose of this practice, but New Yorkers might have aimed thereby to prevent grave robbing by medical students — a crime that ignited New York City's infamous "Doctors' Riot of 1788." House opponents of a motion to strike the clause argued that providing corpses "was making those who had injured society, contribute to its advantage by furnishing subjects of experimental surgery." Hugh Williamson of North Carolina, a physician by training, not surprisingly alluded to "the very great and important improvements which had been made in Surgery from experiment." Virginia's John Page, whose own reputation lay in the field of physics rather than the biological sciences, averred that the idea "renders anatomy disgusting." After

---

[40] *DHFFC*, 4:671, 12:138.
[41] Ibid., 12:136, 138.

two afternoons' debate, the motion to strike was defeated and the clause was retained.[42]

Public Morality

The connection between public morality and national character in 1790 may be easily imagined, even if what were understood as matters of public morality at that time seem quaint or outmoded today. It was with real alarm, for example, that representatives such as Theodore Sedgwick of Massachusetts voiced concern over excessive investment in national debt certificates. Diverting capital in this way was referred to disparagingly as "speculation" and was considered "in no way useful in encreasing the labor of the community." Sedgwick equated it to "a spirit of gambling . . . of such evil tendency, that every legislative endeavor should be made to suppress it." Similarly, when James Jackson of Georgia argued against setting impost duties too high, he was doing more than protecting southern interests heavily dependent on foreign imports. He was warning Congress that the resultant incentives to smuggling would lead to a general corruption of morals.[43]

The importation of European luxury goods also was viewed as a very definite corrupter of morals. Pennsylvania Rep. Thomas Scott in particular lamented their polluting influence among his frontier neighbors in the vicinity of Pittsburgh, claiming, "though I am sorry to say it, there exists as great a rage for every species of luxury . . . as there does even in the city of New-York; and how should it be otherwise? have they not the example of yourselves?" Boston's Rep. Fisher Ames defended both his lifestyle and a moderate impost by pointing out that "all the enjoyments of life might be considered in a certain degree as luxuries."[44]

As the First Congress neared the end of its first session, several congressmen supported a measure intended in part to evoke the spirit of America's more spartan roots. On September 25, 1789, Elias Boudinot of New Jersey rose to move that Congress request the president

---

[42]Ibid., 13:968, 969, 970.
[43]Ibid., 12:111, 10:289, 290.
[44]Ibid., 10:191, 551.

to "recommend to the people of the United States, a day of public Thanksgiving and prayer."[45] Observing public thanksgivings had been a custom in New England since the days of its Puritan theocracy; throughout the Revolutionary War, the Confederation Congress had called on all the states to set aside time for such an occasion. Resurrecting the holiday would stimulate a recognition of the blessings of the Constitution and conjure the national myth of the recently consummated Revolution as an Old Testament war of liberation.

Aedanus Burke resented "this mimicking European customs," while fellow South Carolina Antifederalist Thomas Tudor Tucker thought it was "a business with which Congress have nothing to do; it is a religious matter, and, as such, is proscribed by us." Besides opposing it on constitutional grounds, Tucker advanced the eminently reasonable objection that the president should not direct the people to do "what, perhaps, they have no mind to do." Let them wait "to return thanks for a constitution, until they have experienced that it promoted their safety and happiness." Father Sherman, recalling Solomon's thanksgiving announcement for the completion of his Temple, thought the idea "worthy of christian imitation" and seconded Boudinot's motion, after which it passed by a great majority.[46]

The impact of European values, like the impact of European luxury goods, attracted the attention of the First Congress on a number of fronts. Creating a unitary national identity against the backdrop of a plurality of ethnic identities remains perhaps the quintessential theme of the American experiment. How the laws of property ownership and naturalization facilitated the influx of immigrants was clearly understood by the members of the First Congress as a critical factor in the evolution of American national character.

During the December 1790 debate over the land office bill (HR-114), Thomas Scott of Pennsylvania urged his colleagues "to let everyone purchase [land] when he pleased and as much or as little as he chose." In favoring modest farm plots, Scott denigrated speculating European land companies, mostly French. He did not welcome the

---

[45]Ibid., 3:232.

[46]Ibid., vol. 11 (Charlene Bangs Bickford, Kenneth R. Bowling, and Helen E. Veit, eds.), pp. 1500–1501.

idea of large French colonies in the middle of the American wilderness where, he said, immigrants would "preserve their language and manners 2000 years perhaps; this would not be for the true interest of the country, all its inhabitants should by mutual intercourse become assimilated and no name be known but that of Americans." The House agreed to limit the number of acres allowed to each settler, but the entire bill was ultimately postponed to the Second Congress.[47]

The second session House debate on the Naturalization Act (HR-40) involved significant constitutional questions over states' rights, especially regarding immigrants' qualifications for holding state office. While these engaged the ideological orientation of every congressman, support for easy naturalization standards broke down only loosely along sectional lines. Among representatives of the Deep South, hungry for settlers to fill its vacant backlands, South Carolina's Tucker argued against a one-year residency requirement. Representatives of the New England states objected that lowering the bars "made our citizenship too cheap." Predictably, Thomas Hartley, from the middle state of Pennsylvania, advocated intermediate measures. A brief residency, he maintained, would serve as "some security for their fidelity and allegiance" and give immigrants an opportunity to learn about the government and appreciate its "intrinsic value."[48]

The exceptions to this sectional breakdown were notable. Charleston's William Smith favored high restrictions, as did James Jackson of Georgia, himself an immigrant. Jackson's fear was such that "rather than have the common class of vagrants, paupers, and other out-casts of Europe . . . we had better be as we are, and trust to the natural increase of our population for inhabitants." New York City's John Laurance, on the other hand, was against high restrictions on suffrage, reminding his colleagues of their own Revolutionary War slogan, "taxation without representation is tyranny." The House finally rejected Tucker's motion to strike a probationary residency, but resisted an effort to raise it from two years to three. It also struck out wording that would have required an applicant for citizenship to submit proof of his "good moral character." Under the Naturalization Act of March 1790,

---

[47]Ibid., 14:192, 193.
[48]Ibid., 12:162, 146.

the only proof of satisfactory character was an oath or affirmation to support the Constitution.[49]

First Congress petitions to standardize reprints of the Bible, moderate alcohol consumption, and regulate the slave trade each presumed that deficiencies in the national character constituted legitimate grievances that could be corrected by national legislation. No other group of petitions so directly and dramatically challenged Congress to assert its role in promoting public morality under its "implied powers" to provide for the general welfare. By 1789 the individual states were already well practiced in wielding such powers. For example, every state had passed laws regulating slavery or the slave trade, and some of the New England state constitutions contained religious establishment clauses. At question was not whether government enjoyed the right to legislate public morality, but how much the federal government would be allowed to do so under the Constitution's necessary and proper clause of Article I, section 8.

In May 1790 a convention of Congregational ministers meeting in Boston appointed a five-member committee to petition Congress "to secure the public from impositions by inaccurate editions of the Holy Scriptures." It also authorized them to call upon other Christian denominations "to confer & unite with us in one Petition, & thus to concentrate the whole Christian interest in America." Rhode Island Quakers expressed an intention "to Unite . . . to preserve the Bibles Printed in America from Error," but they are not known to have drafted a petition. The Congregationalists' petition of June 1790 was followed in the third session by petitions from several New England Baptist Associations. All were read and tabled.[50]

The First Congress's inaction contrasts starkly with two related initiatives in the Confederation Congress. In response to a petition of Presbyterian ministers in 1777, Congress agreed to import twenty thousand Bibles from Europe. It avoided authorizing an official American

---

[49]Ibid., 12:151, 148. For the evolution of the language of the Naturalization Act (HR-40), see 6:1516–22.

[50]Petition to Congress, June 14, 1790, Petitions and Memorials: Various Subjects, Senate Records, RG 46, NARA; Committee of Congregational Ministers to Rev. Dr. Parker, June 24, 1790, Miscellaneous Collection, Massachusetts Historical Society, Boston, Mass.; Moses Brown to the Committee [Dec. 1790], Almy Brown Papers, Brown University, Providence, R.I.

imprint only because of the impracticability of securing paper and type, not because of ideological scruples about the separation of church and state. Three years later, the Confederation Congress did authorize the first English language American edition of the Bible and recruited a board of ministers to verify its accuracy.[51]

Regulation of alcohol consumption was a subject that evoked considerably more comment during the First Congress — much of it critical. During the first session debate on the Impost Act (HR-2), Madison had opposed offering drawbacks on rum. Drawbacks on exported products were reimbursements for duties paid on imported raw materials — in this case molasses. "Of the small proportion [of distilled rum] which went abroad," Madison pointed out, "the greatest part went to Africa; he feared this trade was inconsistent with the good of mankind, and ought to be reprobated instead of encouraged."[52] It was an early instance of injecting humanitarian concerns into foreign trade policy.

When New England congressmen later tried to lower the impost on molasses, one of their arguments was that the increased burden on domestically distilled rum unfairly favored imported spirits. A discrimination between the two had nothing to do with increasing sobriety, observed Fisher Ames. "Pernicious as country Rum is, foreign spirits are little better — All were poisons — and the difference of two balls, or one, through the brain, was not very material." He went on to describe as "idle the visionary notion of reforming the morals of the people by a duty on molasses. We are not to consider ourselves while here as at church or school, to listen to harangues of speculative piety; we are to talk of the political interest committed to our charge." Ames did not deny that the legislator was competent to legislate on morality; but "when we take up the subject of morality, let our system look towards that object, and not confound itself with revenue."[53]

Ames's speech became a virtual manifesto defining the limitations of legislative influence. James Jackson quoted it verbatim during the third session almost two years later, when he attacked the Duties on

---

[51] *JCC,* 8:733–35, 18:979, 19:91, 23:572–74; *LDC,* 7:311–12 n. 1 provides details on these efforts and bibliographic references.

[52] *DHFFC,* 10:222.

[53] Ibid., 10:364–65, 377.

Distilled Spirits Act (HR-110) in part because it tried to do too much: "This wonderful bill is to encourage industry and agriculture, to promote morality, and to raise revenue. Some of which objects are as diametrically opposite to the other as the east is to the west."[54] For Jackson there was no question as to where the priority should lie.

Fueling Jackson's sense of urgency was the petition submitted in both the House and Senate only weeks before by the prestigious College of Physicians of Philadelphia, "praying them to take speedy and effectual means to discourage, as much as possible, the imposition and use of distilled spirituous liquors." The petition was careful to defer "to Men of other Professions to enumerate the pernicious Effects of these Liquors upon Morals and Manners." But a strong moralism inevitably pervades the text. The petitioners "beheld with regret the feeble influence of Reason and Religion in restraining the Evils which they have enumerated." In closing, they based their appeal on Congress's "regard to the Character of our Nation, and to the Rank of our Species in the Scale of Beings."[55]

The petition was read and promptly tabled in each house. But Jackson sought to deflect any lingering force behind the physicians' arguments by postulating that "they might, with as much propriety, present a memorial to Congress to prevent people from over-eating, or to forbid the use of mushrooms, because sometimes ill effects had been produced by eating them." Later, during the last days of debate on the Duties on Distilled Spirits Act (HR-110), Jackson sarcastically proposed referring a controversial amendment to a committee of the same physicians — those "gentlemen of the squirt," as he called them — "who as they had attempted to squirt morality and instruction into the minds of the members, perhaps may also be able to squirt understanding into the house, on *this* subject."[56]

Overall, the petition stimulated more public interest north of the Potomac than in the southern states, where it is not known to have

---

[54] Ibid., vol. 14 (William Charles diGiacomantonio, Kenneth R. Bowling, Charlene Bangs Bickford, and Helen E. Veit, eds.), p. 217.

[55] Minute Books, Records of the College of Physicians, Library of the College of Physicians, Philadelphia, pp. 118–22, 147–49; Petition to Congress, Dec. 29, 1790, Petitions and Memorials: Various Subjects, Senate Records, RG 46, NARA.

[56] *DHFFC*, 14:213, 335–36.

been reprinted. Newspaper editorials expressed a variety of sentiments on the topic. One satirized the southerners' self-proclaimed
right to get drunk. But the majority reproached the College of Physicians for going far beyond the scope of legislators, much less physicians. "A more officious piece of impertinence was never offered to any
legislative body," wrote one critic. Even "A Friend to the College"
advised the petitioners to "be extremely cautious how they meddle,
even more so obliquely, with the diseases of the body politic, which are
much too deep for their inspection. . . . Legislators and Physicians have
nothing to do with the prevention of vices or diseases, 'tis enough to
cure them."[57]

By far the most significant and sustained debate on the First Congress's influence over the improvement of public morality occurred as
the result of three petitions from Quaker groups seeking federal regulation of slavery and the slave trade. Legislation to regulate slavery in
all the colonies had been proposed as early as the First Continental
Congress in 1774. That body's Non-Importation Association pledged
the colonies to discontinue the slave trade after December 1775. Although the association achieved only a temporary cessation of the
slave trade, the antislavery movement went on to obtain numerous vic-
tories at the state level throughout the 1780s. The only other attempt
to adopt national measures occurred in October 1783, when a delegation of Philadelphia Quakers personally presented a petition to the
Confederation Congress seeking the suppression of the slave trade.

The fate of the 1783 petition reveals how the debate over antislavery
legislation was affected by the larger debate over the growth of centralized power in the 1780s. Congress referred the petition to a committee composed of prominent states' rights advocates. Although all
three were generally sympathetic to the antislavery cause, they reported only that "it be recommended" to the individual states to enact
laws in accordance with the antislavery clause of the 1774 Continental
Association. The full Congress voted down the committee report the
next day.[58] On the other hand, the prohibition of slavery in the North-

---

[57]"D," *Pennsylvania Mercury (Philadelphia)*, Feb. 22, 1791; *General Advertiser* (Philadelphia), Jan. 18, 29, 1791.
    [58]*JCC*, 25:660.

west Territory under the Northwest Ordinance of 1787 reveals how far Congress was willing to go to regulate slavery where it had the undisputed authority to do so.

The Quakers' First Congress petition drive followed two unsuccessful attempts to regulate the slave trade by taxing the import of slaves under the authority of Article I, section 9 of the Constitution. Both initiatives were the work of Rep. Josiah Parker of Virginia. His first attempt to lay a duty under the Impost Act (HR-2) was opposed, ironically, on the grounds that it inhumanely lumped people with taxable property and so warranted a separate bill. The second attempt came in the form of the slave trade bill (HR-30), the first antislavery legislation proposed under the Constitution. It was postponed without debate until the second session and was not brought up again.[59]

On February 11, 1790, the Philadelphia and New York Yearly Meetings of Friends submitted antislavery addresses to the First Congress. A memorial from the largely Quaker-controlled Pennsylvania Abolition Society reached Congress the next day. The Yearly Meetings confessed themselves "religiously bound to request your serious christian attention to the deeply interesting subject." But in their Pennsylvania Abolition Society petition many of the same petitioners this time based their appeal on a provision of the Constitution itself. Referring to the Preamble's explicit commitment to " 'promoting the Welfare & *securing the blessings of liberty to the People of the United States,* ' " they prayed Congress to "Step to the very verge of the powers vested in you," to remove "this *Inconsistency from the Character of the American People.*"[60]

No other petitions to the First Congress generated the passion or public rhetoric that these antislavery petitions did. The counterattack waged by the delegations of the southernmost states was quick and tenacious. Their speeches, covering an agonizingly prolonged seven days of debate, amounted to the first documented case of filibustering at a time when congressmen already felt "bewildered," "like a Flight of Land Foul [*sic*] at Sea,"[61] due to the long debate over Madison's controversial proposal to discriminate between primary and secondary

---

[59] For House debate, see *DHFFC*, 10:633–39, 642–51.

[60] Petitions and Memorials: Various Subjects, Senate Records, RG 46, NARA.

[61] *DHFFC*, 9:206.

holders of wartime securities. Avoiding any direct references to "implied powers," congressmen from Georgia and South Carolina initially focused on the constitutional guarantees limiting regulation to the ten-dollar-per-head impost and protecting the trade until at least 1808. The bulk of their attack, and their most virulent language, was directed against the petitioners themselves.

For the first time, a petition's merit was questioned not only on the basis of the prayer it contained but on the identity of the persons bringing it forward and their motivation in doing so. Like the College of Physicians, the Quaker petitioners were pilloried for meddling "in a business with which they have nothing to do; they were volunteering it in the cause of others, who neither expected it nor desired it." The perception of "intemperate and unwarrantable meddling" seemed confirmed by the Quakers' daily attendance in the House gallery, where their silent witness of the proceedings on the floor below prompted one South Carolina representative to liken them to "evil spirits hovering over our heads." Another suggested, to the accompaniment of much laughter and confusion, that the Quaker petitioners were like Milton's Lucifer, who entered paradise in the shape of a cormorant. Their attackers went on to indict the Quakers' "enthusiastic bigotry" in pretending to be concerned with the moral welfare of a country which their treasonous indifference during the Revolutionary War did nothing to help establish.[62]

Members from Georgia and the Carolinas further attacked the petitions on the grounds of nonsectarian disengagement. Many of their speeches emphatically rejected "religious scruples" as a basis for public policy. Thomas Tudor Tucker insisted that it was "a ground that is not admissible and on which no subject ought ever to be taken up in this house. If we are to pay attention to the religious scruples of one sect, we are equally bound to pay attention to all." He then illustrated the threat by reading from a pamphlet on vegetarianism, while his colleague William Smith mentioned the cohabitation practices of the Shakers. Maryland's Michael Jenifer Stone was even more direct. "There never was a [religious] society of any considerable extent

---

[62]Ibid., 12:286, 810, 719; John Pemberton to James Pemberton, Mar. 17, 1790, Pennsylvania Abolition Society Collection, Historical Society of Pennsylvania, Philadelphia.

which did not interfere with the concerns of other people, and this interference has at one time or other deluged the world in blood." Alone among the Quakers' defenders, Scott of Pennsylvania was vehement in combating these objections on their own ground. He rejected the argument that abolition was purely an abstract tenet of a religious minority. "I do not stand in need of religious motives to induce me to reprobate the traffic in human flesh. If there was neither God nor the devil, I should oppose it upon the principles of humanity, and the law of nature."[63]

Just as Ames had predicted about the consumption of rum, the Quakers realistically conceded that the national character would be slow to change. One supporter wrote James Pemberton, president of the Pennsylvania Abolition Society, that the government "must be led on by imperceptible Degrees to what they ought to do at once . . . and the public mind must be taught by a Series of Legislative Interpositions." Pemberton in turn wrote the London Abolition Society while the House was still debating the petitions: "We dare not flatter ourselves with anything more than a very gradual Work. Long Habits & strong Interests are not to be overcome in an Instant."[64]

Public response to the antislavery debates justified Pemberton's caution. Anticipating popular interest, New York City newspapers provided an unusually detailed level of coverage, including reprints of the petitions and the House committee reports. Newspapers up and down the Atlantic coast copied lengthy firsthand accounts of the often colorful debates, while editorials pro and con continued to appear months after the House finally disposed of the petitions by passing a noncommittal report that simply restated Congress's constitutional limitations. Most of the editorials that had appeared during the debate attacked slavery's spokesmen. The most famous of these newspapers articles was the last piece authored for publication by Benjamin Franklin, a satire written under the pseudonym "Historicus." In the ensuing months, editorials became increasingly bitter, less over the Quakers' "meddling" than over Congress's failure to handle more expeditiously what

[63]*DHFFC*, 12:304, 305, 831–32, 307.

[64]William Pinckney to James Pemberton, Jan. 16, 1790; James Pemberton to the London Abolition Society, Feb. 28, 1790, Pennsylvania Abolition Society Collection, Historical Society of Pennsylvania.

many would have agreed with Ames was essentially "a kind of forensic dispute — a matter of moonshine."[65]

The First Federal Congress considered the subject of public morality on one other occasion during the third session. Like the second session debate over antislavery, this debate was prompted by several Quaker petitions that tested Congress's recognition and encouragement of its constituents' "religious scruples" against constitutional guarantees separating church and state. The petitions from Quaker Meetings in Philadelphia, New York, Baltimore, and New England all protested a clause of the militia bill (HR-102) that obligated conscientious objectors to pay an "annual tax" for not performing state militia duty, which was prohibited by the Quakers' well-known peace testimony. The Philadelphia petitioners called attention to the fact that paying a monetary equivalent was no less a contribution to military preparedness than militia training. Citing relevant verses from the fifth chapter of Matthew, their petition closed with the fervent hope that "the glorious gospel day, prophetically declared, may not be retarded . . . and nation shall not lift up sword against nation neither learn war any more."[66]

The debate over exemptions for conscientious objection was part of a larger debate over the economic and sociological impact of calling up various age groups or classes of artisans and professionals. Such exemptions were the subject of one other petition to the First Congress from a Maryland glass manufacturer, as well as at least two other intended petitions from Philadelphia and Baltimore tradesmen and mechanics. All these considerations became bound up with the question of the states' right to define their own militia exemptions. Southern proslavery congressmen were thus able to repeat their attacks against a "peculiar indulgence" for the Quakers, this time on states' rights grounds.[67]

James Jackson in particular feared that the principle of exempting conscientious objectors "will carry us too far. It will exonerate men of

---

[65]Fisher Ames to Richard Minot, Mar. 23, 1790, in W. B. Allen, ed., *The Works of Fisher Ames*, 2 vols. (Indianapolis, 1983), 1:731.

[66]Petition of Dec. 18, 1790, Broadsides Collection, Rare Book Room, Library of Congress, Washington, D.C.

[67]*DHFFC*, 14:180.

weak nerves." In the Quakers' arguments for refusing to pay even an equivalent, William Smith detected a more insidious threat: "In case of war, they might refuse to pay imposts or direct taxes, under an impression, that their money would be appropriated to the expence of the war." Added to these practical considerations was the logistical problem of verifying a genuine objection for reasons of conscience. Jackson predicted that there would be "very few but will wear the mask of Quakerism." In short, announced the Georgia congressman, "we could not more effectually encourage that religion by making it the religion of the land, than we should by annexing these privileges to it." "The constitution places all religions on an equal footing," he later reminded his colleagues. "What right then, have we, the mere creatures of the constitution, to create and give rank and stability to one church more than another?"[68] Stone of Maryland changed the emphasis slightly, but to the same effect: "We lay it down as a legislative principle, that the belief of certain tenets, dissolves so much of the cement of government, as thereby to separate the interests and connexion of the parts: it is allowing principles in direct opposition to the principles under which we act."[69] All religious sects were equal in the eyes of the government; but the tenets of some rendered them "less equal" than others in their claim to protection.

The Committee of the Whole House eventually struck all mention of "persons conscientiously scrupulous of bearing arms." The committee retained a clause exempting "all ministers of religion, actually having the charge of a church or congregation" and later added a clause exempting "persons authorized and received to preach and teach the gospel, by the societies of which they are respectively members."[70]

Madison's objection to the addition of this second clause is noteworthy. During the defense of his own expanded census schedule the session before, Madison admitted that, "as to those employed in teaching and inculcating the duties of religion, there may be some indelicacy in singling them out, as the general government is proscribed from interfering, in any manner whatever, in matters respecting religion." This

---

[68] Ibid., 14:171, 138, 177.
[69] Ibid., 14:186–87.
[70] Ibid., 5:1463, 1470–71.

same position is certainly borne out by Madison's opposition to exempting ministers from militia duty, except that he argued against exemption on the grounds that the motion for exempting ministers "would exempt the whole of some societies, which permitted every member to preach and teach the gospel." Falling under that description were the very same Quakers for whose exemption Madison would only days later advocate on the grounds of conscientious objection.[71]

After seven days of debate, the militia bill was referred to a new committee, whose amendatory militia bill (HR-112) died in the Committee of the Whole House before the end of the last session.

A Mixed Legacy

No American has yet patented a method for determining whether a particular moral tenet ends up as a foundation brick or a brickbat of society. And what one party considers a "matter of moonshine" another may consider a matter of high moral purpose. For these reasons, morality's standing on the political agenda continues to animate the national dialogue. Current debates over abortion and gay rights show that citizens' interest in public morality is hardly diminished; the First Congress's conscious distancing from questions regarding "religious scruples" may even seem timid by today's standards.

Explicit constitutional grants to encourage the arts and sciences, and by inference to support public morality as part of the Preamble's general welfare clause, fundamentally redefined the federal government's authority in 1789. The expectations of some individuals and special interest groups were correspondingly strengthened. The fate of several of the petitions referred to in this paper indicate that Congress was reluctant to use its powers in the manner sought. But Rep. Thomas Scott correctly prophesied the new direction in national politics when he told his colleagues that how they responded to the antislavery petitions of 1790 "will in a degree form the character of the American people on this subject."[72]

---

[71] Ibid., 12:137, 14:99. For the complete text of the Militia Bill (HR-102), see 5: 1458–75.

[72] Ibid., 12:819.

What would John Adams have thought about these first tentative steps toward creating and shaping a national character? Would history vindicate the career plans he had for his children? John Quincy Adams helped establish the Smithsonian Institution and died, virtually on the floor of the House, defending antislavery petitions. Adams's grandson, Charles Francis Adams, was also a noted abolitionist, diplomat, and one of America's early documentary editors. His great-grandson, Henry Adams, in turn became a famous historian as well as a novelist. We might surmise, then, that John Adams's spirit is appeased by their accomplishments and by a sustained, vigorous encouragement of the arts, sciences, and morality.

Herbert M. Druks

Religious Freedom and
the First Federal Congress

$\mathbf{F}$REEDOM OF THOUGHT, freedom of speech, and above all, freedom of religion are barometers of the freedom that the people of a
society or a civilization enjoy. By these standards, the United States has
done well. Often the issue of religious freedom has been interwoven
with a variety of other issues, including the relationship between the
federal government and the states. The question of religious freedom
was and remains one of the most sensitive issues in the American
experience.

Although members of the First Federal Congress were men of faith,
the following survey of the debates and records documented and published in *The Documentary History of the First Federal Congress* demonstrates that one of their uppermost concerns was that every effort be
made to maintain a wall of separation between church and state that
would permit the free exercise of religion.

One of the staunchest defenders of freedom of religion in the First
Federal Congress was Thomas Jefferson's friend and colleague James
Madison, who had fought hard for religious liberty as a member of the
Virginia House of Delegates. Madison opposed all forms of church and
state union. He favored equality and freedom for all religious groups.
Toleration was not sufficient; each and every man was entitled to "lib-
erty—not toleration." The original draft of the Virginia Bill of Rights
of 1776 had referred to "toleration," but thanks largely to Madison's

criticism it was modified to read "all men are equally entitled to the free exercise of religion, according to the dictates of conscience."[1] Jefferson may have been the author of the 1786 Virginia Statute of Religious Freedom, but Madison worked just as vigorously for its adoption.

As a member of the First Congress, Madison generally is given primary credit for passage of the twelve amendments submitted to the states for ratification that became the Bill of Rights — the first ten amendments to the Constitution. The first amendment to be ratified dealt explicitly with the issue of religious freedom: "Congress shall make no law respecting an establishment of religion, or prohibiting the free exercise thereof."[2]

Like Jefferson, Madison insisted that religion was a matter of individual conscience — not the business of civil government: "The religion . . . of every man must be left to the conviction and conscience of every man; and it is the right of every man to exercise it as these may dictate. This right is in its nature an unalienable right." To Madison, an "authority which can force a citizen to contribute threepence only of his property for the support of any one establishment may force him to conform to any other establishment in all cases whatsoever."[3]

Because he wanted to ensure separation of church and state, Madison was concerned that the first federal census not gather information about ministers of religion. The census bill provided for the listing of farmers, mechanics, and other groups, but it did not include the learned professions. When Theodore Sedgwick of Massachusetts suggested that the census should "specify every class of citizens, into which the community was divided, in order to ascertain the actual state of society," Madison expressed concern lest there might be "some indelicacy in singling [out]" those who might be teachers of religion.[4]

Madison likewise opposed paying a congressional chaplain from the

---

[1] A. P. Stokes, *Church and State in the United States* (New York, 1950), p. 55. See also, Robert P. Williams, *The First Congress, March 4, 1789–March 3, 1791* (New York, 1970), chap. 5.

[2] Stokes, *Church and State,* p. 55.

[3] Ibid., p. 60; Elizabeth Fleet, ed., "Madison's Detached Memoranda," *William and Mary Quarterly,* 3d ser. 3 (1946):534–68.

[4] *Documentary History of the First Federal Congress,* 14 vols. to date (Baltimore, 1972–), vol. 12 (Helen E. Veit, Charlene Bangs Bickford, Kenneth R. Bowling, and William Charles diGiacomantonio, eds.), p. 137 (hereafter *DHFFC*).

public purse, asking: "Is the appointment of chaplains to the two Houses of Congress consistent with the Constitution, and the pure principle of religious freedom." He also opposed the incorporation of religious institutions by the federal government, as well as appropriating federal funds for chaplains, whether they would be for the Congress or the military. Such a practice, he feared, might find Congress endorsing one religion as the national religion.[5]

The following pages focus on three issues considered by the First Federal Congress in which the question of religious freedom figured prominently: Quaker antislavery and militia exemption petitions and the naturalization process.

Quaker Antislavery Petitions and Religious Freedom

The House of Representatives agreed to debate antislavery petitions submitted by the Quakers and the Pennsylvania Abolition Society even though some members from South Carolina and Georgia argued that Congress did not have the right to consider the matter because it was within the jurisdiction of the individual states. Moreover, Article I, section 9 of the Constitution prohibited Congress from interfering in the slave trade before 1808. Some southern members saw the antislavery petitions as the beginning of a congressional attempt to end slavery. However, there were a few southern congressmen, such as John Page and Madison of Virginia, who thought it appropriate to debate the issue.

Aedanus Burke of South Carolina argued that the Quakers had no right to interfere with slavery in America on religious or any other grounds. Furthermore, he did not believe that the matter should be discussed. It would be "blowing the trumpet of sedition" and "spreading alarm among the citizens." Congress had no more right to interfere with slave property than it had a right "to take us from our houses, lands or other property. The one attempt is equally extravagant and alarming to us as the other." But that was not all that the Quakers were

---

[5]Stokes, *Church and State*, p. 347.

seeking to do; they were trying "to strip us of the little strength and resources we have; and to weaken the southern states."[6]

Thomas Tudor Tucker of South Carolina likewise did not think that Congress had a right to involve itself in religious political controversies. With these petitions, the Quakers performed a great deal of mischief on the people of the southern states. He knew of nothing that was more likely to create a greater alarm among the people than such antislavery propositions. Tucker asked a series of rhetorical questions seeking the ultimate goal of the petitions: What was the aim of the Quakers? Did they wish the "general emancipation of the slaves?" Did they wish to purchase the slaves? How could the Quakers take this upon themselves? "Are they the only men who have religion and morality?" What would be their next step? Would they then seek "to establish their religion among us."[7]

Richard Bland Lee of Virginia rejected even a discussion of the Quaker petitions.[8] James Jackson of Georgia observed that religion and politics did not mix. He suggested that the members of Congress consult the Bible and see that it did not sanctify slavery.[9]

Peter Silvester of New York was greatly concerned that the issue would offend colleagues from southern states such as Georgia. While he respected the Quakers for their work in the cause of humanity, he did not feel that their petition should be considered by Congress since "he thought the present was not the proper time to enter into a consideration of the subject" and "especially as he conceived it to be a business in the province of the state legislatures."[10]

Others, like Elbridge Gerry of Massachusetts, believed the matter of slavery should be debated by Congress since it was a matter of humanity. He wondered what it would be like if he was taken from his family and made into a slave and his children left to mourn. He believed that Congress had the right to impose a duty of ten dollars per slave if it chose to do so (Article I, section 9 of the Constitution specified

---

[6]*DHFFC*, 12:296, 302, 307–8, 776–78.
[7]Ibid., 12:295, 306.
[8]Ibid., 12:273.
[9]Ibid., 12:296.
[10]Ibid., 12:296, 301, 303, 309.

Congress could impose a duty "not exceeding ten dollars" on each imported slave). Congress might even purchase all the slaves and settle them in the West.[11]

On February 13, 1790, by a vote of forty-three to eleven, the House decided to debate the Quaker petitions. Once the vote was taken, the debate became more acrimonious. Tucker of South Carolina, upset that the Quakers seemed to think they were the only ones possessed with "religion and morality," expressed sorrow and disappointment that "so great a majority of the House favored giving the Quaker Memorial a second reading," for it was a "glaring interference with the Constitution." Moreover, it was "interference in the internal regulations of the particular states" — most particularly, the southern states. Do Quakers expect a general emancipation of the slaves by law? This, Tucker suggested, would lead to civil war.[12]

Jackson of Georgia built upon the theme that the Quaker petitions inevitably might lead to "revolt, insurrection and devastation." The people of the South "will resist one tyranny as soon as another; the other parts of the continent may bear them down by force of arms, but they will never suffer themselves to be divested of their property without a struggle." If the slave trade were given up by Americans it might fall into the hands of the Spanish, and it would be better for the slaves to remain in America than become slaves in Africa. Jackson claimed that in Georgia and some other states there were "guards against oppression" and that the master was "as liable to be punished for the death of his slave as for that of any other person."[13]

Jackson raised the specter of miscegenation in his opposition to the antislavery petitions. He noted that the people of Georgia were opposed to mixture between whites and blacks, but if the Quakers were fond of this mixture "and of giving their daughters to negro sons, and receiving the negro daughters for their sons," he suggested that they might go to Africa and there "marry and be given in marriage, and have a motley race of their own." Sarcastically, he added that they

---

[11]Ibid., 12:298, 305.
[12]Ibid., 12:302–6.
[13]Ibid., 12:307–8, 727.

could even "convert the natives of that continent to the tenets held by themselves."[14]

Like Tucker, Jackson was insulted by the self-righteousness of the petitions. "Is their [the southern slaveowners'] humanity less than that of their more northern neighbors?" he asked. The Quakers may claim that they acted out of their Christian disposition, but "Christianity is not repugnant to slavery." Jesus allowed it in his day as did his apostles. Calling upon the example of the classical past, the Georgia congressman argued that "never was a government on the face of the earth, but what permitted slavery: the purest sons of freedom in the Grecian republics, the citizens of Athens and Lacedaemon all held slaves."[15]

Abraham Baldwin, also of Georgia, stressed the constitutional prohibitions against interfering with slavery. Congress could not interfere with the importation of slaves because the Constitution provided that "the migration or importation of such persons, shall not be prohibited by congress." Moreover, the same section of the Constitution provided "that no capitation or direct tax shall be laid, unless in proportion to the census." Baldwin argued this prohibition "was intended to prevent Congress from laying any special tax upon Negro slaves, as they might, in this way, so burthen the possessors of them, as to induce a general emancipation." While some might claim that this Quaker petition did not call for the abolition of the slave trade, it did just that, and Congress should have "no more to do with it, than if it prayed us to establish an order of nobility or a national religion."[16]

William Smith of South Carolina opposed the Quaker petitions not only on the grounds that the economies of the southern states depended upon slavery, but also because of the inappropriateness of granting a hearing to any one particular religious group. Smith was certain his constituents did not wish or need to be taught morality by outsiders; they had as much morality as their northern neighbors. Quakers could claim no monopoly on morality or religion: "Now, if

---

[14]Ibid., 12:728, 733.

[15]Ibid., 12:729–32.

[16]Ibid., 12:308–9.

these people were to petition Congress to pass a law prohibiting matrimony, I ask, would gentlemen agree to refer such a petition? I think if they would reject one of that nature, as improper, they ought also to reject this."[17]

Both Page and Madison of Virginia argued that the issue should be openly examined. As far as Page was concerned, there was nothing unconstitutional in antislavery petitions presented by a religious group. If a slave would hear that Congress refused even to consider the question, he might infer that the government had shut its ears against the voice of humanity and "he should despair of any alleviation of the miseries he and his posterity had in prospect; if anything could induce him to rebel, it must be a stroke like this, impressing on his mind all the horrors of despair." But if he would hear that Congress was willing to consider a proposition that sought to discourage the further importation of slaves, "he would trust in their justice and humanity, and wait the decision patiently." Page believed that "the most likely way to prevent danger, was to commit the petition."[18]

Madison favored considering the petitions because he contended that the Framers of the Constitution believed Congress had the power to regulate the subject of slavery. He admitted that Congress was "restricted by the Constitution from taking measures to abolish the slave trade," but it could "make some regulations with respect to introducing the trade into the Western territory."[19]

The House debated and rejected the Quaker memorial. While some members of the First Federal Congress were antagonized by the petition and felt that no one had a right to interfere with slavery, others defended the right of the Quakers to express themselves on religious or moral grounds.

The Militia Bill and Religious Freedom

As Congress considered a bill to provide a uniform militia throughout the United States, it received petitions for exemption from military

---

[17]Ibid., 12:310–11.
[18]Ibid., 12:305, 311–12.
[19]Ibid., 12:312.

service. The Society of Friends in particular sought exemption on the grounds of religious convictions.

On December 19, 1790, a Quaker petition to the First Federal Congress asserted their claim of conscientious objection. They believed that if Congress approved the measure to "more effectually provide for the national defence, by establishing an uniform militia throughout the United States," it would "materially affect us, and our fellow members in general, in the free exercise of conscience." Any and every "restraint imposed or attempted by human laws on the free exercise thereof, is not only an infringement on the just rights of men, but also an invasion of the prerogative of Almighty God." Quakers insisted that the teachings of their Christian faith commanded them against "all revenge, animosity, strife, and contention." The Quakers therefore insisted that they not only "uniformly declined joining personally in war," but likewise believed themselves to be "conscientiously bound to refuse the payment of any sum required in lieu of such personal service, or in consideration of an exemption from military employment, however laudable the purposes are, to which the money is intended to be applied, as it manifestly infringes on the rights of conscience."

James Jackson responded to the petition by insisting that the bearing of arms was one of the most important duties owed to society, and all persons exempted from such duty should pay the sum of three dollars. He considered it "highly improper that persons exempted should not make a compensation, as their property and persons were equally to be secured, with those of every other citizen." If everyone who did not wish to bear arms would be excused without paying an equivalent, "what would become of America?" Jackson found the whole subject of conscientious objection fraught with problems: "Who was to know what persons were really conscientiously scrupulous?" Was there a court where they would have to "swear their scruples?" Because other groups also were averse to bearing arms, if Congress did not adopt a measure requiring compensation from the exempted it would lay "the axe to the root of all militia." Individuals should either perform their military duty or pay an equivalent.[20]

---

[20]Ibid., vol. 14 (William Charles diGiacomantonio, Kenneth R. Bowling, Charlene Bangs Bickford, and Helen E. Veit, eds.), p. 81.

Moreover, Jackson thought that it was wrong, "impolitic and unconstitutional," to give one religion preference over another. If the American people were to see that Quakers could "sit at home in the hour of invasion," while their neighbors would be torn from family and exposed to perils and hardships in opposing an enemy, "there are very few but will wear the mask of Quakerism," and then "an invader could march through the country with a single regiment."[21]

Although Jackson professed to believe that Quakers were a "worthy set of men," he hoped that every man would be permitted to worship God in his own way. Therefore, Quakers would be better neighbors if they would keep their principles to themselves. As far as he was concerned, they were "too officious in interposing their good advice, in many cases" where it was not required — or welcomed.[22]

Returning to his social contract argument, Jackson reminded Congress that the signers of the Declaration of Independence mutually agreed to protect and defend each other's lives and property. A tax in place of military service would be "an equivalent for personal service due to society; this personal service is time and labor, and time is money." Some provide military service, others will provide money. Jackson believed that the Quakers wanted to be exempted in order to avoid contributing toward their own defense. This, he concluded, was "an unjust request" and ought not to be granted.[23]

Aedanus Burke thought there were too many categories of exemption, however; unlike Jackson, he thought it was wrong to impose a tax on those who could not serve because of religious scruples. He was against intolerance or violating the rights of conscience and he "felt happiness in being a citizen of the republic, whose glory it was to be the first country on earth, which held out to all the sons of men, the happy privilege of pursuing their own scheme of religion unmolested."[24]

Moreover, Burke thought it cruel to compel such individuals to bear arms and unjust "to require an equivalent of them. If the United States gave liberty of conscience to all men, they ought not to tax the exercise of such rights." Furthermore, no law could be legislated to force Quak-

---

[21]Ibid., 14:123.
[22]Ibid., 14:151.
[23]Ibid., 14:59, 88, 128.
[24]Ibid., 14:128.

ers to "carry the musket." It had been tried, but without success. Burke had seen how the Quaker people of Charleston had refused to bear arms in the city's defense in 1779: "No law or penalty could force them to bear arms . . . and he would not undertake so vain a task as again to try the experiment."[25]

William Branch Giles of Virginia likewise did not wish to grant exemptions to the Quakers. If an individual could not serve by reason of conscience, then he would have to provide the community with reasonable compensation. Since it was not against the conscience of a Quaker to hold and possess property, they should help protect that property: "Every man who receives the protection of the laws ought to contribute his proportion to the support of the laws." Exemptions only served to create "unwarranted distinctions between citizens, throwing a burden on the majority to relieve the minority."[26]

Giles addressed two questions: "the difficulty of finding out who were conscientiously scrupulous" and the principle of religious toleration. On the first question, he stressed that there were no outwardly visible signs by which to judge the sincerity of conscientious objectors: "The inward light, with which they glow does not shine so clearly through every sense and way as to show the officer the indelible mark by which it may be known that they have scruples of conscience against taking up arms." On the question of toleration, Giles wondered how far it had to be taken: "Will the mere sound of toleration induce us to exceed the bounds of discretion? Are we to fix no limits?" "If toleration was carried so far as to subvert good government," Giles argued, "it was the height of intolerance."[27]

Elias Boudinot of New Jersey, on the other hand, supported exempting Quakers from military service, observing that if a man was old or feeble, he would be freed from service; similarly, Quakers, even if compelled, would make poor soldiers. "Could the U.S. depend for their protection on men, whose religious principles precluded the idea even of resistance," he wondered. Congress was obligated to "guard the rights and protect the just privileges" of its citizens, and in this instance

[25] Ibid., 14:115–16, 158.

[26] Ibid., 14:153, 163.

[27] Ibid., 14:154.

Congress should not "infringe the right of conscience." Indeed, Boudinot argued, the power to provide military exemptions clearly rested with Congress and not the states.[28]

In supporting the exemption of Quakers, Madison countered Jackson's argument that it would motivate people to become Quakers to avoid military service. The Virginian was confident that "not a single citizen will be found throughout the United States, who will usurp this privilege by hypocritical pretensions." Moreover, while it was possible to oppress the Quakers, it was impossible "to make them bear arms." He hoped the exemption provision would be granted. "It is the glory of our country that a more sacred regard to the rights of mankind is preserved, than has heretofore been known." He thought it of less importance whether the equivalent was determined then or later, as long as it was generally understood that an equivalent should be required.[29]

Roger Sherman of Connecticut echoed Madison's recommendation to approve the exemption and postpone the decision on an equivalent. He, too, saw the folly of trying to force the "conscientiously scrupulous" to serve in the militia. Conscientious objectors "would rather suffer death than commit what appeared to them a moral evil." They likewise found paying an equivalent to be as disagreeable as having to serve and it was "advisable to exempt them as to both at present," but afterward Congress could obtain some tax that "might not give offense to their consciences."[30]

William Smith of South Carolina returned the debate to Boudinot's claim that Congress had the authority to grant militia exemptions. He thought it proper to make Quakers pay an equivalent, and it made little difference to him whether it was a voluntary or compulsory equivalent, but he wanted the House to settle the question as to whether Congress or the state legislatures should make the exemptions.[31]

Sherman believed that the states possessed the right to make exemptions. He was not concerned, as some members were, that the militias of the various states might not be uniform if the matter of exemptions was left to the states. Madison, on the other hand, argued

[28]Ibid., 14:168–69.
[29]Ibid., 14:127, 149, 162.
[30]Ibid., 14:149.
[31]Ibid., 14:129.

that the establishment of the militia was a federal matter. Benjamin Bourne of Rhode Island pointed out that several states, including New Hampshire, Massachusetts, Rhode Island, and Connecticut, already exempted the Quakers and imposed no fines on them.[32]

Samuel Livermore of New Hampshire insisted that the Constitution provided that "the several states should establish their own militia and that Congress had no further concern in the business, than barely to organize that militia and direct how it should be armed, trained and disciplined." While he thought Congress had the right to exempt federal officeholders, members of Congress, and even seamen, he saw no reason why the federal government should exempt individuals who were conscientiously scrupulous of bearing arms. This was a matter for the states, who should grant them exemption without any "equivalent or compensation."[33]

Thomas Hartley of Pennsylvania warned that every effort had to be made to guard against the abuse of power that might arise in the state governments if they were allowed to decide the question of militia exemptions. He believed the states might provide too extensive exemptions. The federal government had been established to prevent such abuses at the state level. The matter of exemption for religious reasons would be best determined at the federal level. Congress should determine the exemption and then let the exempted either pay a fine or render personal service: "Let us count on men, who will not fight; but let us, in the course of a single year, acquire an accurate knowledge of our real strength."[34]

Jackson and Thomas Scott of Pennsylvania returned the debate to the question of church and state. Jackson argued that if Quakers were exempted then all religions should be put on the same footing and declare that "any one who does not yield his personal service, may pay the equivalent. The Constitution places all religion on an equal footing." By what right, Jackson wondered, did members of Congress try to "create and give rank and stability to one church more than another?"[35]

Scott also thought that religion should not be the subject of legisla-

---

[32]Ibid., 14:165, 168, 175, 185.
[33]Ibid., 14:176.
[34]Ibid., 14:179.
[35]Ibid., 14:177.

tive discussion, unless some sect should seek to destroy the peace of the community. While every man owed equal duty to the community, it was not expected that every man should discharge that debt in the same manner. He hoped that Congress could help ensure the performance of duty "without hurting the religious principles of any society." Furthermore, no man could tell whether the religion that he believed in was "right or wrong," nor could he "decide with respect to any other man's religion." He did not care to support the exemption suggested by the proposed legislation. "Were all men conscientiously scrupulous of shedding human blood, universal happiness would be the consequence of such scruples," but that happy day was not in sight, and it was necessary to examine the world realistically and "provide against hostile attempts."[36]

The First Federal Congress reached no decision regarding the question of exemption from militia service on the grounds of conscientious objection, but the debate reflected the variety of opinions regarding freedom of religion and state versus federal jurisdiction over such matters.

The Naturalization Process and Religion

The issue of freedom of religion came up again in the course of the First Federal Congress debate as to whether Congress or the individual states had the power over the naturalization process. Some members of the House, like Roger Sherman, believed that Congress should control the process in order to prevent some states from accepting individuals who might not be received in other states. This was necessary to "guard against an improper mode of naturalization."[37]

Madison thought that there should be a residency requirement before people could be admitted to citizenship, even though he was not in favor of excluding good people "who really meant to incorporate" themselves into American society. No one should be excluded from these shores who could contribute to "the wealth and strength" of the

[36]Ibid., 14:188.
[37]Ibid., 12:147.

United States.[38] Smith of South Carolina agreed with Madison; how was a man to know the way the government functions unless he spent some time in America. "How then could he ascertain who was a proper person to legislate, or judge of the laws?"[39]

While members like Madison, Smith, and Thomas Hartley of Pennsylvania favored "easy terms of admission" because it would induce immigration, others like Burke of South Carolina preferred to encourage only "useful men, such as farmers, mechanics and manufacturers." These classes of men he would "receive on liberal terms," and he believed there was "room enough for them, and their posterity, for five hundred years to come." But there was one category of immigrants he would not welcome. The merchants who might come to make their fortune and carry it off to Europe. Such individuals "injure us more than they do us good," and Burke considered them to be nothing more than "leeches." Burke likewise preferred to exclude "the convicts and criminals which . . . pour out of British jails." The "privilege of an American citizen, [is an] honorable one, and it ought not to be thrown away upon such people."[40]

John Page brought up the question of exclusions on religious grounds, concerned that the United States might adopt European standards of "bigotry and superstition, or a deep-rooted prejudice against the government, laws, religions, or manners of neighboring nations." Page offered a strong argument for adopting religious toleration; we would be, he believed,

> inconsistent with ourselves, if, after boasting of having opened an asylum for the oppressed of all nations, and established a government which is the admiration of the world, we make the admission, to the full enjoyment of that asylum and government, so hard as is now proposed. It is nothing to us, whether Jews, or Roman Catholics settle among us; whether subjects of Kings, or citizens of free states, wish to reside in the United States, they will find it their interest to be good citizens; and neither their religious or political opinions can injure us, if we have good laws, well executed.[41]

---

[38]Ibid., 12:148–49.
[39]Ibid., 12:149.
[40]Ibid., 12:150, 155.
[41]Ibid., 12:147.

Throughout the First Federal Congress's debates on freedom of religion, the members of the House considered the issues most seriously and carefully. The issues involving freedom of religion inspired debate on the questions of state versus federal jurisdiction and religious conviction as opposed to the duties of citizenship. At times petitions such as those presented by the Quakers against slavery and their request for exemption from military duty on religious grounds stimulated a crossfire of views and opinions regarding the powers and limitations the Constitution placed on Congress. Members like Aedanus Burke, Thomas Tudor Tucker, and James Jackson were deeply concerned lest Congress establish a special privileged class of people if it exempted Quakers from military duty for their religious convictions; others, like James Madison, Elias Boudinot, and Roger Sherman, were prepared to support exemption from military service on just those grounds. Some members of Congress, including Jackson, Burke, William Smith of South Carolina, and Abraham Baldwin, were even more concerned by the Quaker antislavery petitions. They asked the question that would be asked for some two centuries thereafter: Does one segment of society or one section of the country have the right to impose its moral standards upon another? Their arguments reflected the seriousness and the sincerity of conviction and beliefs and the intellectual integrity of the members of the First Federal Congress.

William P. Cowin

The Invisible Smith

The Impact of Adam Smith on the Foundation of
Early American Economic Policy during the
First Federal Congress, 1789–91

O N JULY 4, 1776, when the United States of America claimed its
place among the nations of the world, it was a loose informal
confederation of states clinging for survival in the midst of a revolution. Economic policies that would eventually lead to a four-trillion-
dollar economy were far from the minds of the Founding Fathers
faced with the might of the British military. Nonetheless, the publication four months earlier of the work of a Scottish philosopher laid the
foundation for the formulation of an American economic policy that
would be legislated only thirteen years later during the First Federal
Congress.

Almost immediately after its release, Adam Smith's *An Inquiry into
the Nature and Causes of the Wealth of Nations* was taught in universities as
far from England as Königsberg in eastern Prussia and Princeton in
the United States. Scholars contend that Thomas Jefferson regarded it
as the best book available on political economy, and his contempo-
raries applauded it for "overturning all that interested Sophistry of
Merchants, with which they have confounded the whole subject of
Commerce."[1] Although he would not be found among the members
seated in the first House of Representatives, Adam Smith provided a

---

[1] Hugh Blair, cited in Jerry Z. Muller, *Adam Smith in His Times and Ours* (New York,
1993), p. 15 n. 209.

powerful voice in its debates, added to those of two other Smiths serving in the body—William Smith of Maryland and William Smith of
South Carolina.

Adam Smith (1723–1790) wrote only two full-length books. *The
Wealth of Nations,* published seventeen years after *The Theory of Moral
Sentiments* (1759), can be seen in many ways as an extension of the
earlier work. *Moral Sentiments* postulated that the unique abilities that
separated men from animals required the formation of government,
with its power to advance or hinder economic progress. Within this
context, the significance of *The Wealth of Nations* comes into perspective. It is important for three main reasons.[2] First, it presents an impressive collection of economic data, which Smith used to provide a factual
basis for his frequent ventures into the philosophy or theory of economic development. Second, it was the most comprehensive and ambitious attempt up to Smith's time to present the nature of the economic
process in a predominately "individualistic," "competitive," "market,"
or "capitalistic" society (to use current terminology). Third, it was a
crusading book that sharply criticized existing society and government
and argued strongly for changes in national policy, especially in relation to the extent and nature of government intervention in economic
matters—domestic, colonial, and international.

The Wealth of Nations has had an incredible longevity and influence.
Most recently it was cited in chapter 4 of the 1995 *Economic Report of the
President,* the annual report of the Council of Economic Advisors. Its
genius comes from Smith's ability to understand and organize historical events, including the work of great thinkers, and to formulate an
economic system that has explanations, recommendations, and pre-
dictions for a wide range of political and social factors as diverse as slavery and the educational system. Some have argued that David Hume,
Smith's mentor and friend, was the actual hand behind his genius.[3]

---

[2]"Smith, Adam," in *International Encyclopedia of the Social Sciences,* ed. David L. Sills,
19 vols (New York, 1968), 13:324–26.

[3]For an impressive argument on the influence of Hume, see Stanley Elkins and Eric
McKitrick, *The Age of Federalism: The Early American Republic, 1788–1800* (Oxford,
1993), pp. 85–87, 97, 105–7, 111–12, 201, 258–61, 264, 268, 752. In spite of Elkins
and McKitrick's conclusion that Hume was responsible for much of what this paper
attributes to Adam Smith, the fact remains that Smith was directly cited more than
twenty times during the course of the First Federal Congress debates, and Hume was
not cited once.

Because of the encyclopedic and synthetic nature of Smith's work, it is open to such criticism; during the course of *The Wealth of Nations,* Smith refers to Hume six times, John Locke four times, Charles Davenant twice, and Jacques Necker once. Yet there is more to Smith's work than references to other great intellects; they are mere fragments of his work. *The Wealth of Nations* is not just an economics textbook; it is an encyclopedia of centuries of human experience put into economic perspective.

In spite of Smith's influence, parts of his work are still misunderstood. Like many of the physiocrats, Smith adhered to an economic doctrine known as laissez faire — the belief that a nation's economy can best function when the actions of private agents in the marketplace are free from government interference. This doctrine formed the cornerstone of the economic ideology of the English school of classical economists that Smith founded; yet he was by no means antigovernment. He argued that without government intervention nations would always be provided with desired goods through the natural order of supply and demand. Although various government activities restricted free trade, it was not in the best interest of a nation's economy to do so. The explanation for Smith's opposition to government intervention in private affairs stems from his familiarity with the corruption and massive bureaucracy of the British government. On the other hand, Smith believed that the government should interfere in the private sector when such actions would promote the general welfare through taxation and "protecting the society from the violence and invasion of other independent societies, establishing an exact administration of justice and erecting and maintaining certain public institutions and certain public works."[4] He understood that governments which proved they were capable of using such powers to serve the public good deserved that responsibility. Consequently, in *The Wealth of Nations* Smith proposed a perfect balance between government action and the operations of the private marketplace. From references to ancient Greece and Rome to different time periods of British and American colonial history, Smith demonstrated the successes of his theory and the failures, many of them British, of following other courses of action.

---

[4] Adam Smith, *An Inquiry into the Nature and Causes of the Wealth of Nations* (1776) (New York, 1937), p. 185 (hereafter *WN*).

Smith recognized the need to tax a nation's populace in order to raise revenues for the government's necessary and proper welfare functions. He believed that the "expence of defending the society, and that of supporting the dignity of the chief magistrate, are both laid out for the general benefit of the whole society. It is reasonable, therefore, that they should be defrayed by the general contribution of the whole society, all the different members contributing, as nearly as possible, in proportion to their respective abilities." Smith argued that it was virtually impossible for a government to tax in proportion to income. The best method was a tax imposed on consumable commodities: "The state not knowing how to tax, directly and proportionably, the revenue of its subjects," Smith argued, "[it] endeavors to tax it indirectly by taxing their revenue. Their expence is taxed by taxing the consumable commodities upon which it is laid out."[5]

In deciding the level of the tax, Smith separated consumable commodities into two categories — "necessaries" and luxuries. He defined necessaries not only as the items needed to support life, such as food and water, but also as "whatever the custom of the country renders it indecent for creditable people, even the lowest order, to be without."[6] As an example of a necessary cultural item, Smith cited leather shoes in England. All other nonessential items were defined as luxuries. Smith believed that the state should tax necessities separately and in a manner different from luxuries. Since necessities were consumed by most of the population, they should be moderately taxed. Luxuries, on the other hand, were used only by that proportion of the population that could afford them, and thus a more severe tax should be imposed, especially on products seen as unhealthy. Smith, as several members of the First Congress would argue, believed government could serve an important function by trying to prevent the spread of undesirable habits among its citizens.

Convinced that a healthy population meant increased productivity that would benefit the general welfare, Smith argued that the government should discourage the consumption of products that "tend to ruin the health and corrupt the morals of the common people"; for

---

[5]Ibid., pp. 767, 821.
[6]Ibid.

example, raising taxes on distilleries to reduce the consumption of spirituous liquors.[7] This responsibility to watch over the health and well-being of its citizens demonstrated a much wider range of government intervention in everyday life than would be expected from Smith's laissez-faire reputation.

Smith discussed the issue of smuggling within the context of the taxation of consumable commodities. Two factors increased the likelihood of smuggling; first, the ease of smuggling increased as the size and population of a country made regulation more difficult; second, increased smuggling occurred when duties were high. Smith argued that if moderate duties were imposed, smuggling would not be encouraged because the risk would be too high. When the tax upon a commodity is so moderate as not to encourage smuggling, the merchant who advances it does not actually pay the tax because he gets it back in the price of the commodity. The tax finally is paid by the last purchaser or consumer.

Smith's genius included his ability to analyze explosive issues with a practical eye toward their economic consequences and underlying psychological realities. Following this logic, Smith argued that labor was one of the most interesting evolutions in the development of man because it was actually more profitable to employ the services of a free man than to purchase and maintain the health of a slave: "The experience of all ages and nations, I believe, demonstrates that the work done by slaves, though it appears to cost only their maintenance, is in the end the dearest of any. A person who can acquire no property, can have no other interest but to eat as much, and to labour as little as possible. Whatever work he does beyond what is sufficient to purchase his own maintenance, can be squeezed out of him by violence only, and not by any interest of his own."[8] Nevertheless, the author of *Moral Sentiments* recognized that it was the nature of man to want to control other men and that this passion replaced the cost of lost productivity. Although Smith never envisioned a nation going to war over slavery and thus wrote nothing on the role of the government in such a situation, he spent much time detailing the function of government in

---

[7]Ibid., p. 842.
[8]Ibid., p. 365.

protecting its borders and its peoples. In doing so, the doctor weighed the relative merits of militias and standing armies.

Smith believed that as society advanced it became less warlike; nevertheless, he deemed it necessary to provide for defense in one of two fashions — either form a rigorously trained police force or make the trade of the soldier a separate one. If a state chose the second course of action, which he preferred, it must choose between a militia and a standing army. Smith was convinced that a militia was always inferior to a standing army because it had less training and less discipline. In fact, he argued that the establishment of a military not only provided protection for a nation's borders, but could actually enhance the liberty of its people by providing the government with enough security to render obsolete "that troublesome jealousy, which, in some modern republics, seems to watch over the minutest actions, and to be at all times ready to disturb the peace of every citizen."[9]

Recognizing that defense of any kind was expensive, Smith dealt with the possibility of public debt arising from such expenditures. He argued that public expenditures in times of peace equaled revenues, while government contracted debt in times of war. This sequence forced the government to borrow money. In order to do so at a reasonable rate, it must have established good credit. Consequently, it was government's responsibility to fund the debt in such a manner as to limit its burden on the populace at any given time. When borrowing money from any source, government actually produces a contract by which it binds repayment of the loan. As the financial foundation of a nation was strengthened through the government's promise to guarantee its contracts, the risk to investment decreased and interest rates would fall over time, reducing future interest payments on the current debt.[10]

Smith believed that governments were formed to enforce justice through the various arms of the law. If a government could not be trusted to repay its own debts, how could that same government be responsible for establishing an exact administration of justice, which Smith believed was the second major function of government.[11]

In Smith's system, any activity that promoted the public welfare was

---

[9]Ibid., pp. 659, 668 (quote).
[10]Ibid., pp. 88–98.
[11]*Encyclopedia of Social Sciences,* 13:325.

a proper and necessary function of the government. One of the ways a government could promote the public welfare and ensure justice was to protect the public from perpetual monopolies. Although Smith viewed copyrights and patents as monopolies, he did not consider them dangerous because government had to be able to monitor the length of commercial monopolies so that merchants who took risks to establish new businesses were rewarded and consumers did not pay excessive prices for restricted goods.[12] Such governmental interference promoted the general welfare and justified the cost of interfering in the private market and with individual freedoms. Smith saw two situations in which it was acceptable to restrict free trade by regulations on foreign goods for the encouragement of domestic industries: when a particular industry was necessary for the defense of the country and when a foreign government imposed unfair trade restrictions on imported goods.[13]

Clearly the government played a much larger role in *The Wealth of Nations* than some laissez-faire proponents would have us believe. Consequently, it was not surprising that Smith favored a national bank in spite of the opportunities such an institution provided for government corruption. He argued that the establishment of a national bank was not only an implied power of government, but it also provided stability to the government and stimulated the economy by turning inactive money into productive capital:

> It is not by augmenting the capital of the country, but by rendering a greater part of that capital active and productive that would otherwise not be so, that the most judicious operations of banking can increase the industry of the country. That part of his capital which a dealer is obliged to keep by him unemployed, and in ready money for answering occasional demands, is so much dead stock, which, so long as it remains in this situation, produces nothing either to him to convert this dead stock into active and productive stock; into materials to work upon, into tools to work with, and into provisions and subsistence to work for; into stock which produces something both to himself and to his country.[14]

---

[12] *WN*, p. 712.

[13] Ibid., pp. 429–32. The notion of unfair trade restrictions was a gray area in *The Wealth of Nations* because outside of national security issues, Smith believed that trade should be as free as possible. Consequently, it is assumed that Smith left the decision of what trade practices were reasonable or not up to the governments of nations.

[14] *WN*, pp. 304–5.

Some critics tended to believe the establishment of a national bank would lead to a reduction in a nation's supply of precious metals. Smith argued that the export of precious metals was not due to banks, but to the cost of purchasing foreign goods that were better for the nation's productivity than either gold or silver.[15]

Although the above is by no means a detailed summary of Smith's system proposed in *The Wealth of Nations,* these ideas were a perfect match with the issues faced by the members of the First Federal Congress, the legislative body elected to implement the new U.S. Constitution. Although these lawmakers were former citizens of the British empire, they viewed themselves as pioneers of a new American empire. They had the opportunity to create something as successful as the British system while profiting from its mistakes. In a sense, the success of the American Revolution marked one of the initial failures of the British empire as it began to crumble under its own weight. Members of the First Congress were ready for the challenge of producing legislation that would initiate an American empire unlike that of the British, which pursued a policy of colonial government, but a mercantilistic one closer to the Smithian model based on territorial expansion and the formation of a powerful economic marketplace that was profitable both in domestic production and in foreign trade.

In *The Wealth of Nations* Smith not only served as a valuable critic of British economic policy, but also provided guidance on such specific issues as taxes on salt and liquor to such general ones as banking and trade. It was this attention to detail in Smith's work that formed a coherent theoretical model upon which members of the First Federal Congress could draw in formulating early American economic policy.

The First Session

The three sessions of the First Congress met from March 1789 to March 1791. The sixty-five members of the House of Representatives and the twenty-nine members of the Senate faced the problems of enacting the federal system outlined in the Constitution dividing sov-

---

[15] Ibid., p. 514.

ereignty between the national government and the states. Americans only recently had fought the Revolutionary War; now Congress, among other responsibilities, had to decide how to regulate interstate commerce and raise revenues to pay for the war and the enormous tasks that lay ahead. The First Federal Congress encountered challenges that if dealt with successfully would consolidate the union; but if it failed, some states might secede and the dread possibility of disunion and civil war would become a reality.

Much of the first session of the House of Representatives centered around the issue of how the federal government would raise funds to pay for the costs of a national government, including a large debt from the Revolutionary War. The second session revolved around the commercial issues of copyrights, patents, and trade policy, a small detour to discuss Quaker antislavery petitions, and particularly Secretary of the Treasury Alexander Hamilton's "First Report on the Public Credit," which recommended how the debt should be paid in order to establish sound public credit for the United States. The third and final session focused on Hamilton's proposed national bank and a uniform militia.

On July 4, 1789, President George Washington signed the Impost Act, formally titled "An Act for Laying a Duty on Goods, Wares, and Merchandise Imported into the United States." The purpose of this act was not only to enable the federal government to raise revenue to pay for the debt, but also to protect and encourage various American industries. Debate on the tariff bill began three months earlier on April 8, 1789. Several mechanisms existed for the federal government to raise revenue, but Congress ruled out direct taxation and the poll tax (Article I, section 9 of the Constitution prohibited taxes on exports). It did so not only because of the difficulties discussed by Smith, but also because of the general consensus in the House that the public viewed these types of taxes as odious. Public sentiment, demonstrated in numerous petitions, was a driving force behind policymaking during the First Congress. The future of Congress and the United States depended on its success, and the members depended on the support of the citizens they represented. Consequently, they viewed an impost bill as the most acceptable avenue for revenue.

Rep. James Madison of Virginia, who was quite familiar with *The Wealth of Nations*, took charge of the revenue bill, seeing its purpose as raising as much money as possible while leaving commerce as free as the policy of nations would allow.[16] Although the final impost bill (HR-2) included duties on hundreds of goods, wares, and merchandise, for the purpose of demonstrating the influence of Adam Smith on the First Congress, this discussion centers on the debates over molasses, salt, and slavery. These issues brought the House members into debates over, among other matters, necessity versus luxury, poor versus rich, and North versus South. It was within this context that what might be termed "Adam Smith consciousness" emerged.

The necessity versus luxury issue arose in trying to decide a fair duty on molasses. Rep. Benjamin Goodhue of Massachusetts argued that an eight-cent tax on every gallon of molasses was too high. He not only saw the importation of molasses as an important part of trade for the eastern states, but also that "it was used by many persons as a necessary of life, being a substitute for sugar, and mixed with water for beer." Rep. John Laurance of New York City asked during the April 14 debate if the House should tax necessities equally with luxuries. He noted that in some parts of the country molasses was a necessary commodity for the poor. He was against a high tax because he felt the burden would fall most directly on the class that could least afford it.[17] Laurance's objection to the high duty raised two additional issues that Adam Smith dealt with when discussing taxes on consumable commodities: proportional taxation and the connection between high taxes and smuggling. Both brought heated debate and were essential to understanding the final congressional decision.

If one state, or one class of people, had to bear the burden of a tax,

---

[16]Madison was educated at Princeton, where he certainly read Smith's first book, *The Moral Sentiments,* and was prepared for the appearance of *The Wealth of Nations* after his graduation. Seven years after the latter book's publication, Madison recommended its inclusion in the proposed library of the Confederation Congress (*The Papers of James Madison,* 17 vols. to date [Charlottesville and Chicago, 1962–], vol. 6 [William T. Hutchinson and William M. E. Rachal, eds.], p. 86). In addition, in *Federalist* No. 41 Madison argued in the same manner as Smith that the proper functions of government were defense, justice, and public works.

[17]*Documentary History of the First Federal Congress, 1789–1791,* 14 vols. to date (Baltimore, 1972–), vol. 10 (Charlene Bangs Bickford, Kenneth R. Bowling, and Helen E. Veit, eds.), p. 89 (hereafter *DHFFC*). Edwin Cannan, editor of the edition cited in note 4, makes an interesting note that although Smith denoted beer and ale as luxuries in *The Wealth of Nations,* in his lectures he appeared to regard them as necessities of life (*WN,* p. 822).

then the members of Congress were not properly representing their constituents. At the very outset of the debate on molasses, Madison "insisted with great energy on the propriety of a proportionable duty on so much as was distilled into rum, not only because the consumers of all kinds of ardent liquors ought to contribute toward the revenue, but because if country rum was clear of duty, it would so effectually rival the others, as to prevent the importation, and of consequence lose the United States all that revenue which they relied upon from these articles."[18]

Goodhue offered a compromise by suggesting an excise tax on rum — a product manufactured from molasses. Rep. Roger Sherman of Connecticut, who was undecided on the issue, thought it was absolutely necessary to devise some way for a proportionate duty to be proposed.[19] Sherman's Connecticut colleague in the Senate, William Samuel Johnson, offered a parallel argument. He reasoned that molasses fell into one of two categories: domestic molasses, which was a raw material and thus deserved leniency from any significant duties, and imported molasses, which was consumed by the poor as an inexpensive food replacement for sugar and thus should not be taxed at all.[20]

The possibility of high duties brought the question of smuggling into the debate. House members recognized, like Adam Smith, that a duty should fall on the consumers of products and not on the merchants who provided them. Furthermore, one of the main purposes of the First Federal Congress was to raise revenues. If the duty on imports was so high that it encouraged smuggling, the tariff's effect would be translated into lost revenues for the government, discontent among the people, and failed policies for members of Congress. The debate on the House floor reflected this concern. Thomas Tudor Tucker of South Carolina expressed his concern about smuggling:

> It appears to me that if we lay high duties on the importation of goods, a system of smuggling will be adopted before we can possibly make the necessary provision to prevent it. I take it, sir, that proper regulations respecting the collection, is all our security against illicit trade. From a

---

[18] *DHFFC*, 10:87.

[19] Ibid., 10:335.

[20] Kenneth R. Bowling and Helen E. Veit, eds., *The Diary of William Maclay and Other Notes on Senate Debates* (Baltimore, 1988), p. 66.

variety of circumstances, it appears to me, we shall not only be a long time in completing such a system, but for want of experience, any of the regulations will be of a dubious propriety. Gentlemen will recollect we have an extensive sea coast, accessible at a thousand points, and upon all this coast there are but few custom-houses where officers can be stationed to guard the collection of the duties; therefore we labour under considerably greater disadvantages than a thicker settled country is liable to. But we know in Great Britain, where the duties are high, no expence is spared in the collection, yet smuggling is carried on to a very considerable amount.[21]

Sherman, Fisher Ames of Massachusetts, and many other House members agreed with Tucker. Consequently, the final duty on molasses was designated at two and a half cents per gallon with additional duties on manufactured products made in part from molasses.[22]

Unlike molasses, which some members viewed as a luxury, salt was consumed proportionally more by the poor. Salt was used more in the interior of the country — where many settlers were poor — because cattle could not survive without salt. Consequently, the burden was heaviest on those who could least afford it. Certain members of the House did not see the issue of a salt duty as clearly as Adam Smith, who had argued that "the quantity annually consumed by any individual is so small, and may be purchased so gradually, that nobody, it seems to have been thought, could feel very sensibly even a pretty heavy tax upon it."[23] Tucker argued that one of the principles of raising revenues was to tax every man according to his aggregate value. He was against a duty on salt because the poor consumed more than the rich.

Andrew Moore, representing the southwestern region of Virginia, argued that although salt was a product of general consumption, it was likely that some states had more need for the commodity than others. Therefore, states such as North Carolina would pay an unfair share of the tax. Moore thought that the duty would be very unpopular with the people and hoped that either there would be no duty on the article or a very low one. Aedanus Burke and William Smith, both of South Carolina, and Thomas Scott of western Pennsylvania also favored strik-

---

[21] *DHFFC*, 10:527.
[22] Ibid., 10:528.
[23] *WN*, p. 825.

ing out the duty because it was unjust and, they argued, fell especially hard on the southern states.[24]

On April 17, in an impressive speech employing Adam Smith's arguments, Laurance convinced a majority of House members to vote in favor of a moderate tax on salt. He presumed that it was quite possible that poor citizens living in the interior of the country would share more of the burden of the salt tax. Still, he believed that they "would pay very little on rum, tea, sugar, coffee, &c. and he believed that unless a duty was imposed on salt, they would contribute little or nothing to the support of the general government." In addition, he claimed that although salt was an article of general consumption, the amount consumed was so little that there should be no objection to a moderate tax. Accepting Laurance's arguments, the House passed a duty on salt of six cents per bushel.[25]

Senate debate over the salt duty took a similar tone. Sen. Richard Henry Lee of Virginia argued that of all the articles on which the Senate considered laying a duty, salt was the only one that actually affected the interior parts of the country, whose inhabitants could afford to pay a higher tax on salt. Lee moved for a duty of twelve cents per bushel. William Maclay of Pennsylvania, along with most other senators, had no trouble in agreeing that salt was the most necessary of all the products in the proposed impost bill, but he believed Congress should still act with caution. He argued that in proportion to the original cost of salt, it was the highest taxed of all commodities. In addition, a duty on salt would be a new method of raising revenue in many of the states and therefore it ought "to be touched with a gentle hand, if at all" to avoid the possibility of general discontent.[26]

The most intriguing debate resulted from Virginia Rep. Josiah Parker's motion on May 13 to place a tax of ten dollars on each slave imported to the United States. The debate was short, and the motion did not pass; but the issue brought serious sectional divisions to the forefront. Tension between the North and the South arose as various members prepared for the battle they expected to ensue. In an imme-

---

[24]*DHFFC*, 10:145–47.
[25]Ibid., 10:180.
[26]Bowling and Veit, *Maclay Diary,* p. 59.

diate response to Parker's motion, Sherman said he did not "like to see human beings among goods, wares, and merchandise. [It] seems improper." Tucker, in an attempt to block debate, argued that the Constitution gave the members of the House no power to debate the morality of owning slaves, whom Parker had described as "unhappy wretches." Madison objected to Tucker's proposition that the matter was unconstitutional. It might not be proper to debate a tax on the slave trade under the current title of the bill, but it was quite simple to solve that problem by changing the title. Madison offered his opinion that the House was at "liberty to impose [a] duty of ten dollars," if it was seen as reasonable.[27] Despite Madison's argument that the issue was constitutional, the House reached general agreement that the motion should be withdrawn and brought up under another resolution. This action only delayed the sectional battle over the slavery issue.

Another means for raising revenue was to impose duties on all ships built in the United States and foreign ships sailing into American ports.[28] On July 20, 1789, President Washington signed an act imposing duties on the carrying capacity, or tonnage, of ships entering American ports. Debate on the tonnage bill began in the House in April with the central issue being the delicate balance between raising revenue and encouraging commerce through free trade.

Goodhue contended that there was no reason to lay a duty on American ships. He cited the Impost Act, which imposed duties on imported articles, as sufficient enough to raise revenue from this source. Any further tax would tend to discourage trade. Goodhue went on to point out that any legislation that reduced domestic shipbuilding decreased national security, "which was of the utmost importance to this country." Shipbuilding not only increased trade, which was the lifeline of American merchants, but also formed the basis of the future American naval forces that would protect its borders, ports, and trade interests.[29]

South Carolina's Tucker disagreed with his Massachusetts colleague. Tucker argued that a duty on American ships was not only necessary to

---

[27]*DHFFC,* 10:633 (quote), 634, 636 (quote), 644. Because Madison had been an important member of the Constitutional Convention, he was looked upon as one of the experts in the House of Representatives on constitutional issues.

[28]Charlene Bangs Bickford and Kenneth R. Bowling, *Birth of the Nation: The First Federal Congress, 1789–1791* (Madison, Wis., 1989), p. 31.

[29]*DHFFC,* 10:241.

raise revenue but also proper because the tonnage duty proposed was small. He did not believe, as did some other members, that it constituted an additional duty imposed on the shipping industry. Instead, the burden fell on the consumers who bought the imports. In the end, Tucker's argument carried the day and Congress laid a duty on all American ships at the rate of six cents per ton. The tonnage debate then turned to the higher discriminatory rates on foreign shipping.[30]

Thomas Fitzsimons of Pennsylvania "observed that it had been the policy of all nations to encourage their own shipping, and to obtain every maritime advantage over their neighbors. Surely we ought not to be less attentive to our national interest." In defending that national interest, he contended that the agricultural interest was served directly by the commercial interest. Still, the members had to be careful in the discrimination they placed on vessels of foreign powers. If the additional burden on foreign vessels was too oppressive, the federal government would lose potential revenues because of smuggling or reduced trade. A reasonable tariff would accomplish all that Congress wished to achieve. Tucker agreed that the motion of sixty cents per ton on foreign ships not in alliance with the United States "would be insupportable." He moved for a duty of twenty cents that not only would avoid smuggling and reduced trade, but also would liberally promote the domestic shipbuilding industry.[31]

In a virtual paraphrasing of Adam Smith, Sherman observed that "the objects of these duties was to put American vessels on a footing of superiority to foreign ones — He feared that object could not be answered by large duties, because other powers would increase their burthens on our ships in proportion — neither did he see the policy of discrimination proposed between the ships of nations in alliance, with those who were not."[32] Sherman worried that any duty laid on foreign shipping would only lead to the disadvantage of the American shipping industry through the retaliatory action of foreign governments.

---

[30] Ibid., 10:242.

[31] Ibid., 10:243–44.

[32] Ibid., 10:245. Smith noted that there "are two which are exceptional, when a particular industry is necessary for the defence of the country, like shipping, which is properly encouraged by the act of navigation, a wise act though dictated by animosity, and unfavourable to foreign commerce; and when there is a tax on the produce of the like manufacture" (*WN*, pp. 429–32).

Ironically, the most die-hard free trader of the First Congress favored discrimination against foreign powers, especially Great Britain. Madison claimed not only that American public sentiment favored discrimination, but also that his constituency would be angered at legislation that placed similar restrictions on allies as on other foreign countries. In particular, a comparison of French and British treatment of American shipping was evidence enough to favor discrimination. In France, American ships could be built and sold with only a 5-percent duty. In Britain, American ships could not be built, sold, or even repaired. Furthermore, some of the most valuable British ports in the West Indies were closed to American shipping. In order to level the playing field with the British and attempt to establish fair trade policies in the future, Madison wondered if it was "not good policy to hold out some inducements for nations who are not in alliance with us, to court that alliance?"[33]

Ames argued for discrimination in order to encourage American navigation and manufacture. In taking a Smithian point of view, Ames denied the suggestion that discrimination might favor the northern states more than the southern, and he was disturbed at this "doctrine of jealousy." As representatives of all Americans, Congress must "look with an equal eye to the good of the whole." In fact, the agricultural interests of the southern states would be promoted through the extension of American trade to as many ports across the globe as possible. Ames went on to argue, befitting a dedicated follower of the English school of classical economists, that since "commerce should be at the mercy of every nation," a discrimination in the tonnage act would be in the best interest of all regions of the United States. Furthermore, Ames viewed the origin of the Constitution as rising from "commercial necessity," creating a government whose responsibilities included promoting navigation by assigning tariffs on foreign shipping similar to those applied to American shipping in foreign ports: "If they pass certain restrictions [that] operate in the same way as [a] tonnage duty, we must impose such a tonnage [that] will restore things to universal equality. In the present instance, our ships can't go abroad with as much advantage as foreigners come here. I have no plan to encourage

---

[33] *DHFFC,* 10:246.

a tax more than that. One to protect the national security and to put our [shipping] equal with others."[34]

In rising as always to defend the rights and privileges of the citizens of Georgia, James Jackson pleaded:

> Not only rice and lumber could not be exported, but 5000 hogsheads of tobacco were now lying in ware-houses for want of shipping — Georgia was already borne down by the oppression of foreign impositions, and obliged to ship her produce under every disadvantage — in this humiliating situation she looks to this Congress for relief — should she be disappointed she may be sorry for the prompt and decided part she has taken in the second revolution: The southern produce is not at a low ebb — the specie is leaving the country, and distress stares us in the face at this time to encrease our burdens and difficulties, by encreasing the embarrassments on our produce, our only resource, will be oppressive and discouraging.[35]

The tonnage rate on American shipping was reasonable at twenty cents per ton, even though Georgia was only paying six cents, but Jackson wished to see a large increase in the discrimination duty on foreign shipping: "I will consent not only to fifty cents per ton, but to a total prohibition of foreigners."[36]

There was a similar disagreement in the Senate over whether discriminatory duties on foreign shipping were in the national interest. Senator Maclay argued that discrimination would only damage the interests of Americans in the long run: "The Superior Capital of the Foreigners would enable them to build more Ships lower than Us, and would in time give them the Whole of our Trade." He went on to warn his colleagues that compared to the British Navigation Act of 1696, which he viewed as a national security measure, the tonnage bill was designed to raise revenue to support the government and its large debt. Consequently, discriminatory duties, even at low rates, went against the interests of the American people.[37]

In deciding the final fate of the tonnage bill, the members of the House and Senate easily solved the dilemma, passing a bill that would

---

[34]Ibid., 10:434, 448–49, 435.
[35]Ibid., 10:448.
[36]Ibid., 10:458.
[37]Bowling and Veit, *Maclay Diary*, p. 77.

raise $124,000 as a result of the tonnage from foreign shipping. As Theodore Sedgwick of Massachusetts observed: "The question was, whether a small good was to be preferred to a great one; whether the whole revenue arising from the American navigation should be given up, for the sake of exercising a fanciful predilection and preference of one foreign nation over another."[38]

The first session revenue debate and its outcome demonstrated the influence of Adam Smith's economic and political theories indirectly but nonetheless clearly. Unlike the first session, the second session featured direct references to Adam Smith and *The Wealth of Nations* in its debates on copyrights, patents, trade policy, slave trade regulations, and public credit.[39]

The Second Session

Prior to the Patents Act signed by President Washington on April 10, 1790, and the Copyright Act signed on May 31, 1790, any American author or inventor who wished federal protection for his or her work had no course of action other than to petition Congress for a private bill. One such example was the petition of John Fitch, who claimed he had discovered that the steam engine could be applied to power ships. Fitch planned to put his expertise to work for common use but had already spent more than four years and sixteen hundred pounds inventing something that would greatly increase the wealth and prosperity of the United States. He asked for fourteen years of coverage based on the "established principles of Justice and Equity."[40]

The Patents Act (HR-41) was designed to promote the progress of the useful arts by protecting the inventor or discoverer of "any useful Art, Manufacture, Engine, Machine, or Device, or any improvement therein not before known or used." The law further directed such candidates to apply to the State Department to receive a patent for no

---

[38] *DHFFC,* vol. 11 (Charlene Bangs Bickford, Kenneth R. Bowling, and Helen E. Veit, eds.), p. 1084.

[39] In the index to the *Debates in the House of Representatives* (vols. 12 and 13 of *DHFFC*), Smith is referred to on pages 235, 242, 261 n, 765, 797 n, 1255, 1269–70, 1395, 1422, 1599, 1600 n, 1601 n, 1606–7, 1610.

[40] *DHFFC,* vol. 6 (Charlene Bangs Bickford and Helen E. Veit, eds.), pp. 1638–39.

more than fourteen years with the approval of two of the following administrators: the secretary of state, the secretary of war, or the attorney general. The Copyright Act similarly encouraged learning "by securing the copies of Maps, Charts, and Books to the Authors and Proprietors of such copies." It also granted fourteen years of protection and added the option of renewing such protection for another fourteen-year period if the certificate was renewed six months before the expiration of the first term. In this manner, authors of books ranging from arithmetic and religious tracts to American history and geography were protected under copyright law. Congress thereby not only protected those citizens who had taken significant time and economic risk but also promoted the arts, education, and commerce. Both laws were vital in piecing together the American free-market economic system.

The explosive issue of slavery emerged in the second session as a result of persistent efforts by Quakers from Virginia, Maryland, Delaware, New Jersey, New York, and western New England who petitioned the House and Senate to regulate the slave trade. They were joined by the Pennsylvania Society for the Abolition of Slavery, whose petition, signed by its president, Benjamin Franklin, called upon Congress to "step to the very verge of the Powers vested in you for discouraging the slave trade."[41] In preparing for the anticipated southern opposition, the Quakers and the abolition society made a strong case against slavery, but they failed to use Smith's argument that slaves were more expensive than free labor and that the South and the agricultural industry as a whole would be more productive with the work of free economically motivated men. After all was said and done, neither the members of the House nor the Senate presented a bill to regulate the slave trade, and this explosive issue was left for the future.

On May 17, 1790, a trade and navigation bill was introduced on the floor of the House as a direct result of the petition of the merchants and traders of Portsmouth, New Hampshire. These men and many other Americans like them were concerned that even after the establishment of the sovereign government of the United States, American merchants were still not allowed access to many profitable ports around the

---

[41] Bickford and Bowling, *Birth of the Nation*, p. 68.

globe. The same nations that restricted American trade, however, were allowed free access to American ports. Merchants worried that "the consequence must be a gradual decrease of [American] trade and navigation and a final destruction of both."[42] The resulting bill proposed to raise the duty on foreign ships not in alliance with the United States to one dollar per ton.

James Jackson spoke against the proposed increase because it was based on the principle of retaliation. Furthermore, such action would demonstrate that the maritime interest of the United States was more important than the agricultural interest. "In support of this idea, Mr. Jackson observed, that the best writers on the subject ought to be consulted, and therefore he quoted from Smith's *Wealth of Nations.*" Jackson went on at great length from book 4, chapter 2, "Of Restraints upon the Importation from Foreign Countries of such goods as can be produced at home," and from book 4, chapter 9, "Of the Agricultural Systems, or of those Systems of Political Oeconomy, which represent the Produce of the Land, as either the sole or the principal Source of the Revenue and Wealth of every Country."

In citing "the language of a very great character," Jackson attempted to rally the agricultural interests of the southern states to postpone the bill to another session in the hope it would not be raised again. Jackson contended that in a perfect economic system, freedom of trade would be granted to "artificers, manufacturers, and merchants of all nations." If a certain advantage was given one industry over another it would depress the latter industry unjustly. Furthermore, Jackson noted that the United States was acquiring more shipping daily, and it was possible in a short time that no measures would be necessary to rectify the current situation. He would rather wait and let a natural course take place than to do so by "forced and hostile measures." Moreover, a war appeared to be breaking out in Europe; this would mean increased demand for American products and the likelihood that Great Britain would abolish its previous restrictions on American shipping.[43]

---

[42]*DHFFC,* 6:1970–71.

[43]*DHFFC,* vol. 13 (Helen E. Veit, Charlene Bangs Bickford, Kenneth R. Bowling, and William Charles diGiacomantonio, eds.), pp. 1598–1601. The potential war referred to by Jackson was between the two major European powers of the time, Great Britain and Spain.

John Laurance opposed the one-dollar-a-ton motion, believing that it defeated the purpose of raising revenue in the first place. Such a drastic increase in the duty would certainly be cause for smuggling and drive honest traders from American ports. He also was deeply concerned that if such a bill passed, it would certainly favor one class of citizens while injuring others. This was not a policy the House of Representatives should advocate. Consequently, Laurance made it clear that he did not even want to see the bill amended; he was against all parts and would vote against such a measure "in toto."[44]

Hugh Williamson, who favored the motion, responded to Jackson's complaint that Congress was not taking care of the nation's vital agricultural interest. He believed that by protecting the shipping industry through these duties, and putting the profits of the maritime trade in the hands of Americans rather than foreigners, farmers would profit through a wider domestic market. In following such a course of action, the congressman from North Carolina was confident that he not only had the best interests of his constituents in mind, but also those of the nation and the American shipping industry.[45]

Madison, who sponsored the trade and navigation bill, rose to defend his work. He believed that public opinion favored the legislation because it was based on sound policy and benefited public welfare. Any opposition could be satisfied through amendments in order to save his intended purpose of reciprocity, which would benefit American trade. Such a policy was fair and reasonable since American ships were excluded from British ports, while its shipping was free to sail into the United States. In finishing a Smithian line of reasoning, Sherman added that it "appeared to him to be natural, and nothing more than a proper assertion of the equal rights of this country — It is merely meeting with counter regulations, the regulations of other countries, that are hostile to our interests — this we have a right undoubtedly to do."[46] The trade and navigation bill never passed the House and consequently never went to the Senate for debate.

The House received Alexander Hamilton's "Report of the Secretary

---

[44]Ibid., 13:1601.
[45]Ibid., 13:1603.
[46]Ibid., 13:1626.

of Treasury on Public Credit" on January 14, 1790. The major points of Hamilton's fiscal system called for payment of the federal debt through a long-term funding plan, no discrimination between original and subsequent holders of government certificates, and assumption of the state debts by the federal government. Hamilton believed that implementation of his program would secure solid public credit for the United States. American public credit in the eyes of the European financial world would be determined by how Congress responded. If it did not fund the federal debt, Hamilton argued, America would suffer the consequences of a nation without well-established credit:

> In the affairs of nations, there will be a necessity for borrowing. Loans in times of public danger, especially from foreign war, are found an indispensable resource, even to the wealthiest of them. And that in a country, which, like this, is possessed of little active wealth, it is essential that the credit of a nation be well established. For when the credit of a country is in any degree questionable, it never fails to give an extravagant premium, in one shape or another, upon all the loans it has occasion to make. Nor does the evil end here; the same disadvantage must be sustained upon whatever is to be bought on terms of future payment. From this constant necessity of *borrowing* and *buying dear*, it is easy to conceive how immensely the expences of a nation, in a course of time, will be augmented by an unsound state of the public credit.[47]

Like Adam Smith, Hamilton identified the urgent need of a nation to be prepared for funding future wars. In order to do so under emergency conditions, a nation's public credit must be sound in the view of potential lenders. In arguing for funding the debt, Hamilton raised the issue of the decreased value of cultivated lands since the Revolutionary War, which had fallen 25 to 30 percent and even more in distant areas of the country. Hamilton, like Smith, believed that one of the major factors in this decreased value was the scarcity of money; "consequently whatever produces an augmentation of the monied capital of the country, must have a proportional effect in raising that value. The beneficial tendency of a funded debt, in this respect, has been manifested by the most decisive experience in Great Britain."[48]

---

[47]*DHFFC*, vol. 5 (Charlene Bangs Bickford and Helen E. Veit, eds.), p. 744.
[48]Ibid., 5:747–48.

Hamilton then presented his case for why there should not be a discrimination between original and subsequent holders of public securities. He recognized the argument for discrimination because it would appear unreasonable to pay a speculator twenty shillings when he had not paid more than three or four. In addition, the secretary realized that such a nondiscriminatory policy would only add salt to the wounds of the original owner of the security who probably sold the asset out of a desperate need for money. Nevertheless, Hamilton opposed such action because it was "unjust and impolitic, as highly injurious, even to the original holders of public securities; as ruinous to public credit." Furthermore, he argued against discrimination because it was "inconsistent with justice" and was "a breach of contract; in violation of the rights of a fair purchaser." Hamilton ended his argument against discrimination with an objection that many House members would raise to Madison's discrimination proposal: enforcement likely would prove not only impossible but also more costly than the government could afford.[49]

Finally, Hamilton called for the federal government to assume the state debts. Hamilton reasoned that assumption would "contribute, in an eminent degree, to an orderly, stable and satisfactory arrangement of the national finances."[50] The basis for this conclusion was derived from sound economic policy: "If all the public creditors receive their dues from one source, distributed with an equal hand, their interest will be the same. And having the same interests, they will unite in the support of the fiscal arrangements of the government: As these, too, can be made with more convenience, where there is no competition: These circumstances combined will ensure to the revenue laws a more ready and more satisfactory execution."[51]

In the long run, Hamilton was convinced that interest rates would fall because of the establishment of solid American credit. Consequently, interest payments on the debt would be reduced and an enormous financial burden would be lifted from the government's shoulders. (Smith also argued in *The Wealth of Nations* that in the case of

---

[49]Ibid., 5:749.
[50]Ibid., 5:752.
[51]Ibid., 5:753.

Great Britain, as the financial foundation of a nation was strengthened, risk of investment was lowered and thus interest rates fell over
time.) Hamilton concluded his report with a wish for a rapid legislative
decision on the funding plan. He knew that the longer the United
States waited to establish a solid plan to pay off its debts, the more
financial losses would be incurred as a result of questionable public
credit. Hamilton's report demonstrated the great influence of Adam
Smith on the secretary of the treasury. Although Hamilton made no
direct reference to Smith, the British economist's views on debt, public
credit, and contracts echoed throughout the report.[52]

Once copies of Hamilton's report had been distributed, members
of the House entered into heated debate over Madison's motion to
protect the original holders of government debt. William Smith of
Maryland, like Hamilton, argued against the motion to discriminate
between original owners and subsequent speculators, who paid for a
piece of paper that had no real value at the time of the transaction. If
anything, the speculators provided the original owners with money
they otherwise would not have had to buy necessities.[53] Smith's argument was a detailed sketch of Adam Smith's ideal free-market economy. Speculators paid the market value, substantially lower than the
face value of the security, but the sellers were not forced to accept the
speculator's offer. It was not the responsibility of the government to
interfere with the economic transactions of private individuals.

---

[52]*DHFFC*, 5:760–76. The similarity of Smith and Hamilton could be attributed to
coincidence or to the theory that great minds think alike; but history has shown differently. In *Federalist* No. 29, Hamilton argued for the superiority of a professional army
over a militia in a fashion similar to Smith, among other documented examples of
Hamilton's close familiarity with Smith's work. It appears as if Hamilton prepared his
"Report on Public Credit" and his subsequent report on the establishment of a national bank with a pen in one hand and a copy of *The Wealth of Nations* in the other.
Hamilton wrote an extended commentary, which has since been lost, on Smith's trea-
tise in 1783 (Henry Cabot Lodge, ed., *Works of Alexander Hamilton*, 12 vols. [New York,
1903], 3:417 n). For more on Smith's influence on Hamilton, see John Cunningham
Wood, ed., *Adam Smith: Critical Assessments*, 4 vols. (London, 1984), 4:313 n. Furthermore, Hamilton was familiar with Smithian thought as a result of the influence of his
mentor, Robert Morris, who served as superintendent of finance and later as senator
from Pennsylvania during the First Congress. For Smith's influence on Morris, see *The
Papers of Robert Morris*, 8 vols. (Pittsburgh, 1973–95), vol. 4 (E. James Ferguson, ed.),
p. 39 n.

[53]*DHFFC*, vol. 12 (Helen E. Veit, Charlene Bangs Bickford, Kenneth R. Bowling, and
William Charles diGiacomantonio, eds.), p. 274.

Elias Boudinot echoed Hamilton's concern about the impossibility of the government determining the original holders of government securities. He was convinced adoption of Madison's motion would lead only to "injustice and clamor." Many House members argued that if the United States made a discrimination it would not only interfere with the free-market economy, but also extend government intervention to such a degree that the balance of justice would be lost.[54]

Madison tried to convince his peers to vote in favor of discrimination. The Virginian asserted: "This was the language of the constitution, which expressly declares, that all debts have the same validity against the United States, under their new, as under their old form of government." Madison continued to argue that justice was actually on their side if his peers would vote for discrimination. By paying the original holders of government certificates, the desperate and deserving soldiers who had fought for the nation's independence, how could the government do anything but what was morally right? In a direct attack on Hamilton's report, Madison proclaimed that any comparison of the American economic situation with that of England was absurd. He also believed, contrary to some of his colleagues, that it would be quite easy to identify the original holders from government records.[55]

Laurance objected to Madison's reasoning: "Public justice required a performance of contracts, when there was no fraud on the part of the holder. That the possessor had been guilty of no fraud, no deception; that the contract between him and the original holder was fair, and that a hazard and risk attended the purchase adequate to the advantage."[56]

The discrimination debate could not come to a close without the words of James Jackson, who favored the motion. Jackson considered the debt of the United States as the price of American independence, but he was not convinced of the impracticality of discrimination. "Was it possible for the poor soldier, uninformed, to foresee, when he sold his certificates, that they would rise to the present value? or that he could anticipate the present day, and a second revolution? Equity,

---

[54]Ibid., 12:274.
[55]Ibid., 12:278 (quote), 279, 281.
[56]Ibid., 12:324.

then, requires some mode of justice, and the tribunal exists somewhere, I believe . . . that we are the tribunal; for equity must exist somewhere, or the government is at an end." Jackson went on to refer to the actions of the English Parliament in 1712, when it interfered in the operations of the private Royal African Company to keep it from going bankrupt. He argued that this was the only precedent the House needed to intervene in private affairs. "Public justice," Jackson observed, "had not been done; the soldiers, the original creditors, had not been paid; they had not received the equivalent . . . due them." In spite of Jackson's assertion, the House voted against discrimination thirty-six to thirteen.[57]

The next debate focused on Hamilton's proposal for the federal assumption of state debts. The secretary of the treasury considered assumption necessary if good public credit was to be established and the various state economies were to survive. The proposal created an uproar. Sen. William Maclay, who observed some of the House debates, was stunned and discerned an ulterior motive: "The Secretary's People Scarce disguise their design, Which is to create a Mass of debt, which will Justify them in seizing all the Sources of Government, thus annihilating the State legislatures, and erecting an Empire on the Basis of Consolidation."[58] The House agreed to fund the federal debt essentially as Hamilton proposed, but repeatedly defeated attempts to assume the state debt. When the bill reached the Senate, that body agreed to assumption by a one-vote margin. The House accepted the Senate amendment on July 26 by a vote of thirty-four to twenty-eight. A vital component of Hamilton's public credit plan survived, but only because of the Compromise of 1790 that linked it to the location of the national capital on the Potomac River.[59]

The Third Session

The third session of the First Congress considered another part of Hamilton's plan, the creation of a national bank with a twenty-year

---

[57]Ibid., 12:356–57. Jackson undoubtedly procured his information about the Royal African Company from *The Wealth of Nations.* Smith mentioned it as having been subsidized by Parliament in order to pay off its debts. See *WN,* pp. 700–701.

[58]Bowling and Veit, *Maclay Diary,* p. 240.

[59]Bickford and Bowling, *Birth of the Nation,* pp. 66–75.

charter. Hamilton's report on the establishment of a national bank led to a debate that raised several arguments made by Smith in *The Wealth of Nations*. The report, presented to Congress on December 14, 1790, called for the creation of a bank generally modeled after the Bank of England. Hamilton proposed that one-fifth of its ten-million-dollar capitalization be subscribed by the government with the remainder to be provided by private individuals. He opened the report by stating the utility that public banks had served in the most enlightened commercial nations, including France and England. He argued, like Smith, that the "augmentation of the active or productive capital of a country — Gold and Silver, when they are employed merely as the instruments of exchange and alienation, have been not improperly denominated dead Stock; but when deposited in Banks, to become the basis of a paper circulation, which takes their character and place, as the signs or representatives of value, they then acquire life, or, in other words, an active and productive quality."[60]

Hamilton's report outlined the additional advantages of a national bank. There was a coincidence of interests between the bank's investors, who benefited from the interest on their investments, and the community at large, who benefited from increased trade and commerce stimulated by the bank's loans. In emergency situations government was able to use the mass of capital stored in the bank without disturbing the interest payments on that money. Furthermore, a national bank facilitated the collection of federal revenues and the productivity of commerce through the increased number of transactions and fertility of capital.

Hamilton also discussed the disadvantages of banks, including their tendencies to increase usury; prevent other lending; furnish temptations to overtrading; subsidize fraudulent, foolish, or incompetent merchants who disturbed the natural balance of trade; provide unqualified credit to fraudulent traders; and deplete the nation's gold and silver supply.[61] In refuting these charges, Hamilton used arguments and economic theory that appeared in *The Wealth of Nations*.[62]

The most blatant use of Smithian analysis in Hamilton's report

---

[60]*DHFFC*, vol. 4 (Charlene Bangs Bickford and Helen E. Veit, eds.), pp. 171, 174, 175 (quote).
[61]Ibid., 4:178.
[62]*WN*, pp. 285–309.

came from the explanation of two of the major suspicions about the utility of a national bank: that banks tended to promote fraudulent credit and to increase the export of gold and silver. Hamilton contended that it was in the interest of the bank and its directors to make wise loans its policy. If this were not the case, banks in general could not exist. Loans were valuable to society, Hamilton believed, because the money a bank lent became active and promoted economic expansion. Further, he argued, "the intrinsic wealth of a nation is to be measured, not by the abundance of the precious metals, contained in it, but by the quantity of the productions of its labor and industry."[63]

Hamilton contended, as he had in his "Report on Public Credit," that low interest rates would reduce the burden of the public debt and increase trade and other industries: "Banks," he wrote, "are among the best expedients for lowering the rate of interest in a country; but to have this effect, their capitals must be completely equal to all the demands."[64] In echoing a portion of Smithian laissez-faire principles, Hamilton observed: "To attach full confidence to an institution of this nature, it appears to be an essential ingredient in its structure, that it shall be under a *private* not a *public* Direction, under the guidance of *individual interest*, not of *public policy:* which would be supposed to be, and in certain emergencies, under a feeble or too sanguine administration would, really, be, liable to being too much influenced by *public necessity.* "[65] Hamilton also contended that, although impractical in the United States, the capital of a bank should in theory be backed by gold and silver as Smith had argued in *The Wealth of Nations.*[66] In concluding his proposal for a national bank, Hamilton referred to the prosperity of the Bank of England that arose from loans to the government.

Opposition to the bank was moderate in the Senate. Maclay, who reluctantly supported it perhaps in hope of reelection, considered banks "Machines for promoting the profits of unproductive Men. That the business of the United States so far as respected deposits, could be done in the present banks. That the Whole profit of the Bank ought to belong to the publick provided it was possible to advance the Whole

---

[63]*DHFFC,* 4:182.
[64]Ibid., 4:190.
[65]Ibid., 4:194.
[66]*WN,* p. 285.

Stock on her account. I was sorry That this at present was not possible. I would however take half, or I should rather in the present Case say 1 / 5 of the loaf than no bread." Other senators, including Pierce Butler and Ralph Izard of South Carolina, believed "the publick should have all the advantages of the bank." In the end the bank bill passed the Senate in spite of the implications it had for the location of the capital. Maclay could not resist adding to his diary "a Sincere Wish That the Integrity of the directors may make amends for the Want of it in Many of the Legislators who enacted it. For in the hands of bad Men it May be made a Most Mischievous engine . . . but so may Any, even the best of human Institutions."[67]

In an unusual legislative procedure, the House did not debate the measure until the third reading of the bill.[68] William Smith (probably the South Carolinian) argued that there was no debate over the bank bill during the first two readings because the members of the House were unprepared for discussion when it rather unexpectedly came up on the floor.[69] Once debate was underway, James Jackson argued against the bill, rejecting Hamilton's analogy to the Bank of England. In addition, he believed that the bank would only benefit a small portion of the population and not the large majority Hamilton suggested. Jackson believed the measure served the mercantile interest and not the farmers and yeomanry. Finally, he "urged the unconstitutionality of the plan, and called it a monopoly." Like Adam Smith, he believed it was improper for government to create a monopoly. Indeed, it was one of the functions of government to intervene to eliminate most monopolies because they went against the interest of public welfare.[70]

---

[67]Bowling and Veit, *Maclay Diary*, pp. 362, 359, 364.

[68]The normal legislative process during the First Federal Congress was to raise objections to the constitutionality of a bill, or any other complaints, during the first, or at the latest the second, reading of the bill. The third reading of the bill normally was just a routine ritual before the actual vote on the bill.

[69]Kenneth R. Bowling argues that raising the constitutional issue on the third reading of the bill was a desperate attempt to protect the 1790 decision to locate the capital on the Potomac. See Kenneth R. Bowling, "The Bank Bill, the Capital City and President Washington," *Capital Studies* 1 (1972):59–71. Also see Benjamin B. Klubes, "The First Federal Congress and the First National Bank: A Case Study in Constitutional Interpretation," *Journal of the Early Republic* 10 (1990):19–41. Klubes is convinced that the constitutional issue raised on the third reading was sincere.

[70]*DHFFC*, vol. 14 (William Charles diGiacomantonio, Kenneth R. Bowling, Charlene Bangs Bickford, and Helen E. Veit, eds.), pp. 55–61.

In response to Jackson's constitutional objection, Rep. John Laurance argued that the Constitution gave the government the power to borrow money; consequently, this implied the power to create capital, which in case of an emergency a national bank could loan the government. Fisher Ames also remarked that the constitutionality of the bill should never be raised during a third reading because by such time the issue had become null and void. While the constitutionality of the bill dominated the debate, the House discussed other issues as well.[71]

Madison also opposed the bank because "it was admitted by the most enlightened patrons of banks, particularly by Smith on *The Wealth of Nations,*" that they banish a country's precious metals. Madison, like Hamilton, disagreed with Smith's belief that the return on the lost precious metals was more valuable than the coins themselves. Furthermore, Madison suggested the option of establishing a number of smaller banks that he thought would increase trade in a larger area of the country than one large bank in one location. In offering other alternatives for the government to borrow money, especially in times of emergency, Madison referred to England and the South Sea Company that had been a far greater creditor to England than its national bank. Madison argued that the federal government could subsidize American corporations so that they, and not a national bank, could lend money to the government.[72]

Smith of South Carolina questioned both the validity of Hamilton's argument and Jackson's interpretation of *The Wealth of Nations.* He was convinced that there was no doubt the bank proposed by Hamilton was "a law entirely subversive of the principles laid down in his able defence of the constitution." He also noted that the Constitution required that no preference shall be given to one part of the country over another. Clearly, the bank bill gave preference to the mercantile portion of the American population. Furthermore, regarding Jackson's partial quotation from *The Wealth of Nations,* Smith observed that

---

[71]*DHFFC,* 14:61–65.

[72]Ibid., 14:364–71. Adam Smith also referred to the South-Sea Company, although more to its financial problems than to its assistance to the English government. "It was naturally to be expected, therefore, that folly, negligence, and profusion should prevail in the whole management of their affairs. The knavery and extravagance of their stock-jobbing projects are sufficiently known, and the explication of them would be foreign to the subject" (*WN,* pp. 700–709).

"he could have wished the gentleman had been more copious in his quotations from that author — if he had, he would have found that that author has fully demonstrated their [bank's] utility." In Smith's final observation, a national bank had to be within the power of the Federal Congress because no state could, or should, exercise such power.[73]

Michael Jenifer Stone of Maryland made the Smithian argument that there were times when normal revenues were insufficient for the activities of the government, especially emergencies. Consequently, borrowing would be a necessity and the government should be able to borrow from its own bank, which would serve the general welfare. Boudinot stated that he, like James Jackson, would oppose the bank bill if agricultural interests were to be sacrificed for commercial interests. Yet he was convinced, as Adam Smith had argued, that if one sector of the economy was greatly enhanced, the others could not help but profit as well: "He could not bring his mind to comprehend how the commercial interests of a country could be promoted without greatly advancing the interests of agriculture. Will the farmer have any temptation to labor, if the surplus of what he raises, behind his domestic consumption, is to perish in his barn for want of a market."[74]

Elbridge Gerry countered Jackson's objection that the bank formed a monopoly. He reminded the gentleman that the creation of a national bank would not prevent the individual states, or private individuals, from forming their own banks. Consequently, the government was not advocating a monopoly of the banking industry.[75] In spite of Madison's last stand against the bank bill during the February 8, 1791, debate, the bill passed thirty-nine to twenty. With the help of Adam Smith, another part of Alexander Hamilton's financial program had passed.

In addition to the financial debates, the third session also considered options for national defense. Members of Congress generally agreed that protection of the American people and the nation's borders was one of the government's responsibilities. The dispute arose

---

[73] *DHFFC*, 14:421–22. Representative Smith referred to the apparent contradictions arising from differences in Hamilton's position in various numbers of *The Federalist* and in his report on the establishment of a national bank.

[74] Ibid., 14:435, 439–40 (quote).

[75] Ibid., 14:461.

over how this was to be accomplished — by a standing army or by a plan designed to create uniformity among the state militias. Adam Smith, it will be remembered, favored a standing army over a militia.

Although the First Federal Congress failed to enact a militia plan, the sensitive issue of federalism sparked an interesting debate. Jackson opened with historical arguments in support of a militia, concluding that recently in England the government neglected the militia and the result was the formation of a standing army. He hoped that this same scenario would not be the case in America. "Every man in a republic ought to be a soldier — if it was only to prevent the introduction of the greatest of all evils, a standing army." In constructing the perfect militia, Jackson argued against exempting artificers. Although they devoted their lives to the arts and sciences and created great wealth for the nation, it was for the protection of these very liberties that they must also serve in the militia.[76]

Josiah Parker agreed with Jackson that it was the right and responsibility of the national government to protect the people. Thomas Hartley of Pennsylvania argued that a militia could serve the needs of the interior regions of the country, but that on the "extremes of the empire we shall be obliged to have a standing force." Hugh Williamson hoped the establishment of the militia would be based on the principles of perfect equality: "Every man must do his share of the duty, imposed by the civil compact. We cannot be maintained in our liberties and properties, without either a standing army or an efficient militia: and as all are to be protected, so all are bound to lend their assistance in this great work." In addition, he predicted that a national standing army would eventually replace militias as states gradually exempted a majority of their citizens from taking part in national defense.[77]

Since the House rejected the militia bill, one must return to the second session and the debate over the Military Establishment Act in order to discern the opinion of senators on the issue of national defense. Maclay noted that "this bill seems laying the foundation of a Standing Army. The justifiable Reasons for Using force, seem to be the enforcing of laws, quelling Insurrections, and repelling Invasions. The

---

[76] Ibid., 14:58.
[77] Ibid., 14:110, 134–35.

constitution directs all these to be done by Militia. should the United States unfortunately be involved in War an Army for the Annoyance of an enemy in their own Country will be necessary. This seems the Meaning of the Constitution. & that no Troops should be kept at peace. This Bill certainly aims at different Objects." Richard Henry Lee of Virginia also opposed the bill because he saw it as the egg from which a standing army would be hatched. Rufus King and Philip Schuyler of New York were in favor of the bill as a necessary response to the need to protect the citizens and borders of the country. Butler warned that as the Senate wasted time in debate, he had reliable information that fifty Indians were wreaking havoc in Georgia. The senator threatened that if Congress did not augment state troops, "Georgia would seek protection elsewhere." Oliver Ellsworth of Connecticut agreed that the military establishment bill constituted less than the establishment of a standing army. Ralph Izard of South Carolina observed that he believed the most effective and disciplined method of protecting the states was through a standing army: "No nation ever lost their liberty by a standing army."[78]

Ironically, Adam Smith's preference for a standing army over a militia prevailed by accident. Congress moved on both fronts but could not obtain a consensus on how to establish uniformity among the state militias. Consequently, the size of the standing army was increased in the second session and dramatically enlarged in the third.

The accomplishments of Congress in a mere two years were extraordinary. "In no nation, by no Legislature, was ever so much done in so short a period for the establishment of Government, Order, public credit & general tranquility," a friend wrote to Vice President Adams.[79]

In the 220 years since the publication of *An Inquiry into the Nature and Causes of the Wealth of Nations,* Adam Smith has been credited with virtually everything from being the father of economics to one of the greatest philosophers of all time. Yet this brilliant Scottish intellect has never been adequately recognized as a major contributor to American economic policy as articulated by the First Federal Congress. Only

---

[78]Bowling and Veit, *Maclay Diary,* pp. 231, 243, 250.
[79]John Trumbull to John Adams, 1791, as quoted in Bickford and Bowling, *Birth of the Nation,* p. 100.

thirteen years after its publication, Smith's masterpiece had a dramatic impact on the principal actors and the eventual outcome of many of the major acts in this legislative drama. The accomplishments of the First Federal Congress were extraordinary by any standard, but without the groundwork set by Adam Smith, such a performance could not have been possible.

Contributors

R. B. Bernstein teaches American legal history and law and literature at New York Law School and is Senior Research Fellow at the Council for Citizenship Education, Russell Sage College. He has written, edited, or coedited thirteen books on American constitutional history, including *Are We to Be a Nation? The Making of the Constitution* with Kym S. Rice. *Amending America,* his most recent book, is the first comprehensive history of the Constitution's amending process in nearly a century. He is now completing a book, "Conven'd in Firm Debate: The First Congress as an Experiment in Government, 1789–1791.

Charlene Bangs Bickford is project director of the First Federal Congress Project, affiliated with The George Washington University History Department. She is coeditor of the *Documentary History of the First Federal Congress, 1789–1791,* fourteen volumes of which have been published to date. Ms. Bickford has published on both the First Federal Congress and advocacy for the historical and archival professions, including *Birth of the Nation: The First Federal Congress, 1789–1791* (with Kenneth R. Bowling) and *The Coalition to Save Our Documentary Heritage: An Important Lesson in Historical Advocacy.* She has taught for The George Washington University and George Mason University and is a former president of the Association for Documentary Editing.

William P. Cowin serves as an information specialist for Fox News Channel in New York, working on the national cable newscasts and programs, Internet site, and the closed-captioning initiative. Before joining Fox News, Mr. Cowin worked for Andersen Consulting in Washington, D.C. While attending The George Washington University, he worked for the President's Council of Economic Advisors for three years. He graduated summa cum laude and won the Joshua Evans III prize for political science.

William C. diGiacomantonio is associate editor of the Documentary History of the First Federal Congress, 1789–1791, a project of the National Historical Publications and Records Commission of the National Archives and The George Washington University in Washington, D.C. Past contributions to the field of federal history include published articles on the Quakers' antislavery lobbying and President George Washington's federal city commissioners.

Herbert M. Druks is associate professor of American history in the department of Judaic studies at Brooklyn College and teaches history in the humanities department of the School of Visual Arts. His research and writings in American history include *The Failure to Rescue* (1977), *The U.S. and Israel, 1945–1973: A Diplomatic History* (1979), and *Truman and the Russians* (1981). He is also committed to teaching and writing about the history of the American Revolution and Federal Period. In 1997 he was given an award for excellence in teaching by the Brooklyn College faculty. Professor Druks is currently preparing two book-length manuscripts: "The World of Thomas Jefferson" and "Essays on the U.S. and Israel."

Marie Sauer Lambremont is a fifth-grade teacher in the Chapel Hill–Carrboro City Schools in Chapel Hill, North Carolina. She received her master's degree in elementary education in 1996 from The George Washington University, where she developed her interest in James Jackson's congressional career as an undergraduate history major.

Donald S. Lutz, professor of political science at the University of Houston, works primarily in American political theory and American institutional design. His books include *Colonial Origins of the American Constitution: A Documentary History* (1998), *A Preface to American Political Theory* (1993), *The Origins of American Constitutionalism* (1988), *American Political Writing during the Founding Era* (1984), and *Popular Consent and Popular Control: Whig Political Theory in the Early State Constitutions* (1980). He is currently working on a comparative study of institutional design in national constitutions around the world, entitled "Popular Sovereignty and Principles of Constitutional Design."

Alison G. Olson is professor of history at the University of Maryland, College Park, where her areas of special interest are American colonial history and North Atlantic history, 1600–1815. She has edited two books and is the author of three more, including *Anglo-American Politics, 1660–1775*, and most recently, *Making the Empire Work*. She has received fellowships from the Guggenheim Foundation, the American Council of Learned Societies, the Folger Library, the American Association of University Women, and the University of Maryland. Professor Olson is currently engaged in a study of political humor in eighteenth-century Anglo-America.

Carl J. Richard is associate professor of history at the University of Southwestern Louisiana. His first book, *The Founders and the Classics: Greece, Rome, and the American Enlightenment* (1994), won honorable mention in history from the Association of American Publishers and several other awards. A specialist in American intellectual history, Professor Richard has recently completed a second book manuscript, "A History of American Thought from a Christian Perspective."

Index